IRVING BABBITT
Representative Writings

Irving Babbitt *from a drawing by Johan Bull*

IRVING BABBITT
REPRESENTATIVE WRITINGS

EDITED, WITH AN INTRODUCTION, BY
GEORGE A. PANICHAS

UNIVERSITY OF NEBRASKA PRESS
Lincoln • London

UNP

Copyright ©1981 by the University of Nebraska Press
All rights reserved
Manufactured in the United States of America

Library of Congress Cataloging in Publication Data
Babbitt, Irving, 1865-1933.
    Irving Babbitt, representative writings.

    Bibliography: p.
    Includes index.
    Contents: What I believe—The terms classic and romantic—The rational study of the classics—[etc.]
    1. Literature—Addresses, essays, lectures.
I. Panichas, George Andrew. II. Title.
PN37.B2 1981   809   81-2968
ISBN 0-8032-3655-7   AACR2

CONTENTS

INTRODUCTION

I

BORN IN Dayton, Ohio, on 2 August 1865, Irving Babbitt was the son of Edwin Dwight and Augusta (Darling) Babbitt. He came of a family founded in America by Edward Bobet, or Bobbett (later spelled Babbitt), an Englishman, who settled at Plymouth, Massachusetts, in 1643. In his early years Irving lived in New York City; in East Orange, New Jersey; and in Madisonville, Ohio, where he developed as a country boy after the death of his mother. When his father, a physician, remarried, the family went to live in Cincinnati. Here he attended Woodward High School. He spent two summers working as a reporter in Cincinnati and then a while as a cowboy on an uncle's ranch in Wyoming. Eventually, with help from relatives, he came East to enter Harvard College in 1885. Upon graduation with Final Honors in Classics in 1889, he accepted a position at the College of Montana, in Deer Lodge. Then, in 1891-92, with money he had saved, he went to study in Paris, returning to the Harvard graduate school, where he met Paul Elmer More (1864-1937), who eventually became his lifelong friend and ally. He took the A.M. degree in 1893, in the autumn becoming an instructor in Romance languages at Williams College. In 1894 he received an appointment at Harvard, where he taught for the rest of his life. He was made a full professor of French literature in 1912, though he taught for the most part in the department of comparative literature. In London on 12 June 1900, he married Dora May Drew. Their daughter, Esther, was born in 1901 and their son, Edward

Sturges, in 1903. In 1926 he became a corresponding member of the Institute of France, and in 1930 he was elected to the American Academy of Arts and Letters. He was also a fellow of the American Academy of Arts and Sciences. In June 1932 he received the honorary degree of Doctor of Humane Letters from Bowdoin College. Irving Babbitt died in Cambridge, Massachusetts, on 15 July 1933.

These bare facts hardly suggest the depth and intensity of the life of the mind that Babbitt lived. Nor do they capture the excitement surrounding the movement which, under the name of the New Humanism (or Neohumanism), developed in America during the first three decades of the twentieth century, and of which Babbitt was the chief critical theorist and More the most gifted critical practitioner. (Theirs was a transcendent partnership of principles, sustained "by long association and by a fundamental sympathy of mind not incompatible with clashing differences," as More wrote.) If humanism, as it is said, is never new, it must constantly face new problems in any place and in any age. By humanism Babbitt meant the affirmation of man, of man's world of value, and of the faculty in his nature that sets him apart from "a merely quantitative order" and from the chances and changes of time. Babbitt pitted humanism as a third possible attitude toward life against naturalism and supernaturalism, or as he declared, "The problem is to find some middle ground between Procrustes and Proteus."

The New Humanism was a truly conservative humanism that opposed literary avant-gardists, naturalistic psychologists, uncritical traditionalists, liberals, collectivists, progressivists, and pragmatists. The positive and critical humanist, as Babbitt termed him, though he does not disavow the religious life, for "one must insist that religion is the height of man," lives in the secular realm, which he must strive to save from the defects of humanitarianism (for example, the myth of man's natural goodness, the lack of seriousness in the body politic, and indifference to moral principle). In the *will to refrain* (that is, the need to assert a "veto power" over "the despotism of mood" and an "inner check" upon the expansion of natural impulse, as well as a unifying exercise and expression of "the higher will") he found a mediating point between humanism and religion. Indeed, in Francis Bacon's utilitarianism and in Jean-Jacques Rousseau's romanticism Babbitt discerned the undermining not only of the Judaeo-Christian religious tradition but also of the older tradition of humanism, going back to ancient Greece.

The New Humanism attracted many adherents in colleges and universities, especially among teachers of literature. Gradually a voluminous literature regarding it came to be written by adherents and by antagonists. The high point of the critical debate between the two factions occurred in 1930 with the publication of two books, *Humanism and America: Essays on the Outlook of Modern Civilisation,* edited by Norman Foerster, and *The Critique of Humanism: A Symposium,* edited by C. Hartley Grattan. Inevitably the restrictive essences of New Humanism, which George Santayana wrongly associated with the Genteel Tradition of Massachusetts and which H. L. Mencken chose to deride as "gloomy humors," worked against its popular acceptance. Its austerely conservative diagnosis of social and cultural conditions could hardly compete with public demand for social action at a time that found the United States sinking into the Great Depression. John Dewey (1859–1952) was deemed a more appropriate spokesman of national aspirations. His radical optimism concerning the human capacity for reconstructive change and his view of life as a social experience of "shared good" were found more fitting to the national mood. Bread and butter, not "the aristocracy of true distinctions," or the lessons of caution, or the verdict of tradition, were to win the day. What validity has a humanist "communion" of "angry professors," asked Malcolm Cowley,

> for the mill hands of New Bedford and Gastonia, for the beet-toppers of Colorado, for the men who tighten a single screw in the automobiles that march along Mr. Ford's assembly belt? ... And what, in turn, has Humanism to do with the scene outside my window: with the jobless men who saunter in the dusk, or the dying villages, or the paper mill abandoned across the river—this mill whose owners have gone South where labor is cheap?

On occasion equally harsh reaction from even the intellectual right greeted the critical views of the New Humanists, especially as found in "The Fallacy of Humanism," an essay by Allen Tate which appeared in 1929. "[Their] doctrine of restraint does not look to *unity,*" Tate claimed, "but to abstract and external *control*—not to a solution of the moral problem, but to an attempt to get the moral results of moral unity by main force, by a kind of moral Fascism." Tate also argued that the humanists had no method, no unifying living center of action and judgment, no "definite and living religious background." In short, humanism was not enough: "It is an effort to imitate by rote the natural product of culture; it is a mechanical formula for the recovery of civilization." If, then, the values for which the humanists plead are to be realized, "the background of an objective religion, a universal scheme of reference, is necessary." More himself admitted that Tate "has laid hold of some of the real difficulties inherent in the humanist movement as it is now conducted."

Although the reputation of the New Humanism as a doctrine and a movement faltered, its influence, in ideas and ethics, did not. Even the unusual aggressiveness of those attacking Babbitt ("this drill-sergeant," Rebecca West called him) and More (a "banker-conservative," as he was labeled in the *New Republic*) registers the seriousness with which their analysis of American letters and society was taken. Clearly, the New Humanism had a profound educational impact. Walter Jackson Bate, in placing Babbitt's achievement among the major texts of criticism, concludes, "To a degree unsurpassed by any other writer of the last half century, he made traditional critical issues a vivid and living concern, applicable to almost every aspect of modern life." If, too, the New Humanists were dissatisfied with modern literature, prompting even a friendly critic like F. O. Matthiessen to cite their "inadequate sensibility that is a sign of the divorce between mind and experience," their insistence upon standards of discrimination and taste had a beneficial influence. In this respect Babbitt and More sought to strengthen and dignify the office of the critic in the contexts of selecting, weighing, defining, and "ever checking the enthusiasm of the living by the authority of the dead," as More writes in an important essay, "Criticism." To the critical function they ascribed a higher, sapiential purpose, the Arnoldian belief that a definite end must be kept in view. The critics, More asserted, "stand with the great conservative forces of human nature, having their fame certified by the things that endure amid all the betrayals of time and fashion."

Babbitt never flinched from what he viewed as his commanding office as a teacher and critic. His critical position sanctioned neither retreat nor rerouting. From the start he chose to travel on one road. Like Archilochus's hedgehog, Babbitt knew one big thing, related everything to a central vision, and affirmed a single, universal, organizing principle. He never betrayed his conscience, the truths of which, once he had discovered them, he possessed altogether, avoiding "sudden conversions" and scorning "pistol-shot transformations." His doctrine is characterized not by a program of ambition or even by a rectitude of judgment but by a forthright acceptance of limitation as the law of the manifested world and, consequently, of man's need for self-discipline and self-reliance. Babbitt was to become a lay preacher to Americans whose ministration revolved around conscience rather than grace. His innately protestant sensibility was to be schooled by his classicist and orientalist metaphysics in their assimilated forms and consecrated to "the service of a high, impersonal reason." In the end his humanism became a finely wrought reconciliation of East and West, of Confucius and Aristotle, of Buddha and Christ.

Possessing an absolute and undeceived integrity, Babbitt had no pretensions or poses. He discloses the rigorous workings not only of a "conservative mind" but also of a "universal mind," always speaking directly, with courage of judgment and with that tenacity of character associated with the New England mind and conscience. To be regretted, the dark thought will occur to some readers, is the absence of a compassionate mind, a mind that is ever in intimate dialogue with the heart. Words like "sympathy," "love," "charity," "kindness," "pity" are not a visible part of Babbitt's vocabulary. As critical polemicist and check, he refused to "put on sympathy a burden that it cannot bear" and allowed nothing to muddle his censorious inspection of the conditions of existence. The pitiless facts of human experience, he stressed, were incontrovertible: "If the moral realist seems hard to the idealist, this is because of his refusal to shift, in the name of sympathy or social justice or on any other ground, the struggle between good and evil from the individual to society." Pointing to similarities between the dilemma of ancient Rome and the dilemma confronting modern America, he warns: "We, too, seem to be reaching the acme of our power and are at the same time discarding the standards of the past. This emancipation has been accompanied by an extraordinary increase in luxury and self-indulgence." To treat the ills of modern civilization Babbitt offered what he himself called an "unamiable suggestion": "The democratic contention that everybody should have a chance is excellent provided it means that everybody is to have a chance to measure up to high standards."

In order to measure Babbitt's contribution as a critic, one must first discern his place as a teacher. For him there was no strict division between two interacting ministries, two interdependent disciplines. Neither can exist without the other, though the quality of the combination must depend on the power of the mind in which the two are combined. A teacher who has no critical viewpoint is no teacher; a critic who ignores or tries to conceal his role as a teacher is no critic. As a teacher Babbitt embraced a doctrine, taught and argued it, reinforced it, sustained it. His teachings, his criticism, are imbued with a finality of belief and decision and constitute a law in tone and temper. It can be safely conjectured that, had he not become a teacher, he would have made an excellent theologian. In both his teaching and his criticism one can hear the voice of the theologian expounding the logos of his doctrine. Such a position is not so much to be defended as to be asserted, argued, and affirmed as revealed truth. In the end he gives instruction in the basic doctrines of his catechesis.

Babbitt was no ordinary teacher. He possessed conviction and determination, as well as zest and militancy, seldom seen in the academic world. He made his mark despite the fact that his teachings were intellectually and spiritually incompatible with his time. His influence was as enduring as it was para-digmatic. T. S. Eliot captures its full force when he recalls:

> Yet to have been once a pupil of Babbitt's was to remain always in that position, and to be grateful always for (in my case) a very qualified approval. . . . If one has once had that relationship with Babbitt, he remains permanently an active influence; his ideas are permanently with one, as a measurement and test of one's own. I cannot imagine anyone coming to react *against* Babbitt. Even in the convictions one may feel, the views one may hold, that seem to contradict most important convictions of Babbitt's own, one is aware that he himself was largely the cause of them. The magnitude of the debt that some of us owe to him should be more obvious to posterity than to our contemporaries.

Nor was he an ordinary critic. The most impressive charac-teristic of his criticism is that it contains the voice of a teacher. Its final imprint is its didactic tone, severe, magistrative, un-compromising, urgent—inescapably repetitive, as it must always be in the teaching process. Babbitt's is the style of a teacher ever aware of the dual purpose of nourishing followers and converting enemies. It is a style that is a call to action, a missionary style, for within and beyond the words Babbitt is concerned with the survival of humane civilization.

Education, literature, religion, and politics have a common frontier and constitute the basic area, even the raison d'être, of Babbitt's teaching and criticism. "He had given you theses about literature, about life," Stuart P. Sherman writes of his teacher, "which you would spend a lifetime in verifying." In his critical and intellectual pursuits he was, to use an older designation, a generalist, or, to use more modern usage, a com-paratist. In his cultural outlook he was an ecumenist, a desig-nation that, at least in his day, was neither honored nor hon-oring. Bravely and persistently, for there were—and always are—collegial cynics and adversaries to contend with, he re-fused to see teaching as a one-dimensional task. Teaching was a total process of commitment to creating an ethos and de-fining a critique. Yet, curiously, he has at times been regarded as a sort of rough-hewn provincial, his worth in the meanwhile underestimated or even derided. "Babbitt, one must con-clude," René Wellek writes, "remained an American Republican and a Protestant, however high may have been his regard for the role of the Roman Church, and however far he was from subscribing to any definite Protestant creed."

The reasons for the neglect or the abuse of Babbitt are not difficult to find. The modern age is imperiously scientific and skeptical. To resist this historical fact involves grave risks for a teacher-critic. The risks are apt to be all the more costly when opposition to secular values comes in the form of vigorous protest and argument. At the heart of Babbitt's critique of the main power centers of modern society—utilitarianism, empiricism, positivism, liberalism—is a moral toughness. Against the twentieth-century relativism of the "sociological dreamers and reformers" he set the ancient struggle between good and evil in man rather than in society. This was perhaps his most uncompromising doctrine, as well as the impelling principle of his critique of the Baconian-Rousseauistic point of view.

Babbitt believed that standards have been under attack especially since the eighteenth century, which he identified with Rousseau and with the ascendance of "the temperamental view of life." To obtain general universal standards, then, constitutes an urgent intellectual and spiritual need in a modern world in which relativity and anarchy increasingly supervene. For the critical humanist, having standards is a dual process of selection and rejection and, on the ethical and the aesthetic level, of the "imitation" of a standard. Standards resist the meretricious, the impressionistic, the illusionary, and the merely experimental. They represent what is immutable and transcendent; what is of fixed and permanent worth and yet, as Babbitt unfailingly emphasized, is always tempered by the sense of change and instability. Standards, then, give intrinsic meaning to value, soundness to judgment, and order to vision, are the mediating and unifying formulation of truths that view man in his possibilities and limitations. A bulwark against formlessness, multiplicity, and meaninglessness, they are inevitably centered in a scale of values. "To have standards," he wrote, "means practically to have some principle of unity with which to measure mere manifoldness and change." Babbitt's stress on "analytical intellect," on "power of control," on "poised and proportionate living" was largely derived and sustained by this principle.

The deterioration of the ethical and moral life he saw as a concomitant of the loss of the classical spirit and the resultant "pursuit of strangeness and adventure." Babbitt was protesting against a Benthamite, "causo-mechanical" world in which the life of value receded before the philosophy of change. His affirmation of the life of value is tied to the requirement of *vital control,* which signifies an acceptance of discipline that embodies the presence and application of standards, leads to an avoidance of excess ("nothing too much"), and recognizes an ethical "self" that is capable of exercising control and a natural "self" that needs controlling. Babbitt was an absolutist who believed in making a distinction between moral progress and material progress, between the spirit of permanence and the law of change, between reverence for "the limit" and romantic longing for the infinite. At the center of all distinctions, he placed the eternal opposition of the qualitative and the quantitative views of life. In embracing the latter, he contended, lay the beginning of error, of which a growing absorption in the present, an emphasis on specialization, and a neglect of tradition and of anything related to an identifiable center of values were some of the more alarming manifestations.

In his teaching and criticism Babbitt was continuously exercising a dialectic. His allegiance to it was undeviating, as he connected it with first principles, on which, he claimed, the modern world had gone wrong. Reverence, discipline, wisdom, proportion, decorum, standards: these composed the formative terms of his dialectic. In the best sense, he used a language that belonged to a classical tradition, to the wisdom of the ages, as he liked to put it. Doubtlessly, the Great War of 1914–18 did much to diminish the authority and integrity of such a language. But the fault, Babbitt claimed, did not lie in the credibility of language itself, which he equated with what is universal and human, but with its corruptive conversion into what is local and relative. Cultural breakdown had progressed with the indiscriminating liberalism of an age in which man entered a Rousseauistic dreamland; in which, symptomatically, "the great illusion is not war but humanitarianism." "The results of the material success and spiritual failure of the modern movement are before us. It is becoming obvious to everyone that the power of Occidental man has run very much ahead of his wisdom."

Babbitt adhered to the old struggle between good and evil within man: "The true dualism I take to be the contrast between two wills, one of which is felt as vital impulse (*élan vital*) and the other as vital control (*frein vital*)." In this dualism he recognized an enduring element within man that sets him apart from the everlasting flux, that accentuates a sense of values, and that gives man a purposive character. The acceptance of the dualistic philosophy was for Babbitt a criterion of truth and value. He refused "to shift in the name of sympathy or social justice or on any other ground, the struggle between good and evil from the individual to society." He was no less critical of "pantheistic dreamers" who have sought to substitute "the grace of nature" for "the grace of God," since this substitution discloses the absence of the will to refrain that leads to spiritual anarchy and "endless self-deception." In the political realm, too, Babbitt saw the requirement of the dualistic element. The constitutional democrat's drive for institutions that act as checks on the immediate will of the people, he believed, is an instance of the principle of control. He goes on to say: "The partisan of unlimited democracy on the other hand is an idealist in the sense the term assumed in connection with the so-called romantic movement. His faith in the people is closely related to the doctrine of natural goodness proclaimed by the sentimentalists of the eighteenth century."

For the recovery of the truth of dualism, Babbitt insisted, modern man must begin by exalting the ethical, or higher, will to the first place: "To give the first place to the higher will is another way of declaring that life is an act of faith." The affirmation of this quality of will he saw as a humanistic rather than as a purely religious act of restraint identifying man as a responsible moral agent. Man's "free temperamental overflow" must be subject to a veto power, to an inner human check, or as Babbitt observes with special reference to oriental religious philosophy: "The greatest of vices according to

resort moral." So writes John Middleton Murry in a review of
Rousseau and Romanticism in 1920. His words pinpoint one of
the basic purposes, and values, of Babbitt's contribution.

Yet one must approach this dimension of Babbitt's critical
thinking cautiously. That is, his stress falls on ethical rather
than on metaphysical essences and is rooted in human experience. Though his meaning has appurtenant religious
values, insofar as Babbitt posits his critique of modern life on
unchanging standards, which must revolve around what he
termed a "precise tracing of cause and effect," it is in the end
not theologically oriented. Babbitt affirmed a perspective
inseparable from the kind of religious empiricism for which he
admired Buddha. Such a perspective, containing a "path," he
conceived of as leading to a "higher will," revealed in the act of
concentration. Specifically human and ultimately religious, it
disposed one to acts of a "spiritual strenuousness," which
Babbitt called the chief virtue of Buddhism.

His admiration of Christian tradition, with its implicit
vision of order and continuity, did not at the same time soften
his distrust of its doctrine of salvation, attended as it can be by
enticing forms of procrastination. (Babbitt much preferred "a
rest that comes through striving.") Hence he was especially
sensitive to any shifting of standards, whether the shifting
originated with a romanticizing and emotional religionism or
with an insidious utilitarianism "inclined to eliminate the will
to refrain and the inner effort it involves in favour of a mere
outer working." The moral process was for Babbitt one of self-
restraint, which meant the simultaneous need to resist metaphysical illusion, a rarefying but corruptive form of the tendencies of human expansiveness. In holding to his concepts,
Babbitt sought to support the case of a true spirituality: "Men
cannot come together in a common sympathy, but only in a
common discipline." At the core of this discipline he placed a
highly concentrated humanism which he himself both qualifies
and clarifies when he declares: "I am concerned . . . less with
the meditation in which true religion always culminates, than
in the mediation or observance of the law of measure that
should govern man in his secular relations."

This concern was critical rather than metaphysical. "Why

do you keep wishing me to be a theologian?" he asks one of his followers. "I am merely a critic." For him the moral spirit and the critical spirit are symbiotic. The growth and the refinement of one depends on and informs the other. The critical act is a judgmental act with implications of a prescriptive character. It enables participation in human life, which Babbitt differentiated from the religious experience that he respected but that he saw as potentially static. The critic must create standards in opposition to what is relativistic. He must affirm limits that are moral in their significance. Since there is a law for man and a law for thing, the critic continually makes distinctions and emphasizes the need "for the sharply drawn line of demarcation, for the firm and fast distinction." He constantly engages in "the application of standards of judgment" and searches for *la vraie vérité*. The critical process is inherently moral in its demands and conditions. As Babbitt states, "The greater a man's moral seriousness, the more he will be concerned with doing rather than dreaming (and I include right meditation among the forms of doing)."

Critical judgment epitomizes the capacity for distinction. Babbitt saw it as a basic feature of the humanistic idea of discipline, as an act of choice that translates into the highest critical function, reinforcing the principle of restriction and selection implicit in a standard. Critical judgment also serves as a refining process of concentration, which he believed to be operable or inoperable according to the way in which vital impulse is submitted to vital control. Babbitt was not a casuist. His approach was direct and concrete, rational and never problematic; and his precepts were clear-cut. In delineating his valuations—valuation being one of his most enduring critical preoccupations—he was compelled by conscience. The main task, he asserted, was to avoid, or at least to mitigate, confusions and false analyses and syntheses. Babbitt's position, in keeping with his set of principles, was inherently combative. The issues that he attacked stemmed from the modern tendency, fast becoming a habit, to compromise moral value by glorifying the "new" values of doubt, questioning, relativism—those qualities that culminate in paradox and ambivalence and that dull the line between man and nature.

The imperative of moral discipline is antecedent to the continuity of moral order. It acts as a defense against the expansive tendencies that Babbitt associated with the decay of cultural standards: "Every doctrine of genuine worth is disciplinary and men in the mass do not desire discipline." Without the "disciplinary virtues" no person, and certainly no civilization, can participate in the universal life or be liberated from nonessentials. "Civilization is something that must be deliberately willed; it is not something that gushes up spontaneously from the depths of the unconscious." Humanistic discipline, as it creates and establishes standards of order, is protection against the Bergsonian apostles of flux and evolution, the "votaries of the god Whirl" and of "a universal relativity."

In its critical context Babbitt's world view is inclusive, particularly as this inclusiveness is revealed in his valuations of literature and of the theory of literature as well. His critical theory and practice never deviated from his perception of right order as the source of moral feeling. This line of his critical thought is classical and conservative in its basic premises and formulations and canonic and cosmopolitan in spirit. There is some truth to the charge that Babbitt's work bears the mark of a heresy hunt. Tough and zealous, he was clear about the war that he was fighting and the enemy he was facing. His treatment of intellectual and moral problems was invariably in a state of vigorous, even fierce, reaction, which must maintain active, steady opposition to ideologues who refuse to see the duality of human experience and who subordinate all standards to the doctrine of flux and relativity. "I would react in the name of the modern spirit," Babbitt asserts, in qualifying the forms and the relevance of his own reaction as a "modern of moderns." "For the modern spirit does not necessarily coincide with the naturalistic spirit; it is simply the positive and critical spirit, the spirit that refuses to submit tamely to authority, but would try out and test everything according to the facts." He was particularly alert to any movement that leads to the obfuscation of the sharp judgment and to the encouragement of sophistry. Though Rousseau marks the beginning of the modern "naturalistic imbroglio," Babbitt saw other enemy faces. Never one to hide behind an academic mask, he confronted his enemy with zealousness and honesty, without a shadow of deflection:

> The critics have lost traditional standards and have failed as yet to find inner standards to take their place; they have, in short, become impressionists. Those critical impressionists are ... closely related to philosophers like James and Bergson who revel in the infinite otherness of things, the warm immediacy of individual impulse, and dismiss everything that makes for unity as cold, inert, merely conceptual.

> The scientist who tries to stretch his observation of natural law to cover the whole of human nature is really being drawn away from the positive and critical attitude into some phantasmagoria of the intellect.... What the present situation would seem to require is not the transcendentalist, but the spiritual positivist who will plant himself on the facts of the human law as firmly as the true scientist does on the facts of the natural law, and who would look with equal disdain on the apriorist and the metaphysician.

One finds in these statements an unhesitating power that invests Babbitt's critical thought with a clarity that is commensurate with moral instruction. He combined the tasks of a diagnostician with those of a pathologist discoursing on the nature and causes of the diseases of modernism. His main function was that of delineating his perception of human dualism. His devotion to this function permanently informed his approach. In it one discovers the value-creating principle of unity that Babbitt adhered to in his critical theory and that undergirds his achievement with the same sureness of purpose that he sees as being at the core of *The Masters of Modern French Criticism*: "My whole volume is meant as a protest against the romantic tendency to withdraw into the tower of ivory—in other words, to treat art and literature as something apart from life." He never deviated from this principle of unity, from this criterion, which, if the critic is to have any responsible standards—if he is to be a critic at all—signifies the attainment of the truths of dualism. Babbitt's moral sense is ancillary to a criticism which "can only come from a progressive knowledge of the inner check."

"If art is to be humanized," Babbitt says, "it must not simply flow with nature but be checked and tempered by some perception of the One." The critic must be vigilant against what Babbitt considered a paramount cause of the fall of cultural standards: anarchy of the emotions and of the imagination. In this respect he was in the vanguard of critical theorists refusing to separate a literary situation from a cultural situation. "Thus to study English with reference to its intellectual content," he writes, "will do more than anything to make it a serious cultural discipline." Babbitt's literary standards interknit with his cultural standards. "The best type of critic may therefore be said to be creative in the sense that he creates standards. It is in their common allegiance to standards that critic and creator really come together." Babbitt's emphasis on classical and religious tradition is in keeping with his task as a conservator. To those living in an age of expansion, the catechistical nature of his critical expression was no doubt exasperating. A critic counseling mediation between appreciation and judgment, let alone repeatedly emphasizing the need for retrenchment, individual and national, could hardly expect a receptive audience. The call to discipline and the affirmation of standards of taste are hardly tolerable in an increasingly pluralistic age in which "creative spontaneity" becomes gospel.

His doctrine of the New Humanism sought to moderate the worst, and the easiest, habits of modern man, or what Babbitt terms "the expansive lusts of the natural man." But his penchant for words like "mediation" and "moderation" was perhaps an unconscious disciplining of his own innermost feeling, and anger. Mediation and moderation were rational antidotes to conditions that struck him as "nothing less than pernicious." But it was for the eradication of these conditions that, intuitively, he worked. That his enemies detected his motives accounts for their fulminations, crystallized in Edmund Wilson's denunciation of Babbitt for conveying opinions which are "the mere unexamined prejudice of a bigoted Puritan heritage . . . [which he] never succeeded in sloughing off." Babbitt's theory and practice of criticism can be likened to "spiritual exercises," the demanding asceticism of which dictates attitudes of discipline and emphasizes the universality of duty. But asceticism, whether spiritual or intellectual, has never been one of the goals of modernism, and even the most sensitive critics have chosen to err on the side of naturalism rather than of asceticism. Babbitt recognized precisely this clinging to naturalistic postulates in the ideas of his student Walter Lippmann; and when, in the *Forum*, he reviewed the latter's *A Preface to Morals* (1929), he singled out "the modernist's dilemma" of which this book was a sign: "The modernist has achieved the emancipation from the traditional faith for which he has been striving and is disillusioned regarding the results of his own rebellion."

Moral criteria inform Babbitt's critical theory and practice. These criteria, the guide and impulse to his criticism, revolve around moral effort. (Babbitt unqualifiedly endorses Buddha's words: "Self is the lord of self. Who else can be the lord? . . . You yourself must make the effort.") Babbitt opposes "the moral real" to "the moral ideal," which he identifies with "anarchy of the imagination": with moral indolence, whether in the form of the romantic confusion of values or of the failure, either as evasiveness or escapism, to exercise restraint. He finds the ideal of romantic morality summarized in Lord Byron's words (from "The Island"): "The wish—which ages have not yet subdued / In man—to have no master save his mood." An aesthetic morality that lacks a universal and ethical quality leads to anarchical attitudes and, hence, to an art of shifting illusions. In the realm of the imagination, Babbitt believes, the inner check acts as a moral law against an unbounded aesthetic temperament. Man's moral sense reveals and refines itself in art as a perception of the struggle between good and evil in the individual. This perception is Babbitt's fundamental moral criterion, which in effect announces that the artist attains breadth "not by throwing off but by taking on limitations, and what he limits is above all his imagination." The imagination is an important part of the burden of moral responsibility insofar as it resists the utilitarian and sentimental tendencies of naturalist ethics and also searches for distinctions and definitions. From the tensive interplay of this resistance and this search, Babbitt is saying, arise the standards of "an art of clear and firm outlines."

Whatever the weaknesses or the irritations of his critical methods, it is clear that one is in contact with a powerful and distinguished mind in complete possession of its purpose and pursuing it with firmness and wholesome clearness. Not unlike the Matthew Arnold who, as Babbitt was to write, was misunderstood by his contemporaries not because he was less but because he was more modern than they, Babbitt made judgments out of his relentless concern with the menace of moral and cultural anarchy. His criticism is a censure of art that, lacking the principles of selection, results in the triumph of formlessness over form and of diffuseness over concentration. The good critic must be watchful of two rhythms, the naturalistic and the romantic, that is to say, of two influences and effects, in modern art: "decadent aestheticism" and the "emancipation of the imagination from any allegiance to standards, from any central control." The criteria that Babbitt employs in his judgment of art are those that he honors in Arnold:

> Arnold always assumes a core of normal experience, a permanent self in man, and rates a writer according to the degree of his insight into this something that abides through all the flux of circumstance, or, as he himself would say, according to the depth and soundness of this writer's criticism of life.

III

The failure to penetrate the moral qualities of Babbitt's criticism has long led to a misunderstanding of his work. Thus, though a perceptive scrutiny of Babbitt's criticism, R. P. Blackmur's essay "Humanism and Symbolic Imagination" fails precisely because, in adhering to what Brooks Adams called "the comfortable muddle," it cannot grasp the moral essences and exigencies of Babbitt's criticism. Blackmur's argument is that the tragedy of Babbitt was his isolation, "the utter desolateness of the center"; that Babbitt was unable to deal with the symbolic imagination without reducing it to an intellectual level:

> He never saw afresh in the imaginative field. He never ... at-

tempted to revive the turbulence of the flesh—the fury and the mire, to use Yeats's phrase, in human veins. . . . He never realized that we inherit only in the flesh, that the spirit is nothing without the letter. He knew nothing, in short, or at any rate never took account of the chthonic underside of things which the topside only keeps down. His interest . . . lay almost entirely in what could be made to seem exemplary within the terms of a formula.

Blackmur's essay underlines what is symptomatic of so much modern criticism, even as it points to those habits that Babbitt tirelessly inveighed against. His critical valuations, far from having the disability that Blackmur believes they have, are stringent and in their ethical aim free from any confusion— the outgrowth of an active critical intelligence whose mission is to mobilize the moral sensibility.

Babbitt's aesthetic valuations ultimately emerge, taking their critical shape from his indictment of a romantic imagination that fails to distinguish between the fictitious and the real worlds and perpetuates vision at the expense of discipline. It is an imagination that lingers in the primitivistic, the idyllic, the passional, the illusionary, and ends in retreat into a "land of chimeras," into "an endless and aimless vagabondage of the emotions with the imagination as their free accomplice." Adventure and spontaneity, dreamland and revery are constituents of this imagination. The real gives way to the ideal, obligations and constraints to fantasy, to sentiment, to nostalgia as "the pursuit of pure illusion." Distinctions separating the different literary genres and also the different arts deteriorate. The romantic, or eccentric, imagination has no center and fails, Babbitt writes, "to disengage the real from the welter of the actual and so achieve something that strikes one still as nature but a selected and ennobled nature." Such an imagination, absolved of restraints or limits, wars against two great traditions and the sustaining ethos of each: against both classical decorum and Christian humility.

Aesthetic romanticism was equated by Babbitt with the evasion of moral responsibility. It points to the victory of shifting illusion over an art of clear and firm outlines as unity of insight becomes unity of instinct. Babbitt insists on the need to deal with both art and life from an ethical center. Art discloses "the high seriousness of the ethical imagination"; it cannot absolve itself from universal values and from common intellectual and moral judgments. The artist can neither ignore nor reject those traditional forms that comprise "the funded experience of any particular community." When he does, the result is one of disconnection. Babbitt shares Edmund Burke's belief that individualism should be humanistic and religious rather than, as Rousseau argued, naturalistic. "If the individual," writes Babbitt, "condemns the general sense, and trusts unduly his private self, he will have no model; and a man's first need is to look up to a sound model and imitate it." With Burke, he believed that much of the wisdom of life consists in the imaginative re-creation of past experience in such a way as to bring it into connection with the present: "The very model that one looks up to and imitates is an imaginative creation." If Rousseau emboldens the imagination of wonder, Burke emboldens the imagination of reverence. The latter imagination is drawn back to an ethical center and supplies a standard "with reference to which the individual may set bounds to the lawless expansion of his natural self (which includes his intellect as well as his emotions)."

The artist, if he is to proffer a humanistic value of wisdom, according to Babbitt, must strive to mediate between the intuition of the Many, when dealing with the natural order, and the intuition of the One, when dealing with man's peculiar domain. Only then does the artist recognize the potentiality in man of a spontaneousness that resists the flux and yet also imposes upon it a human purpose and satisfies a higher standard: "Unless there is something that abides in the midst of change and serves to measure it, it is obvious that there can be no standards." There is, then, an imagination that gives access to the supersensuous and becomes an organ of insight and an imagination that does not rise above sense impressions.

In the philosophy and aesthetic theory of Benedetto Croce (1866–1952), though Babbitt found some merits—for instance, Croce's indictment of intellectual anarchy, of unbridled individualism, of scientific intellectualism—he also found a central wrongness and void: "In general, nothing could be more ro-

mantic than Croce's cult of intuition in the sense of pure spontaneity and untrammelled expression, his tendency to reduce
art to a sort of lyrical overflow that is not disciplined to any
permanent centre of judgment in either creator or critic and
the consequent identification of genius and taste." Croce, said
Babbitt, failed to see the One in the Many; denied the validity
of genres in literature and art; rejected the Aristotelian view of
poetry as a creative imitation of the universal in favor of a
view of poetry as expression and lyrical spontaneity. Above
all, he found lacking in Crocean aesthetics an effective counterpoise to the expansionist desires, "to the love, namely, of
change and motion for their own sake, to the psychic restlessness that is the inner equivalent of the unparalleled increase of
power and speed in the outer world."

Following Aristotle, Babbitt taught that centrality of
vision is necessary if the creative imagination is to be able to
separate unity and purpose from the welter of the actual.
Man's craving for the marvelous is, to be sure, necessary, but
it must not sacrifice truth to the universal. Coleridge's *The
Rime of the Ancient Mariner,* for example, represented for
Babbitt the sacrifice of the verisimilar to the marvelous, radically removed from the Aristotelian high seriousness requir-
ing relevancy to normal experience and a relevancy tested in
terms of action. Coleridge's poem lacks, he goes on to emphasize, a serious ethical purport and an adequate concern with
moral choices as they bear on the problem that finally counts,
"that of man's happiness or misery." Imagination that fails to
cooperate with reason in the service of the higher self can
scarcely create values that have a human significance. In the
artist's tendency to exalt the differences between man and
man and to denigrate the identities Babbitt detected a confusion between individuality and personality, the latter being
something that man must consciously win with reference to a
disciplining and humanizing standard set above his temperamental self. In viewing in the literary cults of his time what he
regarded as the increasing surrender of discrimination, of control, of human substance to pure spontaneity, Babbitt viewed
what he believed to be a drift towards unintelligibility. His pre-
diction, first made in the thirties, has been amply proved: "If

we are to judge by *surréalisme* and other recent literary cults the time is approaching when each writer will, in the name of his genius conceived as self-expression, retire so completely into his own private dream that communication will become impossible."

Life gives, and, indeed, man himself is, Babbitt notes, a "oneness that is always changing." Oneness and change are inseparable, a fact which means "that such reality as man can know positively is inextricably mixed up with illusion." If life is but a web of illusions, "a dream within a dream," there is, Babbitt demurs, at the center of all change a unity, as also there are "standards with reference to which the dream of life may be rightly managed only through a veil of illusion." The problem of the One and the Many can be solved only by the right use of illusion, that illusion which, in Joubert's phrase, "is an integral part of reality" and which, if left out of human experience, prompts one to "see the fact or 'law' in hard isolation and not in its mysterious interconnection with the whole." Deeper insight into the role of the imagination can lead to a perception of an abiding unity and provide an organ of insight that achieves "the illusion of higher reality," remaining true to the idea of the universal, that is, something that has purpose, or constraint and effort. There is a right use of illusion, but there is also a wrong use when man hungers for sensual or metaphysical illusions—for instance, the glamour of an earthly paradise or the ecstasy of a "false finality." This wrong use Babbitt connects with "reverie," the intense and prolonged enjoyment of a physical impulse and the yearning to live subjectively in an element of fiction that absolves one from "the real labor of thinking" and glorifies half-truths. The undiscriminating use of illusion is still another form of an expansionist tendency. Babbitt tied the element of illusion, in the framework of the play of the imagination, to an essential question that is to be asked of all men: whether one regards liberty as "a taking on or as a throwing off of limitations." Again echoing Aristotle, Babbitt observes, "One may be rightly imitative . . . and so have access to a superior truth and give access to it only by being a master of illusion."

The mystery of the creative process, of those dimensions

of art which are gratuitous and autotelic and manifest creativity as a "magic synthesis," hardly impressed Babbitt. He
viewed as unsound the free and virtuosic aspects of art (arising
from high spirits, the gratuitous instinct of play, the need for
beauty and delight and fantasy, the irresponsible spirit of
comedy, of fervor, of mischief). Not the "passion for origins" in
creativity and in the study of literature but rather a preoccupation with ends comprised his critical orientation. This concern also marked the intense moral character of Babbitt's critical sensibility. What his antagonists have taken to be his
deficiency of aesthetic understanding, he took to be the core and
strength of his critical ideas: unswerving commitment to the
moral consciousness, to which literature as a criticism of life
must address itself. Bravely and with perseverance, he pronounced those criteria of literary culture, always in close relation to the social-political situation, that neither in his time nor
in ours make popular the critic as moralist. To disabuse one of
one's illusions, to break into, tamper with, and overturn one's
dreamland, as Babbitt did with ferocious diagnostic power,
became a denounceable breach, a violation, a violence, which
others do not easily condone or forget, and from which they do
not easily recover. To judge by the interminable hostility to
Babbitt it is not at all hard to conclude that he penetrated into
areas of life and thought too vulnerable to tolerate interven-
tion—the vulnerability all too often symptomatic of both individual and national infirmity.

Babbitt never ceased to state the case for criticism. Nor
did he ever relent in affirming the active interdependence of, if
not the parity between, the creative and the critical states of
mind. He refused to accept or to tolerate the aesthetic contention that, as it has been representatively and exuberantly
stated, "the work of art assumes the existence of the perfect
spectator, and is indifferent to the fact that no such person
exists. It does not allow for our ignorance and it does not cater
to our knowledge." He dismissed such an aesthetic response
as a surrender to unchecked expansiveness, to romantic and
emotional aestheticism, to "a rampant naturalism." "Man will
always crave a view of life to which perception lends immediacy and the imaginative infinitude," Babbitt was to remark

of a desire that he found wanting in discrimination and wisdom. The imagination, he believed, reaches out, seizes likenesses, and helps to establish certain constant factors in human experience. "The obvious reply to those who call for more creation and less criticism," he writes, "is that one needs to be critical above all in examining what now passes for creation." For the critic the act of selection constitutes a constant process, which he saw as a counterpoise to excess of the sympathetic and appreciative temper and to what he labeled "the romantic confusion of the arts." "What we see in America to-day, for instance, is an endless procession of bad or mediocre books, each one saluted on its way to oblivion by epithets that would be deserved only by a masterpiece," he writes in 1912, his words even more applicable to present circumstances that continue to underline "an undue tolerance for indeterminate enthusiasms and vapid emotionalism." Art and literature that pass from the domain of action into that of revery exhibit the pursuit of illusion for its own sake and the victory of the senses over intellect, character, and will. In art and literature one must look for strict causal connections and seek to maintain a balance between the analytic and the synthetic elements of one's thought.

How can the creator be saved from "the romanticism of nympholeptic longing" and from "the insurrection from below"? This was a question that Babbitt never ceased to ask—and to answer: "If the arts lack dignity, centrality, repose, it is because the men of the present have no centre, no sense of anything fixed or permanent either within or without themselves, that they may oppose to the flux of phenomena and the torrent of impressions." What he attacked was an imagination set free "to wander wild in its own empire of chimeras": "To assert that the creativeness of the imagination is incompatible with centrality or, what amounts to the same thing, with purpose, is to assert that the creativeness of the imagination is incompatible with reality or at least such reality as man may attain." The creative imagination cannot be excused for defying boundaries and spurning definition: "Both the imagination and the emotion that enter into the romantic symbol are undisciplined. . . . Great literature is an imagi-

native and symbolical interpretation of an infinite that is
accessible only to those who possess in some degree the same
imagination."

The distinction between the two main types, or qualities,
of imagination was a distinction between what Babbitt termed
an ethical, or permanent, type, which gives high seriousness to
creative writing, and an Arcadian, or dalliant, type, which fails
to rise above the recreative level. The latter type, which he
viewed as a religion of art, represents a sham religion. It is an
imagination in which illusion is not disciplined to the higher
reality and which leads to a confusion of values and to "anarchy of the imagination." Sound imagination no less than
sound individualism must look to a center and a model and
grasp the abiding human element: "A knowledge of it results
from experience—experience vivified by the imagination."
Man tends to be immersed in his personal conceit and in the
kind of illusion peculiar to his time, though there is always,
Babbitt notes, the question of degree: "Man realizes that immensity of being of which Joubert speaks only in so far as he
ceases to be the thrall of his own ego. This human breadth he
achieves not by throwing off but by taking on limitations, and
what he limits is above all his imagination."

IV

It is the critic's responsibility to uphold the idea of value and
to defend its viability in an age of doubt. Babbitt recognized
both the immediate and the extensive nature of this responsibility in terms of the aristocratic principle of standards that
must be established. His perhaps most preeminent standard
relates to the critic's mission, of which the controlling goal is
that of making moral sense of things. An understanding of
Babbitt's criticism must be looked for in this fundamental
aspect of his mission. That he refused to exempt literature
from moral categories: this pivotal principle empowers his
critical thought. It is its propelling constituent, its final
measure, and its signifying authority. For Babbitt criticism
requires expending a mental effort of precise analysis, which
kindles into spiritual insight and refers human experience to a

moral center: "Experience after all has other uses than to supply furnishings for the tower of ivory; it should control the judgment and guide the will; it is in short the necessary basis of conduct." Babbitt upheld and illustrated two catechistical truths: that without character there is no intelligence and that without honesty there is no clarity.

Put simply, his mission was that of a critic expounding the humanistic values of "moderation, common sense, and common decency." He saw his mission as imposing on him a destiny, a work of life, as it were. The intrinsic requirement of this mission was unconditional, particularly if discipline and standards were to attain any viable place in cultural life. "One should not be," he cries, "moderate in dealing with error," words that portend the form and scope of his mission. Babbitt himself was aware of the rearguard action he was fighting, if one is to judge by his *Democracy and Leadership* (1924), which can be read as a valedictory statement that has yet to find its audience. Here his message is simple and cogent: the crisis of civilization is inseparable from the crisis of spirit in the modern world. The main source of this crisis is the denial of the dualism of spirit and nature. And the main and most frightening consequence is that, morally and intellectually, the spirit of indolence and conceit spreads through all parts of the body politic. Evil is its most destructive agent. Civilization, as a striving for right order and a way to the hierarchy of values, is its most vulnerable object. In *Democracy and Leadership* he uses as one of the epigraphs the following words of Burke, which could easily serve as an epigraph for the whole of Babbitt's thought and work:

> Society cannot exist unless a controlling power upon will and appetite be placed somewhere, and the less of it there is within, the more there must be without. It is ordained in the eternal constitution of things, that men of intemperate minds cannot be free.

Babbitt rejected dogmatic and revealed religion, as well as ecclesiastical authority and forms of worship. "What you get in the churches nowadays," he said, "is religiosity, the religion of feeling, aestheticism, the cult of nature, official optimism, talk about progress, humanitarian sympathy for the poor."

Though he attacked religious obscurantism and enthusiasm, he had strong intellectual respect for orthodox religion, particularly Roman Catholicism, that maintained clearly defined beliefs and civilized standards. The humanist, he said, "does not seek to define God and is chary of ultimates." But he also admitted that humanism "gains immensely when it has a background of religious insight." A balanced religious sympathy braces Babbitt's critical mission, and repeatedly he pleads for uniting humanistic and religious values. He stresses that humanistic mediation which has the support of meditation has a religious background. "Mediation and meditation are after all only different stages in the same ascending 'path' and should not be arbitrarily separated." His critical idiom, even when cursorily surveyed, is replete with religious essences, although his use of religious language never becomes opportunistic. He is careful, for example, to point to the romantic corruption of the idea of the infinite: "No distinction is more important than that between the man who feels the divine discontent of religion, and the man who is suffering from mere romantic restlessness." In a large sense Babbitt belongs to "the old criticism," which is tied to the old definitions and categories, to criticism that participates in a moral vision and that proceeds "in multiplying sharp distinctions, and . . . then put[s] these distinctions into the service of the character and will."

He practiced a religious criticism, though he himself was not a religious critic. "But it is always the human reason, not the revelation of the supernatural, upon which Mr. Babbitt insists," Eliot writes in 1927. Babbitt revealed, at its best, the cooperation between the critical and the religious spirit. He nevertheless stressed that criticism must respond to the "immediate data of consciousness," that the significance of human life must develop from a religious empiricism: "No inconsiderable part of wisdom consists in just this: not to allow the mind to dwell on questions that are unprofitable in themselves or else entirely beyond its grasp." Babbitt contended that no critical pursuit can ever be genuine if in any way it surrenders to Rousseau's counsel, "Let us begin by setting aside all the facts." The germs of Babbitt's criticism are social and moral in direct relation to his fundamental concern with the eclipse of the idea of value in modern literature—and civilization. The theory and the practice of criticism require concentration and selection, even in those same contexts that Babbitt respects in Joubert's view of religion: "Religion is neither a theology or a theosophy; it is more than all that: a discipline, a law, a yoke, an indissoluble engagement." Far from making a "war on literature," as his detractors charged, Babbitt examined the experience of literature as ethical and moral experience. He refused to place criticism in an aesthetic or metaphysical vacuum. The critic reveals his moral sense and validates his relevance through a dedication to standards. Criticism must be a "faith free from illusion."

For his seriousness and commitment Babbitt dared the displeasure of the greater powers. His own university was neglectful in its treatment of him. In particular his feud with the "philological syndicate" was painful and damaging. His categorization of senior colleagues as "intellectual voluptuaries" who "philologize everything" and sacrifice judgment and selection to "the excess of dry analysis and fact-collecting"; his attacks on Harvard's President Charles W. Eliot for breaking down educational tradition in favor of humanitarian conceptions; his indictment of the study of literature as being "rather aimless and just a bit unmanly"; his demand that Ph.D. study, which he saw as an imitation of German scholarship, be rehabilitated so as to include a "right training in ideas"—in all these contentions Babbitt no doubt provoked the "super-professors" and gained the enmity of the academic establishment. At a crucial point in his life it was not quite certain that he would even be able to go on with his teaching. "I wonder how long," he writes to More in 1910, "Harvard will continue its present policy of giving me first-rate responsibility with second-rate recognition." One has a strong sense of his deepening isolation as a result of the "warfare of principles" to which he was committed: "Fighting a whole generation is not exactly a happy task." Edmund Wilson's remark that the intransigent ukases of Babbitt "strike us with a chill even more mortal than that of reason" is typical of the critical opinion which he had to confront. Today it is not unusual for the literary politicians of revolution to single him out as a "suzerain of [an] elite-university literature department." Yet, whatever the virulence of the attacks on him or the unpopularity of the principles for which he struggled, Babbitt did not weaken: "I should prefer never to get any recognition at all than to get it by flattering the enormous humanitarian illusions of the age."

When so many other teachers and critics were, as they are still, involved in propagating the gospel of progress and reform, Babbitt strived to submit all the important issues to "a perfectly pitiless dialectic." To this dialectic he gave a stylistic form not unlike that which he praised in Hippolyte Taine, "real virility of thought and expression." The style, like the man, reflected a growth in assurance, unfailing in its commitment to principles of order, discipline, control. Characteristically, Babbitt remained adamant against appeals from some of his followers to open his "circle of ideas" so that he would attract more sympathizers. "Smartness and journalistic over-emphasis" he refused, seeing these as constituents of the leveling process that he coupled with surrender to a "cheap contemporaneousness." "It is the critic's business," he declares, "to grapple with the age in which he lives and give it what he sees it needs."

One cannot appraise Babbitt's writings in chronological order. His books have a concentric design. They form an unbroken circle; and they become, intellectually, morally, and emotionally, a configuration, returning always to his central idea of life. One could as easily begin with *On Being Creative* (1932) as with *Literature and the American College* (1908). There is no pattern of development and inner changes in Babbitt's criticism; in this connection, More remarks: "He seems to have sprung up, like Minerva, fully grown and fully armed. No doubt he made vast additions to his knowledge and acquired by practice a deadly dexterity in wielding it, but there is something almost inhuman in the immobility of his central ideas." Babbitt's criticism as a whole announces, repeats, and returns to fundamental tenets. There is not really a clear line of demarcation between his essays and books—between his fugitive pieces (articles, reviews, review-essays) and his collections of essays. Throughout there is a concentrated and a recurrent insistence on, rather than an expanding movement of, criticism as "a discipline of ideas." Analytical argument forms the substance of and gives momentum to his criticism, delighting in repartee and written in a masculine, sometimes racy and aphoristic style. Protest and warning inform the intensity of his critical judgments and contemplations. Babbitt was inescapably aware of evil and the antithetic vices. "Poets and reformers need not waste time speculating about the *origin* of evil," he writes, "but they surely cannot be blind to the *fact* of evil." And though he is a critic and not a prophet, it is equally true that his criticism, as an exercise of judgment and a judgment of value, is prophetic in its insistent tone and its repetitive accent. His response to Rousseau and romanticism, not unlike Edmund Burke's response to Rousseau and the Jacobins, was in the nature of prophecy: the response of a critic's whole being, rational and emotional, but never abstract or scientific. Babbitt combines the critic's clarity of aim with the prophet's spiritual insight.

He was a brave man whose example must remind us that nothing else is worth having. Perhaps one of his most extraordinary characteristics is that he was a man without doubts. Some teachers confess, reproachfully, to themselves, or perhaps to their students or to their colleagues, doubts concerning the worth or the influence of their work. Some critics, and some great artists, come to see their writings as just so many words to be forgotten or to be preserved, in Babbitt's words, for "the throng of scholiasts and commentators whom Voltaire saw pressing about the outer gates of the Temple of Taste." These confessions may come out of humility, or exhaustion, or disappointment. But whatever their source, they stem from self-doubt. Feelings of meaninglessness are often the prelude to gestures of renunciation. For Babbitt such confessions would have constituted escapism and self-indulgent solace unworthy of and unwelcome to one who taught the Socratic, the humanistic, doctrine—"the discipline of a central standard"—and who affirmed Goethe's admonition that "anything that emancipates the spirit without a corresponding growth in self-mastery, is pernicious."

It could be said that Babbitt never lost his vision of the One, in the absence of which there is inevitably, as he declares, "a disquieting vagueness and lack of grip in dealing with particulars." While other teachers and critics and thinkers were questioning, even dismantling, the traditional values, and at the same time producing new abstractions or an avoidance of valuations, Babbitt admonished that it was urgent to create "that aristocracy of character and intelligence that is needed in a community like ours to take the place of an aristocracy of birth." He realized fully the difficulty of advocating the aristocratic principle at a time when "all the ideas which I know to be most vital for man have more and more declined." His stress on discerning and observing distinctions and on the selective "truths of the inner life" did not find favor in an age glorifying the gospels of progress and bigness and even promising to open "the gates of Eden." That he would neither substitute miscellaneous sympathies for firm principles of judgment nor view the human problem as merely a socio-economic problem—these were brave refusals which distinguished Babbitt from his contemporaries. The act of valuation, when dictated by prudence, courage, and honor, was for him an act that stamped not only the character of an individual but also that of society. He chose to fulfill unequivocally the function of the critic that Arnold had formulated: "Whoever sets himself to see things as they are will find himself one of a very small circle; but it is only by this small circle resolutely doing its own work that adequate ideas will ever get current at all."

Much as it is, it is not enough to say that he was our last great teacher-saint. "Oh, Babbitt," a Hindu exclaimed to More, "he is a holy man, a great saint!" That Babbitt's achievement is of the spirit is to underline an important quality of his thought. But we must be willing to go beyond even this to discover the source of his real importance: that his criticism is an expression of the spirit, its offshoot and concomitant, all the more to be admired for loyalty to "the permanent things" in a time of distraction and dissolution. Even this late in the season and in this most unpropitious of times, we may say straight out that Babbitt stands among the masters of modern American criticism. A reading of the following selections from his writings should corroborate such a claim and signal the reader to the neglected value and the ignored wisdom that reside in Babbitt's writings. What has prompted the editing of this book instances the kind of critical and humanistic opportunity that must be taken if we are to meet the violent conditions of change that are upon us, even more violent than they were when Babbitt was meeting them. *Irving Babbitt: Representative Writings*, it is hoped, will mark a just appreciation as well as the beginning of an act of reparation.

A Note on the Text

The sources of the texts reprinted in this book are specified in the headnote of each selection. Babbitt's own footnotes (and also those to my Introduction) are included in the section entitled Reference Notes, located at the back of the book, and are arranged according to the pagination. It seems to me that Babbitt's writings receive a more felicitous reading and direct critical response when they are unencumbered by interruptive apparatus of any kind. Both Babbitt's texts and footnotes are reproduced in their original form, with a few exceptions of detail; however, in order to achieve a measure of uniformity, I have italicized all titles of books referred to in the text. The capitalization, punctuation, and spelling are Babbitt's. In an unusually few cases I have corrected typographical errors. In a few cases, too, I have omitted transitional material within the texts when I have found it unnecessary to the particular purposes of this book. These omissions are indicated by asterisks (* * *). Brackets indicate my own few interpolations and translations, the responsibility for which is mine.

GEORGE A. PANICHAS

University of Maryland, College Park

PART I

OUTLOOK AND OVERVIEW

In this creedal statement Babbitt summarizes the principles of the New Humanism. He sets the tone of his indictment of the two main forms of naturalism: the scientific and utilitarian and the emotional. He also reveals his critical style and vision. In Baconian and Rousseauistic ideas he sees the radical sources, the errors, of a modern humanitarianism exalting the materialistic, especially in the assumption that man is naturally good. This assumption, Babbitt claims, undermines the humanistic tradition going back to ancient Greece. Standards that create human significance and a principle of unity that measures manifoldness and change surrender to vital impulse (élan vital). *The elimination of the will to refrain* (frein vital), *that is, the "veto power" or "inner check," leads to "free temperamental overflow" and denies the higher will, by which man is a moral agent. Babbitt insists upon moderation, common sense, and common decency, which he associates with a positive, critical humanism and, hence, with the spirit of the gentleman and the spirit of religion. In opposing the modern movement, Babbitt singles out Rousseau: "To debate Rousseau is really to debate the main issues of our contemporary life in literature, politics, education, and, above all, religion."* (From Spanish Character and Other Essays, ed. Frederick Manchester, Rachel Giese, and William F. Giese [Boston and New York: Houghton Mifflin Co., 1940], pp. 225-47, under title "What I Believe: Rousseau and Religion"; originally printed in the Forum 83 [1930]:80-87, as "What I Believe.")*

WHAT I BELIEVE

I

Rousseau is commonly accounted the most influential writer of the past two hundred years. Lord Acton, indeed, is reported to have said, with a touch of exaggeration, that "Rousseau produced more effect with his pen than Aristotle or Cicero or Saint Augustine or Saint Thomas Aquinas or any other man who ever lived." At all events this saying needs to be interpreted in the light of the saying of Madame de Staël that "Rousseau invented nothing but set everything on fire." His leading ideas were abundantly anticipated, especially in England. These ideas made their chief appeal to a middle class which, in the eighteenth century, was gaining rapidly in power and prestige, and has been dominant ever since.

The Rousseauistic outlook on life has also persisted, with many surface modifications, to be sure, but without any serious questioning on the part of most men of its underlying assumptions. To debate Rousseau is really to debate the main issues of our contemporary life in literature, politics, education, and, above all, religion. It is not surprising, therefore, that his reputation and writings have from the outset to the present day been a sort of international battleground. One cannot afford to be merely partisan in this strife, to be blind to Rousseau's numerous merits—for example, to all he did to quicken man's sense of the beauties of nature, especially wild nature. Neither should one forget that there is involved in all the strife a central issue toward which one must finally assume a clear-cut attitude.

Regarding this central issue—the source of the fundamental clash between Rousseauist and anti-Rousseauist—there has been and continues to be much confusion. A chief source of this confusion has been the fact that in Rousseau as in other great writers, and more than in most, there are elements that run counter to the main tendency. Rousseau has, for example, his rationalistic side. On the basis of this fact one professor of French has just set out to prove that, instead of being the arch-sentimentalist he has usually been taken to be, "the real Rousseau is at bottom a rationalist in his ethics, politics, and theology."

Again, there are utterances in Rousseau quite in line with traditional morality. Another American scholar has therefore set out to show that it is a mistake to make Rousseau responsible for a revolution in ethics. Still another of our scholars has managed to convince himself on similar lines that Rousseau is not primarily a primitivist in his *Discourse on Inequality*.

Most remarkable of all is a book that has just appeared, the author of which covers with contumely practically all his predecessors in this field on the ground that they have been blinded by partisanship, and promises to give us at last the true meaning of Rousseau. Yet this writer does not even cite the passage that, as Rousseau himself correctly tells us, gives the key to his major writings. It is to this passage that every interpreter of Rousseau who is not academic in the bad sense will give prominence: for the thesis it sums up has actually wrought mightily upon the world. It has thus wrought because it has behind it an imaginative and emotional drive not found behind other passages of Rousseau that might in themselves have served to correct it.

The passage to which I refer is one that occurs in Rousseau's account of the sudden vision that came to him by the roadside on a hot summer day in 1749 in the course of a walk from Paris to Vincennes. This vision has an importance for the main modern movement comparable to that of Saint Paul's vision on the road to Damascus for the future development of Christianity. Among the multitude of "truths" that flashed upon Rousseau in the sort of trance into which he was rapt at this moment, the truth of overshadowing importance was, in his own words, that "man is naturally good and that it is by our institutions alone that men become wicked."

The consequences that have flowed from this new "myth" of man's natural goodness have been almost incalculable. Its first effect was to discredit the theological view of human nature, with its insistence that man has fallen, not from Nature as Rousseau asserts, but from God, and that the chief virtue it behooves man to cultivate in this fallen state is humility. According to the Christian, the true opposition between good and evil is in the heart of the individual: the law of the spirit can scarcely prevail, he holds, over the law of the members without a greater or lesser degree of succor in the form of divine grace. The new dualism which Rousseau sets up—that between man naturally good and his institutions—has tended not only to substitute sociology for theology, but to discredit the older dualism in any form whatsoever.

Practically, the warfare of the Rousseauistic crusader has been even less against institutions than against those who control and administer them—kings and priests in the earlier stages of the movement, capitalists in our own day. "We are approaching," Rousseau declared, "the era of crises, and the age of revolutions." He not only made the prophecy but did more than any other one man to insure its fulfillment. There are conservative and even timid elements in his writings; but as a result of the superior imaginative appeal of the new dualism based on the myth of man's natural goodness, the rôle he has actually played has been that of arch-radical. In one of the best-balanced estimates that have appeared, the French critic Gustave Lanson, after doing justice to the various minor trends in Rousseau's work, sums up accurately its major influence: "It exasperates and inspires revolt and fires enthusiasms and irritates hatreds; it is the mother of violence, the source of all that is uncompromising; it launches the simple souls who give themselves up to its strange virtue upon the desperate quest of the absolute, an absolute to be realized now by anarchy and now by social despotism."

I have said that there has been in connection with this Rousseauistic influence a steady yielding of the theological to the sociological or, as it may also be termed, the humanitarian view of life. One should add that there enters into the total philosophy of humanitarianism an ingredient that antedates Rousseau and that may be defined as utilitarian. Utilitarianism already had its prophet in Francis Bacon. Very diverse elements enter into the writings of Bacon as into those of Rousseau, but, like those of Rousseau, they have a central drive: they always have encouraged and, one may safely say, always will encourage the substitution of a kingdom of man for the traditional Kingdom of God—the exaltation of material over spiritual "comfort," the glorification of man's increasing control over the forces of nature under the name of progress.

Rousseauist and Baconian, though often superficially at odds with one another, have co-operated in undermining, not merely religious tradition, but another tradition which in the Occident goes back finally, not to Judea, but to ancient Greece. This older tradition may be defined as humanistic. The goal of the humanist is poised and proportionate living. This he hopes to accomplish by observing the law of measure. Anyone who has bridged successfully the gap between this general precept and some specific emergency has to that extent achieved the fitting and the decorous. Decorum is supreme for the humanist even as humility takes precedence over all other virtues in the eyes of the Christian. Traditionally the idea of decorum has been associated, often with a considerable admixture of mere formalism, with the idea of the gentleman. Humanism and religion in their various forms have at times conflicted, but have more often been in alliance with one another. As Burke says in a well-known passage: "Nothing is more certain than that our manners, our civilization, and all the good things that are connected with manners and with civilization, have, in this European world of ours, depended for ages upon two principles; and were indeed the result of both combined; I mean the spirit of a gentleman and the spirit of religion."

II

All the points of view I have been distinguishing—Baconian, Rousseauist, Christian, humanistic—often mingle confusedly. From all the confusion, however, there finally emerges a clearcut issue—namely, whether humanitarianism, or, if one prefers, the utilitarian-sentimental movement, has supplied any effective equivalent for Burke's two principles. As for the "spirit of a gentleman," its decline is so obvious as scarcely to admit of argument. It has even been maintained that in America, the country in which the collapse of traditional standards has been most complete, the gentleman is at a positive disadvantage in the world of practical affairs; he is likely to get on more quickly if he assumes the "mucker pose." According to William James, usually taken to be the representative American philosopher, the very idea of the gentleman has about it something slightly satanic. "The prince of darkness," says James, "may be a gentleman, as we are told he is, but, whatever the God of earth and heaven is, he can surely be no gentleman."

As to the spirit of religion, though its decline has in my opinion been at least as great as that of the spirit of a gentleman, it is far from being so obvious. In any case, everything in our modern substitutes for religion—whether Baconian or Rousseauistic—will be found to converge upon the idea of service. The crucial question is whether one is safe in assuming that the immense machinery of power that has resulted from activity of the utilitarian type can be made, on anything like

present lines, to serve disinterested ends; whether it will not
rather minister to the egoistic aims either of national groups or
of individuals.

One's answer to this question will depend on one's view of
the Rousseauistic theory of brotherhood. It is at this point, if
anywhere, that the whole movement is pseudo-religious. I can
give only in barest outline the reasons for my own conviction
that it *is* pseudo-religious. It can be shown that the nature
from which man has fallen, according to Rousseau, does not
correspond to anything real, but is a projection of the idyllic
imagination. To assert that man in a state of nature, or some
similar state thus projected, is good, is to discredit the traditional controls in the actual world. Humility, conversion, decorum—all go by the board in favor of free temperamental
overflow. Does man thus emancipated exude spontaneously an
affection for his fellows that will be an effective counterpoise
to the sheer expansion of his egoistic impulses? If so, one may
safely side with all the altruists from the Third Earl of Shaftes-
bury to John Dewey. One may then assume that there has been
no vital omission in the passage from the service of God to the
service of man, from salvation by divine grace to salvation by
the grace of nature.

Unfortunately, the facts have persistently refused to conform to humanitarian theory. There has been an ever-growing
body of evidence from the eighteenth century to the Great War
that in the natural man, as he exists in the real world and not
in some romantic dreamland, the will to power is, on the whole,
more than a match for the will to service. To be sure, many
remain unconvinced by this evidence. Stubborn facts, it has
been rightly remarked, are as nothing compared with a stubborn theory. Altruistic theory is likely to prove peculiarly
stubborn, because, probably more than any other theory ever
conceived, it is flattering: it holds out the hope of the highest
spiritual benefits—for example, peace and fraternal union—
without any corresponding spiritual effort.

If we conclude that humanitarian service cannot take the
place of the spirit of religion and that of a gentleman—Burke's
"two principles"—what then? One should at least be able to
understand the point of view of those who simply reject the

modern movement and revert to a more or less purely traditionalist attitude. Dogmatic and revealed Christianity, they hold, has in it a supernatural element for which altruism is no equivalent. Religion of this type, they argue, alone availed to save the ancient world from a decadent naturalism; it alone can cope with a similar situation that confronts the world today.

But does it follow, because one's choice between the religious-humanistic and the utilitarian-sentimental view of life should, as I have said, be clear-cut, one is therefore forced to choose between being a pure traditionalist or a mere modernist? At bottom the issue involved is that of individualism. The Roman Catholic, the typical traditionalist, has in matters religious simply repudiated individualism. In this domain at least, he submits to an authority that is "anterior, superior, and exterior" to the individual. The opposite case is that of the man who has emancipated himself from outer authority in the name of the critical spirit (which will be found to be identical with the modern spirit), but has made use of his emancipation, not to work out standards, but to fall into sheer spiritual anarchy. Anyone, on the other hand, who worked out standards critically would be a sound individualist and at the same time a thoroughgoing modern. He would run the risk, to be sure, of antagonizing both traditionalists and modernists; of suffering, in short, the fate of Mr. Pickwick when he intervened between the two angry combatants. This hostility, at least so far as the traditionalist is concerned, would seem to be ill-advised. The true modern, as I am seeking to define him, is prepared to go no small distance with him in the defense of tradition.

At all events, anyone who seeks to deal in modern fashion—in other words, critically—with the religious problem, will be brought back at once to Rousseau. He will have to make his clear-cut choice, not between dogmatic and revealed religion, on the one hand, and mere modernism, on the other, but between a dualism that affirms a struggle between good and evil in the heart of the individual and a dualism which, like that of Rousseau, transfers the struggle to society.

Let us ask ourselves what it is the modern man has tended to lose with the decline of the older dualism. According to Mr.

Walter Lippmann, the belief the modern man has lost is "that there is an immortal essence presiding like a king over his appetites." This immortal essence of which Mr. Lippmann speaks is, judged experimentally and by its fruits, a higher will. But why leave the affirmation of such a will to the pure traditionalist? Why not affirm it first of all as a psychological fact, one of the immediate data of consciousness, a perception so primordial that, compared with it, the denial of man's moral freedom by the determinist is only a metaphysical dream? The way would thus be open for a swift flanking movement on the behaviorists and other naturalistic psychologists, who are to be accounted at present among the chief enemies of human nature.

This transcendent quality of will—which is the source of humility and is, at the same time, immediate and intuitive—has often been associated traditionally with the operation of God's will in the form of grace. For this higher immediacy, Rousseau—at least the Rousseau who has influenced the world—tended to substitute the lower immediacy of feeling, thus setting up a sort of sub-rational parody of grace. In order to make this substitution plausible, he—and, in his wake, the sentimentalists—have resorted to the usual arts of the sophist, chief among which are a juggling with half-truths and a tampering with general terms. For example, in their use of words like "virtue" and "conscience," they have eliminated more or less completely, in favor of vital impulse (*élan vital*), the equally vital principle of control (*frein vital*)—in short, the dualistic element that both religion and humanism require.

The half-truth that has been used to compromise religion in particular is that, though religion is in itself something quite distinct from emotion, it is in its ordinary manifestations very much mixed up with emotion. I give an example of this error in its latest and fashionable form. In a very learned and, in some respects, able book, the Reverend N. P. Williams seeks to show that Saint Augustine's experience of grace or, what amounts to the same thing, his love of God, was only a "sublimation" of his "lust." Saint Augustine was a very passionate man and his passionateness no doubt entered into his love of God. But if it could be shown that the love of God was in Saint Augustine or any other of the major saints merely emotion, sublimated or unsublimated, religion would be only the "illusion" that Freud himself has declared it to be. The psychoanalytical divine, who is, I am told, a fairly frequent type in England, is about the worst *mélange des genres* that has appeared even in the present age of confusion.

Another example of prevailing misapprehensions in this field, and that not merely from the point of view of dogma but of keen psychological observation, is the standard treatment of Rousseau's religion by P. M. Masson, a work which has been almost universally acclaimed by scholars and which has, as a matter of fact, distinguished merits as a historical investigation. M. Masson admits that this religion is "without redemption or repentance or sense of sin," and then proceeds to speak of Rousseau's "profound Christianity"!

Religion has suffered not only from the Rousseauist but also from the pseudo-scientist. If the Rousseauist gives to emotion a primacy that does not belong to it, the pseudo-scientist claims for physical science a hegemony to which it is not entitled. A science that has thus aspired out of its due place runs the risk of becoming not only a "wild Pallas from the brain" but, in connection with its use in war, "procuress to the Lords of Hell." Mr. Walter Lippmann seeks to persuade us in his *Preface to Morals* that if one becomes "disinterested" after the fashion of the scientific investigator, one will have the equivalent not only of "humanism" but of "high religion." Certain scientific investigators are busy in their laboratories at this very moment devising poison gases of formidable potency. What proof is there that, so far as the scientific type of "disinterestedness" is concerned, these gases will not be pressed into the service of the will to power? In seeking to base ethics on monistic postulates, Mr. Lippmann has simply revived the error of Spinoza, who himself revived the error of the Stoics. This error becomes not less but more dangerous when associated with the methods of science. The question involved is at all events that of the will and finally of dualism. One cannot insist too often that "the immortal essence presiding like a king over man's appetites" is transcendent—in other words, set above "nature," not only in Rousseau's sense, but also in the sense that is given to the term by the man of science.

This higher will is felt in its relation to the impressions and impulses and expansive desires of the natural man as a will to refrain. In the great traditional religions, notably in Christianity and Buddhism, the will to refrain has been pushed to the point of renunciation. The modern movement, on the other hand, has been marked since the eighteenth century and in some respects since the Renaissance by a growing discredit of the will to refrain. The very word "renunciation" has been rarely pronounced by those who have entered into the movement. The chief exception that occurs to one is Goethe (echoed at times by Carlyle). Anyone who thinks of the series of Goethe's love affairs prolonged into the seventies is scarcely likely to maintain that his *Entsagung* was of a very austere character even for the man of the world, not to speak of the saint.

III

One must admit that genuine renunciation was none too common even in the ages of faith. As for the typical modern, he is not only at an infinite remove from anything resembling renunciation, but is increasingly unable to accept the will to refrain or anything else on a basis of mere tradition and authority. Yet the failure to exercise the will to refrain in some form or degree means spiritual anarchy. A combination such as we are getting more and more at present of spiritual anarchy with an ever-increasing material efficiency—power without wisdom, as one is tempted to put it—is not likely to work either for the happiness of the individual or for the welfare of society. That the drift toward spiritual anarchy has been largely a result of the decline of dogmatic and revealed religion is scarcely open to question. It does not follow that the only hope of recovering spiritual discipline is in a return to this type of religion. Both naturalists and supernaturalists have been too prone to underestimate the value of the third possible attitude toward life, which I have defined as the humanistic.

The humanist exercises the will to refrain, but the end that he has in view is not the renunciation of the expansive desires but the subduing of them to the law of measure. The humanistic virtues—moderation, common sense, and common decency—though much more accessible than those of the saint, still go against the grain of the natural man—terribly against the grain, one is forced to conclude from a cool survey of the facts of history. Such, indeed, is the difficulty of getting men to practice even humanistic control that one is led, not necessarily to revive the dogma of original sin, but to suspect that the humanitarians, both Baconian and Rousseauistic, are hopelessly superficial in their treatment of the problem of evil. The social dualism they have set up tends in its ultimate development to substitute the class war for what Diderot termed in his denunciation of the older dualism the "civil war in the cave."

One reason that Rousseau gave for his abandonment of his five children was that he had been robbed by the rich of the wherewithal to feed them. The ease with which multitudes have been persuaded to follow Rousseau in this evasion of moral responsibility puts one on the track of a human trait that one may actually observe in oneself and others, and that gives some positive justification to the theological emphasis on the old Adam. This trait may be defined as spiritual indolence, a disinclination to oppose to one's expansive desires any will to refrain, and a naïve willingness to shift the blame on something or somebody else for the unpleasant consequences.

It is evident that in the eyes of anyone who believes in the existence in man of a higher will, with reference to which he may be a responsible moral agent, the characteristic modern malady is not plain and unvarnished materialism but sham spirituality. The remedy would seem to be in a reaffirmation in some form of the true dualism rather than in the merely cynical and "hard-boiled" attitude so prevalent nowadays among those who have become convinced of the final inanity of the humanitarian type of idealism. Joubert wrote over a century ago: "To all tender, ardent, and elevated natures, I say: Only Rousseau can detach you from religion, and only true religion can cure you of Rousseau." I have already made plain that in my judgment one may not only oppose Rousseau on human-

istic as well as religious grounds, but that, while making abundant use of the wisdom of the past, one may come at humanism
itself in a more positive and critical fashion than has been customary heretofore.

IV

I can scarcely hope, within the limits of an article, to make entirely clear what I mean by a positive and critical humanism.
This, to judge by certain current misunderstandings of my
position, is a feat I have been unable to accomplish in a series
of volumes. I may, however, touch briefly on a few of the main
issues. A consideration of Rousseau and his influence will be
found to converge on two main problems—the problem of the
will, of which I have already spoken, and, of lesser though still
major importance, the problem of the intellect. That Rousseau
is at the headwaters of an anti-intellectualist trend extending
down to James and Bergson and beyond is generally recognized. This trend is prefigured in his saying that "the man who
thinks is a depraved animal." At bottom the protest of this
type of anti-intellectualist is against the mechanizing of the
world by a scientific or pseudo-scientific rationalism. He seeks
to escape from mechanism by the pathway of romantic spontaneity. This means practically that he is ready to surrender to
the naturalistic flux in the hope of thus becoming "creative."
Unfortunately this surrender involves a sacrifice of the standards and the conscious control that are needed to give to creation genuine human significance.

It is above all in dealing with the problems of the intellect
and the will that I have sought to be positive and critical. As
against the Rousseauistic emotionalist, it seems to me imperative to re-establish the true dualism—that between vital impulse and vital control—and to this end to affirm the higher
will first of all as a psychological fact. The individual needs,
however, to go beyond this fact if he is to decide how far he is
to exercise control in any particular instance with a primary
view to his own happiness: in short, he needs standards. To
secure standards, at least critically, he cannot afford, like the
Rousseauist, to disparage the intellect. One needs to turn its

keen power of analysis to an entirely different order of experience from that envisaged by physical science.

To have standards means practically to have some principle of unity with which to measure mere manifoldness and change. There is a power in man, often termed imagination, that reaches out and seizes likenesses and analogies and so tends to establish unity. The unity thus apprehended needs, however, to be tested from the point of view of its reality by the analytical intellect—the power that discriminates—working not abstractly but on the actual data of experience. The fraternal union that the Rousseauist would establish among men on the basis of expansive emotion is found, when tested in this way, to involve an imaginative flight from the reality of both the human and the natural order, and so to exist only in dreamland. An inspection of all the facts of human experience, past and present, would seem to show that what unity a man may achieve either within himself or with his fellow men must be based primarily, not upon feeling, but upon an exercise of the higher will.

One's conception of the constant and unifying factor in life will appear in one's use of general terms. It is plain that the humanist and the Rousseauist clash radically in their definitions. As a result of his elimination of the dualistic element, the Rousseauist has, as I have remarked, set up a "virtue" that, in the eyes of the humanist, is not true virtue; and so likewise for such terms as "justice" and "liberty," and above all (at least in its application to man) "nature." If there is to be a reintegration of the dualistic element into these words, there would seem to be needed an art of inductive defining somewhat similar to that which Socrates brought to bear upon the sophists. It is precisely at this point that the keen discrimination of which I have spoken would have its fullest play. At all events one may say that the standards that result from the co-operation of the imagination and the analytical intellect, and that are reflected in one's definitions, are finally pressed by the humanist into the service of the higher will with a view to imposing a right direction upon the impulses and expansive desires of the natural man.

The humanist is rather distrustful of sudden conversions

and pistol-shot transformations of human nature. Hence his supreme emphasis on education. If the humanistic goal is to be attained, if the adult is to like and dislike the things he should—according to Plato, the ultimate aim of ethical endeavor—he must be trained in the appropriate habits almost from infancy. Occasional humanists may appear under present conditions, but if there is to be anything resembling a humanistic movement, the first stage would, as I have said, be that of Socratic definition; the second stage would be the coming together of a group of persons on the basis of this definition—the working out, in short, in the literal sense of that unjustly discredited word, of a convention; the third stage would almost inevitably be the attempt to make this convention effective through education.

V

The mention of education brings the whole discussion home to America. Our educators are more completely and more naïvely Rousseauistic than those of almost any other country. For example, there is an important survival of the religious-humanistic conception of education in France and Germany and, above all, England; whereas the assumption is all but universal among those who control our educational policies from the elementary grades to the university that anything that sets bounds to the free unfolding of the temperamental proclivities of the young, to their right of self-expression, as one may say, is outworn prejudice. Discipline, so far as it exists, is not of the humanistic or the religious type, but of the kind that one gets in training for a vocation or a specialty. The standards of a genuinely liberal education, as they have been understood, more or less from the time of Aristotle, are being progressively undermined by the utilitarians and the sentimentalists. If the Baconian-Rousseauistic formula is as unsound in certain of its postulates as I myself believe, we are in danger of witnessing in this country one of the great cultural tragedies of the ages.

Moreover Rousseauism not only dominates our education but has been eating into the very vitals of the Protestant religion. Practically, this means that Protestantism is ceasing to be a religion of the inner life and is becoming more and more a religion of "uplift." The result of the attempt to deal with evil socially rather than at its source in the individual, to substitute an outer for an inner control of appetite, has been a monstrous legalism, of which the Eighteenth Amendment is only the most notable example. Those Protestants who have allied themselves with an organization like the Anti-Saloon League have been violating one of the most necessary of Christian precepts—that which warns against confounding the things of God with the things of Caesar.

The multiplication of laws, attended by a growing lawlessness—the present situation in this country—is, as every student of history knows, a very sinister symptom. It may mean that our democratic experiment is, like similar experiments in the past, to end in a decadent imperialism. Nothing is farther from my thought than to suggest that we are on a fatal descending curve. I do not believe in any such fatality, and am in general skeptical of every possible philosophy of history—of the Spenglerian variety most of all. The all-important factor that the Spenglers are wont to overlook or deny in favor of collective tendencies is the moral choices of individuals. For example, the majority in the United States seems just now to be careless of the higher cultural values, to desire nothing better than a continuation of the present type of material prosperity based on the miracles of mass production. Individuals, however, are already standing aside from the majority and assuming a critical attitude toward its "ideals."

Whether this remnant will become sufficiently large to make itself felt in an important way, remains of course a question. At all events, there is an increasing number of persons in this country who can at least see the point of view of the rest of the world. This point of view may be defined as a curious blend of admiration for our efficiency and of disdain for our materialism. The foreigner is, however, far too prone to make America the universal scapegoat for the present domination of man by the machine.

Though the utilitarian-sentimental movement may have triumphed more completely in America than elsewhere, it has been extending its conquests over the whole of the Occident and is now invading the Orient. The issues it raises are, in short, international. That the peripheral merits of this movement are almost innumerable I should be the first to admit: indeed, almost everything in it seems plausible until one penetrates to its very center, and then one discovers an omission that unless corrected vitiates all the rest—the omission, namely, as I have been trying to show, of any reference to a higher will or power of control.

Without making any pretense to a prophetic rôle, I am yet willing to express the conviction that unless there is a recovery of the true dualism or, what amounts to the same thing, a reaffirmation of the truths of the inner life in some form—traditional or critical, religious or humanistic—civilization in any sense that has been attached to that term hitherto is threatened at its base. I speak of the interests of civilization, though my own prime objection to Rousseauism is that it is found finally not to make for the happiness of the individual.

Babbitt's emphasis on a definition of terms appears in this chapter from Rousseau and Romanticism. *In a chaotic era, and with words like "romantic" and "classic," confused usages need to be resisted. Romantic, for Babbitt, "violates the normal sequence of cause and effect in favor of adventure." Classical is ascribed to something "when it belongs to a high class or to the best class." Here Babbitt's historical orientation, insofar as he traces the main currents in his search for principles to oppose to naturalism, interacts with his critical discrimination as he examines the underlying ideas of romanticism. He notes that the classical spirit was cheapened in neoclassical times, especially in France. He strives to show why reason, as logic or as good sense, became superficial and thus oppressive to the imagination in the eighteenth century. He sees in all romanticism the attempt to extend "the law of thing." The warfare against romanticism can no more cease than can the classical warfare against sin. Babbitt has something to say about both aberrations. (From* Rousseau and Romanticism *[Boston and New York: Houghton Mifflin Co., 1919], pp. 1–31.)*

THE TERMS CLASSIC AND ROMANTIC

The words classic and romantic, we are often told, cannot be defined at all, and even if they could be defined, some would add, we should not be much profited. But this inability or unwillingness to define may itself turn out to be only one aspect of a movement that from Rousseau to Bergson has sought to discredit the analytical intellect—what Wordsworth calls "the false secondary power by which we multiply distinctions." However, those who are with Socrates rather than with Rousseau or Wordsworth in this matter, will insist on the importance of definition, especially in a chaotic era like the present; for nothing is more characteristic of such an era than its irresponsible use of general terms. Now to measure up to the Socratic standard, a definition must not be abstract and metaphysical, but experimental; it must not, that is, reflect our opinion of what a word should mean, but what it actually has meant. Mathematicians may be free at times to frame their own definitions, but in the case of words like classic and romantic, that have been used innumerable times, and used not in one but in many countries, such a method is inadmissible. One must keep one's eye on actual usage. One should indeed allow for a certain amount of freakishness in this usage. Beaumarchais, for example, makes classic synonymous with barbaric. One may disregard an occasional aberration of this kind, but if one can find only confusion and inconsistency in all the main uses of words like classic and romantic, the only procedure for those who speak or write in order to be understood is to banish the words from their vocabulary.

Now to define in a Socratic way two things are necessary: one must learn to see a common element in things that are apparently different and also to discriminate between things that are apparently similar. A Newton, to take the familiar instance of the former process, saw a common element in the fall of an apple and the motion of a planet; and one may perhaps without being a literary Newton discover a common element in all the main uses of the word romantic as well as in all the main uses of the word classic; though some of the things to which the word romantic in particular has been applied seem, it must be admitted, at least as far apart as the fall of an apple and the motion of a planet. The first step is to perceive the something that connects two or more of these things apparently so diverse, and then it may be found necessary to refer this unifying trait itself back to something still more general, and so on until we arrive, not indeed at anything absolute—the absolute will always elude us—but at what Goethe calls the original or underlying phenomenon (*Urphänomen*). A fruitful source of false definition is to take as primary in a more or less closely allied group of facts what is actually secondary—for example, to fix upon the return to the Middle Ages as the central fact in romanticism, whereas this return is only symptomatic; it is very far from being the original phenomenon. Confused and incomplete definitions of romanticism have indeed just that origin—they seek to put at the centre something that though romantic is not central but peripheral, and so the whole subject is thrown out of perspective.

My plan then is to determine to the best of my ability, in

connection with a brief historical survey, the common element in the various uses of the words classic and romantic; and then, having thus disposed of the similarities, to turn to the second part of the art of defining and deal, also historically, with the differences. For my subject is not romanticism in general, but only a particular type of romanticism, and this type of romanticism needs to be seen as a recoil, not from classicism in general, but from a particular type of classicism.

I

The word romantic when traced historically is found to go back to the old French *roman* of which still older forms are *romans* and *romant.* These and similar formations derive ultimately from the mediaeval Latin adverb *romanice. Roman* and like words meant originally the various vernaculars derived from Latin, just as the French still speak of these vernaculars as *les langues romanes;* and then the word *roman* came to be applied to tales written in the various vernaculars, especially in old French. Now with what features of these tales were people most struck? The reply to this question is found in a passage of a fifteenth-century Latin manuscript: "From the reading of certain romantics, that is, books of poetry composed in French on military deeds which are for the most part fictitious." Here the term romantic is applied to books that we should still call romantic and for the very same reason, namely, because of the predominance in these books of the element of fiction over reality.

In general a thing is romantic when, as Aristotle would say, it is wonderful rather than probable; in other words, when it violates the normal sequence of cause and effect in favor of adventure. Here is the fundamental contrast between the words classic and romantic which meets us at the outset and in some form or other persists in all the uses of the word down to the present day. A thing is romantic when it is strange, unexpected, intense, superlative, extreme, unique, etc. A thing is classical, on the other hand, when it is not unique, but representative of a class. In this sense medical men may speak correctly of a classic case of typhoid fever, or a classic case of hysteria. One is even justified in speaking of a classic example of romanticism. By an easy extension of meaning a thing is classical when it belongs to a high class or to the best class.

The type of romanticism referred to in the fifteenth-century manuscript was, it will be observed, the spontaneous product of the popular imagination of the Middle Ages. We may go further and say that the uncultivated human imagination in all times and places is romantic in the same way. It hungers for the thrilling and the marvellous and is, in short, incurably melodramatic. All students of the past know how, when the popular imagination is left free to work on actual historical characters and events, it quickly introduces into these characters and events the themes of universal folk-lore, and makes a ruthless sacrifice of reality to the love of melodramatic surprise. For example, the original nucleus of historical fact has almost disappeared in the lurid melodramatic tale *Les quatre fils Aymon,* which has continued, as presented in the *Bibliothèque Bleue,* to appeal to the French peasant down to our own times. Those who look with alarm on recent attacks upon romanticism should therefore be comforted. All children, nearly all women and the vast majority of men always have been, are and probably always will be romantic. This is true even of a classical period like the second half of the seventeenth century in France. Boileau is supposed to have killed the vogue of the interminable romances of the early seventeenth century which themselves continue the spirit of the mediaeval romances. But recent investigations have shown that the vogue of these romances continued until well on into the eighteenth century. They influenced the imagination of Rousseau, the great modern romancer.

But to return to the history of the word romantic. The first printed examples of the word in any modern tongue are, it would seem, to be found in English. The Oxford Dictionary cites the following from F. Greville's *Life of Sidney* (written before 1628, published in 1652): "Doe not his Arcadian romantics live after him?"—meaning apparently ideas or features suggestive of romance. Of extreme interest is the use of the word in Evelyn's *Diary* (3 August, 1654): "Were Sir Guy's grot improved as it might be, it were capable of being made a most romantic and pleasant place." The word is not only used in a favorable sense, but it is applied to nature; and it is this use of the word in connection with outer nature that French and German literatures are going to derive later from England. Among the early English uses of the word romantic may be noted: "There happened this extraordinary case—one of the most romantique that ever I heard in my life and could not have believed," etc. "Most other authors that I ever read either have wild romantic tales wherein they strain Love and Honor to that ridiculous height that it becomes burlesque," etc. The word becomes fairly common by the year 1700 and thousands of examples could be collected from English writers in the eighteenth century. Here are two early eighteenth-century instances:

> "The gentleman I am married to made love to me in rapture but it was the rapture of a Christian and a man of Honor, not a romantic hero or a whining coxcomb."

> Whether the charmer sinner it or saint it
> If folly grow romantick I must paint it.

The early French and German uses of the word romantic seem to derive from England. One important point is to be noted as to France. Before using the word *romantique* the French used the word *romanesque* in the sense of wild, unusual, adventurous—especially in matters of sentiment, and they have continued to employ *romanesque* alongside *romantique,* which is now practically used only of the romantic school. A great deal of confusion is thus avoided into which we fall in English from having only the one word romantic, which must do duty for both *romantique* and *romanesque.* An example of *romantique* is found in French as early as 1675; but the word owed its vogue practically to the anglomania that set in about the middle of the eighteenth century. The first very influential French example of the word is appropriately found in Rousseau in the *Fifth Promenade* (1777): "The shores of the Lake of Bienne are more wild and romantic than those of the Lake of Geneva." The word *romantique* was fashionable in France especially as applied to scenery from about the year 1785, but without any thought as yet of applying it to a literary school.

In Germany the word *romantisch* as an equivalent of the French *romanesque* and modern German *romanhaft*, appears at the end of the seventeenth century and plainly as a borrowing from the French. Heidigger, a Swiss, used it several times in his *Mythoscopia romantica*, an attack on romances and the wild and vain imaginings they engender. According to Heidigger the only resource against romanticism in this sense is religion. In Germany as in France the association of romantic with natural scenery comes from England, especially from the imitations and translations of Thomson's *Seasons*.

In the second half of the eighteenth century the increasingly favorable use of words like Gothic and enthusiastic as well as the emergence of words like sentimental and picturesque are among the symptoms of a new movement, and the fortunes of the word romantic were more or less bound up with this movement. Still, apart from its application to natural scenery, the word is as yet far from having acquired a favorable connotation if we are to believe an essay by John Foster on the "Application of the Epithet Romantic" (1805). Foster's point of view is not unlike that of Heidigger. Romantic, he says, had come to be used as a term of vague abuse, whereas it can be used rightly only of the ascendency of imagination over judgment, and is therefore synonymous with such words as wild, visionary, extravagant. "A man possessing so strong a judgment and so subordinate a fancy as Dean Swift would hardly have been made romantic . . . if he had studied all the books in Don Quixote's library." It is not, Foster admits, a sign of high endowment for a youth to be too coldly judicial, too deaf to the blandishments of imaginative illusion. Yet in general a man should strive to bring his imagination under the control of sound reason. But how is it possible thus to prevail against the deceits of fancy? Right knowing, he asserts very un-Socratically, is not enough to ensure right doing. At this point Foster changes from the tone of a literary essay to that of a sermon, and, maintaining a thesis somewhat similar to that of Pascal in the seventeenth century and Heidigger in the eighteenth, he concludes that a man's imagination will run away with his judgment or reason unless he have the aid of divine grace.

II

When Foster wrote his essay there was no question as yet in England of a romantic school. Before considering how the word came to be applied to a particular movement we need first to bring out more fully certain broad conflicts of tendency during the seventeenth and eighteenth centuries, conflicts that are not sufficiently revealed by the occasional uses during this period of the word romantic. In the contrast Foster established between judgment and imagination he is merely following a long series of neo-classical critics and this contrast not only seemed to him and these critics, but still seems to many, the essential contrast between classicism and romanticism. We shall be helped in understanding how judgment (or reason) and imagination came thus to be sharply contrasted if we consider briefly the changes in the meaning of the word wit during the neo-classical period, and also if we recollect that the contrast between judgment and imagination is closely related to the contrast the French are so fond of establishing between the general sense (*le sens commun*) and the private sense or sense of the individual (*le sens propre*).

In the sixteenth century prime emphasis was put not upon common sense, but upon wit or conceit or ingenuity (in the sense of quickness of imagination). The typical Elizabethan strove to excel less by judgment than by invention, by "high-flying liberty of conceit"; like Falstaff he would have a brain "apprehensive, quick, forgetive, full of nimble, fiery, and delectable shapes." Wit at this time, it should be remembered, was synonymous not only with imagination but with intellect (in opposition to will). The result of the worship of wit in this twofold sense was a sort of intellectual romanticism. Though its origins are no doubt mediaeval, it differs from the ordinary romanticism of the Middle Ages to which I have already referred in being thus concerned with thought rather than with action. Towards the end of the Renaissance and in the early seventeenth century especially, people were ready to pursue the strange and surprising thought even at the risk of getting too far away from the workings of the normal mind. Hence the "points" and "conceits" that spread, as Lowell put it, like a "cutaneous eruption" over the face of Europe; hence the Gongorists, and Cultists, the Marinists and Euphuists, the *précieux* and the "metaphysical" poets. And then came the inevitable swing away from all this fantasticality towards common sense. A demand arose for something that was less rare and "precious" and more representative.

This struggle between the general sense and the sense of the individual stands out with special clearness in France. A model was gradually worked out by aid of the classics, especially the Latin classics, as to what man should be. Those who were in the main movement of the time elaborated a great convention, that is they *came together* about certain things. They condemned in the name of their convention those who were too indulgent of their private sense, in other words, too eccentric in their imaginings. A Théophile, for example, fell into disesteem for refusing to restrain his imagination, for asserting the type of "spontaneity" that would have won him favor in any romantic period.

The swing away from intellectual romanticism can also be traced in the changes that took place in the meaning of the word wit in both France and England. One of the main tasks of the French critics of the seventeenth century and of English critics, largely under the lead of the French, was to distinguish between true and false wit. The work that would have been complimented a little earlier as "witty" and "conceited" is now censured as fantastic and far-fetched, as lacking in judicial control over the imagination, and therefore in general appeal. The movement away from the sense of the individual towards common sense goes on steadily from the time of Malherbe to that of Boileau. Balzac attacks Ronsard for his individualistic excess, especially for his audacity in inventing words without reference to usage. Balzac himself is attacked by Boileau for his affectation, for his straining to say things differently from other people. In so far his wit was not true but false. La Bruyère, in substantial accord with Boileau, defines false wit as wit which is lacking in good sense and judgment and "in which the imagination has too large a share."

What the metaphysical poets in England understood by wit, according to Dr. Johnson, was the pursuit of their thoughts to their last ramifications, and in this pursuit of the singular and the novel they lost the "grandeur of generality." This imaginative quest of rarity led to the same recoil as in France, to a demand for common sense and judgment. The opposite extreme from the metaphysical excess is reached when the element of invention is eliminated entirely from wit and it is reduced, as it is by Pope, to rendering happily the general sense—

What oft was thought but ne'er so well expressed.

Dr. Johnson says that the decisive change in the meaning of the word wit took place about the time of Cowley. Important evidence of this change and also of the new tendency to depreciate the imagination is also found in certain passages of Hobbes. Hobbes identifies the imagination with the memory of outer images and so looks on it as "decaying sense." "They who observe similitudes," he remarks elsewhere, making a distinction that was to be developed by Locke and accepted by Addison, "in case they be such as are but rarely observed by others are said to have a good wit; by which, in this occasion, is meant a good fancy" (wit has here the older meaning). "But they who distinguish and observe differences," he continues, "are said to have a good judgment. Fancy without the help of judgment is not worthy of commendation, whereas judgment is commended for itself without the help of fancy. Indeed without steadiness and direction to some end, a great fancy is one kind of madness." "Judgment without fancy," he concludes, "is wit" (this anticipates the extreme neo-classical use of the word wit), "but fancy without judgment, not."

Dryden betrays the influence of Hobbes when he says of the period of incubation of his *Rival Ladies*: "Fancy was yet in its first work, moving the sleeping images of things towards the light, there to be distinguished and either chosen or rejected by judgment." Fancy or imagination (the words were still synonymous), as conceived by the English neo-classicists, often shows a strange vivacity for a faculty that is after all only "decaying sense." "Fancy without judgment," says Dryden, "is a hot-mouthed jade without a curb." "Fancy," writes Rymer in a similar vein, "leaps and frisks, and away she's gone; whilst reason rattles the chain and follows after." The following lines of Mulgrave are typical of the neo-classical notion of the relation between fancy and judgment:

> As all is dullness when the Fancy's bad,
> So without Judgment, Fancy is but mad.
> Reason is that substantial, useful part
> Which gains the Head, while t'other wins the Heart.

The opposition established by the neo-classicist in passages of this kind is too mechanical. Fancy and judgment do not seem to coöperate but to war with one another. In case of doubt the neo-classicist is always ready to sacrifice fancy to the "substantial, useful part," and so he seems too negative and cool and prosaic in his reason, and this is because his reason is so largely a protest against a previous romantic excess. What had been considered genius in the time of the "metaphysicals" had too often turned out to be only oddity. With this warning before them men kept their eyes fixed very closely on the model of normal human nature that had been set up, and imitated it very literally and timorously. A man was haunted by the fear that he might be "monstrous," and so, as Rymer put it, "satisfy nobody's maggot but his own." Correctness thus became a sort of tyranny. We suffer to the present day from this neo-classical failure to work out a sound conception of the imagination in its relation to good sense. Because the neo-classicist held the imagination lightly as compared with good sense the romantic rebels were led to hold good sense lightly as compared with imagination. The romantic view in short is too much the neo-classical view turned upside down; and, as Sainte-Beuve says, nothing resembles a hollow so much as a swelling.

III

Because the classicism against which romanticism rebelled was inadequate it does not follow that every type of classicism suffers from a similar inadequacy. The great movement away from imaginative unrestraint towards regularity and good sense took place in the main under French auspices. In general the French have been the chief exponents of the classic spirit in modern times. They themselves feel this so strongly that a certain group in France has of late years inclined to use interchangeably the words classicist and nationalist. But this is a grave confusion, for if the classic spirit is anything at all it is in its essence not local and national, but universal and human. To be sure, any particular manifestation of classicism will of necessity contain elements that are less universal, elements that reflect merely a certain person or persons, or a certain age and country. This is a truth that we scarcely need to have preached to us; for with the growth of the historical method we have come to fix our attention almost exclusively on these local and relative elements. The complete critic will accept the historical method but be on his guard against its excess. He will see an element in man that is set above the local and the relative; he will learn to detect this abiding element through all the flux of circumstance; in Platonic language, he will perceive the One in the Many.

Formerly, it must be admitted, critics were not historical enough. They took to be of the essence of classicism what was merely its local coloring, especially the coloring it received from the French of the seventeenth century. If we wish to distinguish between essence and accident in the classic spirit we must get behind the French of the seventeenth century, behind the Italians of the sixteenth century who laid the foundations of neo-classical theory, behind the Romans who were the immediate models of most neo-classicists, to the source of classicism in Greece. Even in Greece the classic spirit is very much implicated in the local and the relative, yet in the life of no other people perhaps does what is universal in man shine forth more clearly from what is only local and relative. We still need, therefore, to return to Greece, not merely for the best practice, but for the best theory of classicism; for this is still found in spite of all its obscurities and incompleteness in the *Poetics* of Aristotle. If we have recourse to this treatise, however, it must be on condition that we do not, like the critics of the Renaissance, deal with it in an abstract and dogmatic way (the form of the treatise it must be confessed gave them no slight encouragement), but in a spirit akin to Aristotle's own as revealed in the total body of his writings—a spirit that is at its best positive and experimental.

Aristotle not only deals positively and experimentally with the natural order and with man so far as he is a part of this order, but he deals in a similar fashion with a side of man that the modern positivist often overlooks. Like all the great Greeks Aristotle recognizes that man is the creature of two laws: he has an ordinary or natural self of impulse and desire and a human self that is known practically as a power of control over impulse and desire. If man is to become human he must not let impulse and desire run wild, but must oppose to everything excessive in his ordinary self, whether in thought or deed or emotion, the law of measure. This insistence on restraint and proportion is rightly taken to be of the essence not merely of the Greek spirit but of the classical spirit in general. The norm or standard that is to set bounds to the ordinary self is got at by different types of classicists in different ways and described variously: for example, as the human law, or the better self, or reason (a word to be discussed more fully later), or nature. Thus when Boileau says, "Let nature be your only study," he does not mean outer nature, nor again the nature of this or that individual, but representative human nature. Having decided what is normal either for man or some particular class of men the classicist takes this normal "nature" for his model and proceeds to imitate it. Whatever accords with the model he has thus set up he pronounces natural or probable, whatever on the other hand departs too far from what he conceives to be the normal type or the normal sequence of cause and effect he holds to be "improbable" and unnatural or even, if it attains an extreme of abnormality, "monstrous." Whatever in conduct or character is duly restrained and proportionate with reference to the model is said to observe decorum. Probability and decorum are identical in some of their aspects and closely related in all. To recapitulate, a general nature, a core of normal experience, is affirmed by all classicists. From this central affirmation derives the doctrine of imitation, and from imitation in turn the doctrines of probability and decorum.

But though all classicists are alike in insisting on nature, imitation, probability and decorum, they differ widely, as I have already intimated, in what they understand by these terms. Let us consider first what Aristotle and the Greeks understand by them. The first point to observe is that according to Aristotle one is to get his general nature not on authority or second hand, but is to disengage it directly for himself from the jumble of particulars that he has before his eyes. He is not, says Aristotle, to imitate things as they are, but as they ought to be. Thus conceived imitation is a creative act. Through all the welter of the actual one penetrates to the real and so succeeds without ceasing to be individual in suggesting the universal. Poetry that is imitative in this sense is, according to Aristotle, more "serious" and "philosophical" than history. History deals merely with what has happened, whereas poetry deals with what may happen according to probability or necessity. Poetry, that is, does not portray life literally but extricates the deeper or ideal truth from the flux of circumstance. One may add with Sydney that if poetry is thus superior to history in being more serious and philosophical it resembles history and is superior to philosophy in being concrete.

The One that the great poet or artist perceives in the Many and that gives to his work its high seriousness is not a fixed absolute. In general the model that the highly serious man (ὁ σπουδαῖος) imitates and that keeps his ordinary self within the bounds of decorum is not to be taken as anything finite, as anything that can be formulated once for all. This point is important for on it hinges every right distinction not merely between the classic and the romantic, but between the classic and the pseudo-classic. Romanticism has claimed for itself a monopoly of imagination and infinitude, but on closer examination, as I hope to show later, this claim, at least so far as genuine classicism is concerned, will be found to be quite unjustified. For the present it is enough to say that true classicism does not rest on the observance of rules or the imitation of models but on an immediate insight into the universal. Aristotle is especially admirable in the account he gives of this insight and of the way it may manifest itself in art and literature. One may be rightly imitative, he says, and so have access to a superior truth and give others access to it only by being a master of illusion. Though the great poet "breathes immortal air," though he sees behind the shows of sense a world of more abiding relationships, he can convey his vision not directly but only imaginatively. Aristotle, one should observe, does not establish any hard and fast opposition between judgment and imagination, an opposition that pervades not only the neo-classical movement but also the romantic revolt from it. He simply affirms a supersensuous order which one can perceive only with the help of fiction. The best art, says Goethe in the true spirit of Aristotle, gives us the "illusion of a higher reality." This has the advantage of being experimental. It is merely a statement of what one feels in the presence of a great painting, let us say, or in reading a great poem.

IV

After this attempt to define briefly with the help of the Greeks the classical spirit in its essence we should be prepared to understand more clearly the way in which this spirit was modi-fied in neo-classical times, especially in France. The first thing that strikes one about the classicism of this period is that it does not rest on immediate perception like that of the Greeks but on outer authority. The merely dogmatic and traditional classicist gave a somewhat un-Greek meaning to the doctrines of nature and imitation. Why imitate nature directly, said Scaliger, when we have in Virgil a second nature? Imitation thus came to mean the imitation of certain outer models and the following of rules based on these models. Now it is well that one who aims at excellence in any field should begin by a thorough assimilation of the achievements of his great prede-cessors in this field. Unfortunately the neo-classical theorist tended to impose a multitude of precepts that were based on what was external rather than on what was vital in the prac-tice of his models. In so far the lesson of form that the great ancients can always teach any one who approaches them in the right spirit degenerated into formalism. This formalistic turn given to the doctrine of imitation was felt from the outset to be a menace to originality; to be incompatible, and everything hinges at last on this point, with the spontaneity of the imagi-nation. There was an important reaction headed by men like

Boileau, within the neo-classical movement itself, against the oppression of the intuitive side of human nature by mere dogma and authority, above all against the notion that "regularity" is in itself any guarantee of literary excellence. A school of rules was succeeded by a school of taste. Yet even to the end the neo-classicist was too prone to reject as unnatural or even monstrous everything that did not fit into one of the traditional pigeon-holes. One must grant, indeed, that much noble work was achieved under the neo-classical dispensation, work that shows a genuine insight into the universal, but it is none the less evident that the view of the imagination held during this period has a formalistic taint.

This taint in neo-classicism is due not merely to its dogmatic and mechanical way of dealing with the doctrine of imitation but also to the fact that it had to reconcile classical with Christian dogma; and the two antiquities, classical and Christian, if interpreted vitally and in the spirit, were in many respects divergent and in some respects contradictory. The general outcome of the attempts at reconciliation made by the literary casuists of Italy and France was that Christianity should have a monopoly of truth and classicism a monopoly of fiction. For the true classicist, it will be remembered, the two things are inseparable—he gets at his truth through a veil of fiction. Many of the neo-classicists came to conceive of art as many romanticists were to conceive of it later as a sort of irresponsible game or play, but they were, it must be confessed, very inferior to the romanticists in the spontaneity of their fiction. They went for this fiction as for everything else to the models, and this meant in practice that they employed the pagan myths, not as imaginative symbols of a higher reality— it is still possible to employ them in that way—but merely in Boileau's phrase as "traditional ornaments" (*ornements reçus*). The neo-classicist to be sure might so employ his "fiction" as to inculcate a moral; in that case he is only too likely to give us instead of the living symbol, dead allegory; instead of high seriousness, its caricature, didacticism. The traditional stock of fiction became at last so intolerably trite as to be rejected even by some of the late neo-classicists. "The rejection and contempt of fiction," said Dr. Johnson (who indulged in it himself on occasion) "is rational and manly." But to reject fiction in the larger sense is to miss the true driving power in human nature—the imagination. Before concluding, however, that Dr. Johnson had no notion of the rôle of the imagination one should read his attack on the theory of the three unities which was later to be turned to account by the romanticists.

Now the three unities may be defended on an entirely legitimate ground—on the ground namely that they make for concentration, a prime virtue in the drama; but the grounds on which they were actually imposed on the drama, especially in connection with the Quarrel of the Cid, illustrate the corruption of another main classical doctrine, that of probability or verisimilitude. In his dealings with probability as in his dealings with imitation, the neo-classical formalist did not allow sufficiently for the element of illusion. What he required from the drama in the name of probability was not the "illusion of a high reality," but strict logic or even literal deception. He was not capable of a poetic faith, not willing to suspend his disbelief on passing from the world of ordinary fact to the world of artistic creation. Goethe was thinking especially of the neo-classical French when he said: "As for the French, they will always be arrested by their reason. They do not recognize that the imagination has its own laws which are and always must be problematic for the reason."

It was also largely under French influence that the doctrine of decorum, which touches probability at many points, was turned aside from its true meaning. Decorum is in a way the peculiar doctrine of the classicist, is in Milton's phrase "the grand masterpiece to observe." The doctrines of the universal and the imitation of the universal go deeper indeed than decorum, so much deeper that they are shared by classicism with religion. The man who aspires to live religiously must no less than the humanist look to some model set above his ordinary self and imitate it. But though the classicist at his best meditates, he does not, like the seeker after religious perfection, see in meditation an end in itself but rather a support for the mediatory virtues, the virtues of the man who would live to the best advantage in this world rather than renounce it; and these virtues may be said to be summed up in decorum. For the best type of Greek humanist, a Sophocles let us say, decorum was a vital and immediate thing. But there enters into decorum even from the time of the Alexandrian Greeks, and still more into French neo-classical decorum, a marked element of artificiality. The all-roundness and fine symmetry, the poise and dignity that come from working within the bounds of the human law, were taken to be the privilege not of man in general but of a special social class. Take for instance verbal decorum: the French neo-classicists assumed that if the speech of poetry is to be noble and highly serious it must coincide with the speech of the aristocracy. As Nisard puts it, they confused nobility of language with the language of the nobility. Decorum was thus more or less merged with etiquette, so that the standards of the stage and of literature in general came to coincide, as Rousseau complains, with those of the drawing-room. More than anything else this narrowing of decorum marks the decline from the classic to the pseudo-classic, from form to formalism.

While condemning pseudo-decorum one should remember that even a Greek would have seen something paradoxical in a poem like Goethe's *Hermann und Dorothea* and its attempt to invest with epic grandeur the affairs of villagers and peasants. After all, dignity and elevation and especially the opportunity for important action, which is the point on which the classicist puts prime emphasis, are normally though not invariably associated with a high rather than with a mean social estate. In general one should insist that the decorum worked out under French auspices was far from being merely artificial. The French gentleman (*honnête homme*) of the seventeenth century often showed a moderation and freedom from over-emphasis, an exquisite tact and urbanity that did not fall too far short of his immediate model, Horace, and related him to the all-round man of the Greeks (καλὸς κἀγαθός). To be sure an ascetic Christian like Pascal sees in decorum a disguise of one's ordinary self rather than a real curb upon it, and feels that the gap is not sufficiently wide between even the best type of the man of the world and the mere worldling. One needs, however, to be very austere to disdain the art of living that has been fostered by decorum from the Greeks down. Something of this art

of living survives even in a Chesterfield, who falls far short of
the best type of French gentleman and reminds one very remotely indeed of a Pericles. Chesterfield's half-jesting definition of decorum as the art of combining the useful appearances of virtue with the solid satisfactions of vice points the
way to its ultimate corruption. Talleyrand, who marks perhaps
this last stage, was defined by Napoleon as "a silk stocking
filled with mud." In some of its late exemplars decorum had
actually become, as Rousseau complains, the "mask of hypocrisy" and the "varnish of vice."

One should not however, like Rousseau and the romanticists, judge of decorum by what it degenerated into. Every
doctrine of genuine worth is disciplinary and men in the mass
do not desire discipline. "Most men," says Aristotle, "would
rather live in a disorderly than in a sober manner." But most
men do not admit any such preference—that would be crude
and inartistic. They incline rather to substitute for the reality
of discipline some art of going through the motions. Every
great doctrine is thus in constant peril of passing over into
some hollow semblance or even, it may be, into some mere
caricature of itself. When one wishes therefore to determine
the nature of decorum one should think of a Milton, let us say,
and not of a Talleyrand or even of a Chesterfield.

Milton imitated the models, like any other neo-classicist,
but his imitation was not, in Joubert's phrase, that of one book
by another book, but of one soul by another soul. His decorum
is therefore imaginative; and it is the privilege of the imagination to give the sense of spaciousness and infinitude. On the
other hand, the unimaginative way in which many of the neo-
classicists held their main tenets—nature, imitation, probability, decorum—narrowed unduly the scope of the human
spirit and appeared to close the gates of the future. "Art and
diligence have now done their best," says Dr. Johnson of the
versification of Pope, "and what shall be added will be the
effort of tedious toil and needless curiosity." Nothing is more
perilous than thus to seem to confine man in some pinfold;
there is something in him that refuses to acquiesce in any position as final; he is in Nietzsche's phrase the being who must
always surpass himself. The attempt to oppose external and

mechanical barriers to the freedom of the spirit will create in the long run an atmosphere of stuffiness and smugness, and nothing is more intolerable than smugness. Men were guillotined in the French Revolution, as Bagehot suggests, simply because either they or their ancestors had been smug. Inert acceptance of tradition and routine will be met sooner or later by the cry of Faust: *Hinaus ins Freie!* [Out into freedom!].

Before considering the value of the method chosen by Rousseau and the romanticists for breaking up the "tiresome old heavens" and escaping from smugness and stuffiness, one should note that the lack of originality and genius which they lamented in the eighteenth century—especially in that part of it known as the Enlightenment—was not due entirely to pseudo-classic formalism. At least two other main currents entered into the Enlightenment: first the empirical and utilitarian current that goes back to Francis Bacon, and some would say to Roger Bacon; and secondly the rationalistic current that goes back to Descartes. English empiricism gained international vogue in the philosophy of Locke, and Locke denies any supersensuous element in human nature to which one may have access with the aid of the imagination or in any other way. Locke's method of precise naturalistic observation is in itself legitimate; for man is plainly subject to the natural law. What is not truly empirical is to bring the whole of human nature under this law. One can do this only by piecing out precise observation and experiment with dogmatic rationalism. One side of Locke may therefore be properly associated with the father of modern rationalists, Descartes. The attempt of the rationalist to lock up life in some set of formulae produces in the imaginative man a feeling of oppression. He gasps for light and air. The very tracing of cause and effect and in general the use of the analytical faculties—and this is to fly to the opposite extreme—came to be condemned by the romanticists as inimical to the imagination. Not only do they make endless attacks on Locke, but at times they assail even Newton for having mechanized life, though Newton's comparison of himself to a child picking up pebbles on the seashore would seem to show that he had experienced "the feeling infinite."

The elaboration of science into a closed system with the

aid of logic and pure mathematics is as a matter of fact to be associated with Descartes rather than with Newton. Neither Newton nor Descartes, one scarcely needs add, wished to subject man entirely to the natural law and the nexus of physical causes; they were not in short determinists. Yet the superficial rationalism of the Enlightenment was in the main of Cartesian origin. This Cartesian influence ramifies in so many directions and is related at so many points to the literary movement, and there has been so much confusion about this relationship, that we need to pause here to make a few distinctions.

Perhaps what most strikes one in the philosophy of Descartes is its faith in logic and abstract reasoning and the closely allied processes of mathematical demonstration. Anything that is not susceptible of clear proof in this logical and almost mathematical sense is to be rejected. Now this Cartesian notion of clearness is fatal to a true classicism. The higher reality, the true classicist maintains, cannot be thus demonstrated; it can only be grasped, and then never completely, through a veil of imaginative illusion. Boileau is reported to have said that Descartes had cut the throat of poetry; and this charge is justified in so far as the Cartesian requires from poetry a merely logical clearness. This conception of clearness was also a menace to the classicism of the seventeenth century which rested in the final analysis not on logic but on tradition. This appeared very clearly in the early phases of the quarrel between ancients and moderns when literary Cartesians like Perrault and Fontenelle attacked classical dogma in the name of reason. In fact one may ask if any doctrine has ever appeared so fatal to every form of tradition—not merely literary but also religious and political—as Cartesianism. The rationalist of the eighteenth century was for dismissing as "prejudice" everything that could not give a clear account of itself in the Cartesian sense. This riot of abstract reasoning (*la raison raisonnante*) that prepared the way for the Revolution has been identified by Taine and others with the classic spirit. A more vicious confusion has seldom gained currency in criticism. It is true that the French have mixed a great deal of logic with their conception of the classic spirit, but that is because they have mixed a great deal of logic with everything. I have already mentioned their tendency to substitute a logical for an imaginative verisimilitude; and strenuously logical classicists may be found in France from Chapelain to Brunetière. Yet the distinction that should keep us from confusing mere logic with the classic spirit was made by a Frenchman who was himself violently logical and also a great geometrician—Pascal. One should keep distinct, says Pascal, the *esprit de géométrie* and the *esprit de finesse*. The *esprit de finesse* is not, like the *esprit de géométrie,* abstract, but very concrete. So far as a man possesses the *esprit de finesse* he is enabled to judge correctly of the ordinary facts of life and of the relationships between man and man. But these judgments rest upon such a multitude of delicate perceptions that he is frequently unable to account for them logically. It is to intuitive good sense and not to the *esprit de géométrie* that the gentleman (*honnête homme*) of the neo-classical period owed his fine tact. Pascal himself finally took a stand against reason as understood both by the Cartesian and by the man of the world. Unaided reason he held is unable to prevail against the deceits of the imagination; it needs the support of intuition—an intuition that he identifies with grace, thus making it inseparable from the most austere form of Christianity. The "heart," he says, and this is the name he gives to intuition, "has reasons of which the reason knows nothing." A Plato or an Aristotle would not have understood this divorce between reason and intuition.

Pascal seems to get his insight only by flouting ordinary good sense. He identifies this insight with a type of theological dogma of which good sense was determined to be rid; and so it tended to get rid of the insight along with the dogma. Classical dogma also seemed at times to be in opposition to the intuitive good sense of the man of the world. The man of the world therefore often inclined to assail both the classical and the Christian tradition in the name of good sense, just as the Cartesian inclined to assail these traditions in the name of abstract reason. Perhaps the best exponent of anti-traditional good sense in the seventeenth century was Molière. He vindicated nature, and by nature he still meant in the main normal human nature, from arbitrary constraints of every kind whether imposed by an ascetic Christianity or by a narrow and pedantic classicism. Unfortunately Molière is too much on the side of the opposition. He does not seem to put his good sense into the service of some positive insight of his own. Good sense may be of many degrees according to the order of facts of which it has a correct perception. The order of facts in human nature that Molière's good sense perceived is not the highest and so this good sense appears at times too ready to justify the bourgeois against the man who has less timid and conventional views. So at least Rousseau thought when he made his famous attack on Molière. Rousseau assailed Molière in the name of instinct as Pascal would have assailed him in the name of insight, and fought sense with sensibility. The hostility of Rousseau to Molière, according to M. Faguet, is that of a romantic Bohemian to a philistine of genius. One hesitates to call Molière a philistine, but one may at least grant M. Faguet that Molière's good sense is not always sufficiently inspired.

I have been trying to build up a background that will make clear why the reason of the eighteenth century (whether we understand by reason logic or good sense) had come to be superficial and therefore oppressive to the imagination. It is only with reference to this "reason" that one can understand the romantic revolt. But neo-classical reason itself can be understood only with reference to its background—as a recoil namely from a previous romantic excess. This excess was manifested not only in the intellectual romanticism of which I have already spoken, but in the cult of the romantic deed that had flourished in the Middle Ages. This cult and the literature that reflected it continued to appeal, even to the cultivated, well on into the neo-classical period. It was therefore felt necessary to frame a definition of reason that should be a rebuke to the extravagance and improbability of the mediaeval romances. When men became conscious in the eighteenth century of the neo-classical meagerness on the imaginative side they began to look back with a certain envy to the free efflorescence of fiction in the Middle Ages. They began to ask themselves with Hurd whether the reason and correctness they had won were worth the sacrifice of a "world of fine fabling." We must not, however, like Heine and many others, look on the romantic movement as merely a return to the Middle Ages. We have seen that the men of the Middle Ages themselves understood by romance not simply their own kind of speech and writing in contrast with what was written in Latin, but a kind of writing in which the pursuit of strangeness and adventure predominated. This pursuit of strangeness and adventure will be found to predominate in all types of romanticism. The type of romanticism, however, which came in towards the end of the eighteenth century did not, even when professedly mediaeval, simply revert to the older types. It was primarily not a romanticism of thought or of action, the types we have encountered thus far, but a romanticism of feeling. The beginnings of this emotional romanticism antedate considerably the application of the word romantic to a particular literary school* * *

This essay, which marked Babbitt's first appearance in print, contains the seeds of all his thinking. It underlines his view of education, which uncompromisingly indicts the retreat from the classics and the increasing reliance on German research methods. In the disintegration, which he couples with "an epidemic of pedantry" and with "the cheap and noisy tendencies of the passing hour," Babbitt sees the decline of the classical spirit, epitomized by Hellenism. The study of the classics now gives way to the study of decadent contemporary literature. The emphasis on specialization leads to a loss of restraint and proportion, with which a formative and salutary classicism is identified. The man of literal fact defeats the man of general fact; philological minutiae, the "dead-weight of information," attain primacy over the relevance of classical literature, particularly as it fuses reason and imagination and illustrates the interdependence of life, literature, and thought. Education surrenders to the values of the marketplace: to a new rationalism and to positivistic empiricism. For Babbitt the study of the classics constitutes a disciplined assimilation rather than an accumulation of knowledge. Culture and erudition are meaningless if they do not form mind and character. This essay is one of Babbitt's great prophetic utterances, its warnings no less urgent today than in 1897 when it appeared. (From Literature and the American College: Essays in Defense of the Humanities *[Boston and New York: Houghton Mifflin Co., 1908], pp. 150–80; originally printed in the* Atlantic Monthly *79 [1897]: 355–65.)*

THE RATIONAL STUDY OF THE CLASSICS

Dean Swift, in his description of the battle between the ancient and modern books in the king's library, has very wisely refrained from telling the outcome of the encounter. The conflict is not even yet fought to a finish, but the advantage is more and more on the side of the moderns. By its unconscious drift not less than by its conscious choice of direction, the world seems to be moving away from the classics. The modern mind, as the number of subjects that solicit attention increases, tends, by an instinct of self-preservation, to reject everything that has even the appearance of being non-essential.

If, then, the teacher of the classics is thus put on the defensive, the question arises how far his position is inevitable, and how far it springs from a failure to conform his methods to existing needs. Present methods of classical teaching reflect the change that has taken place during the past thirty years in our whole higher education. This period has seen the rise of graduate schools organized with a view to the training of specialists on the German plan, and superimposed on undergraduate systems belonging to an entirely different tradition. The establishment of the first of these graduate schools, that of the Johns Hopkins University, and the impulse there given to work of the type leading to the German doctor's degree, is an event of capital importance in American educational history. President Gilman contemplated with something akin to enthusiasm the introduction of the German scientific spirit, of *strengwissenschaftliche Methode,* the instinct for research and original work, into the intellectual life of the American student. The results have more than justified his expectations. In all that relates to accurate grasp of the subject in hand, to strenuous application and mastery of detail, the standard of American scholarship has risen immensely during the last few years, and will continue to rise. Our universities are turning out a race of patient and laborious investigators, who may claim to have rivaled the Germans on their own ground, as Horace said the Romans had come to rival the Greeks:—

Venimus ad summum fortunae; pingimus atque
Psallimus et luctamur Achivis doctius unctis.

[We have come to the peak of our fortune; we paint and we sing to the lyre, and we wrestle more expertly than the anointed Greeks.]

There are, however, even among those who recognize the benefits of the German scientific spirit, many who feel at the same time its dangers and drawbacks. A reaction is beginning against a too crude application of German methods to American educational needs. There are persons at present who do not believe that a man is fitted to fill a chair of French literature in an American college simply because he has made a critical study of the text of a dozen mediaeval beast fables and written a thesis on the Picard dialect, and who deny that a man is necessarily qualified to interpret the humanities to American undergraduates because he has composed a dissertation on the use of the present participle in Ammianus Marcellinus. It is held by others, who put the matter on broader grounds, that German science is beginning to show signs of a decadence similar to the decadence that overtook Greek science in the schools of Alexandria. Matthew Arnold declares the great Anglo-Saxon failing during the present century to have been an excessive faith in machinery and material appliances. May we not with equal truth say that the great German failing during the same period has been an excessive faith in intellectual machinery and intellectual appliances? What else but intellectual machinery is that immense mass of partial results which has grown out of the tendency of modern science to an ever minuter subdivision and analysis? The heaping up of volumes of special research and of investigations of infinitesimal detail has kept pace in Germany with the multiplication of mechanical contrivances in the Anglo-Saxon world. One sometimes asks in moments of despondency whether the main achievement of the nineteenth century will not have been to accumulate a mass of machinery that will break the twentieth century's back. The Cornell University library already contains, for the special study of Dante alone, over seven thousand volumes; about three fourths of which, it may be remarked in passing, are nearly or quite worthless, and only tend to the confusion of good counsel. Merely to master the special apparatus for the study of Dante and his times, the student, if he conforms to the standard set for the modern specialist, will run the risk of losing his intellectual symmetry and sense of proportion, precisely the qualities of which he will stand most in need for the higher interpretation of Dante.

Nowhere, perhaps, is this disposition to forget the end of knowledge in the pursuit of its means and appliances more apparent than in the study of the classics. There is no intention, in saying this, to underrate the services that nineteenth-century scholars, especially those of Germany, have rendered the cause of classical learning. In their philological research and minute criticism of texts they are only following a method which, though first formulated and systematically applied by Bentley, goes back in its main features to the great scholars of the Renaissance. Is there not, however, a fallacy in assuming that material so strictly limited in amount as that remaining to us from classical antiquity is forever to be primarily the subject of scientific investigation? The feudal institutions which saved France from anarchy during the Middle Ages had come, in the eighteenth century, to be the worst of anachronisms; and in like manner the type of scholarship which was needed at the beginning of the Renaissance to rescue and restore the texts of the classical writers will come to be a no less flagrant anachronism if persisted in after that work has been thoroughly done. The method which in the sixteenth century produced a Stephanus or a Casaubon will only give us to-day the spectacle of the "German doctor desperate with the task of saying something where everything has been said, and eager to apply his new theory of fog as an illuminating medium." As the field of ancient literature is more and more completely covered, the vision of the special investigator must become more and more microscopic. The present generation of classical philologists, indeed, reminds one of a certain sect of Japanese Buddhists which believes that salvation is to be attained by arriving at a knowledge of the infinitely small. Men have recently shown their fitness for teaching the humanities by writing theses on the ancient horse-bridle and the Roman doorknob.

Doubtless the time has not yet come for what may be called the age of research in the ancient languages to be finally brought to a close. Of Greek literature especially we may say, in the words of La Fontaine, "That is a field which cannot be so harvested that there will not be something left for the latest comer to glean." But while there may still be subjects of research in the classics that will reward the advanced student, it is doubtful whether there are many such whose study the beginner may profitably undertake as a part of his preparation in his specialty. In doing the work necessary under existing conditions to obtain the doctor's degree in the classics, it may be questioned whether a man has chosen the best means of getting at the spirit, or even the letter, of ancient literature, or of qualifying himself to become an exponent of that literature to others. It is claimed by the advocates of research that the training the student gets in his investigation, even though he fail to arrive at any important result, is in itself valuable and formative to a high degree. He is at least initiated into that *strengwissenschaftliche Methode* on which President Gilman lays such particular stress. We must recognize a large measure of truth in the claims thus put forward by the advocates of research. It is by his power to gather himself together, to work within limits, as Goethe has told us in a well-known phrase, that the master is first revealed. In so far, then, as the German scientific method forces us to gather ourselves together and to work within limits, thereby increasing our power of concentration, our ability to lay firm hold upon the specific fact, we cannot esteem it too highly. There can be no more salutary discipline for a person who is afflicted with what may be termed a loose literary habit of mind than to be put through a course of exact research. The lack of the power to work within limits, to lay firm hold upon the specific fact, is a fault of the gravest character, even when it appears in a mind like that of Emerson.

The question arises, however, whether an unduly high price has not been paid for accuracy and scientific method when these qualities have been obtained at the sacrifice of breadth. Would it not be possible to devise a series of examinations, somewhat similar in character, perhaps, to those now held for honors at Oxford and Cambridge,—examinations which would touch upon ancient life and literature at the largest possible number of points, and which might serve to reveal, as the writing of a doctor's thesis does not, the range as well as the exactness of a student's knowledge? Some test is certainly needed which shall go to show the general culture of a candidate as well as his special proficiency, his familiarity with ideas as well as with words, and his mastery of the spirit, as well as of the mechanism, of the ancient languages.

It is precisely in the failure to distinguish between the spirit and the mechanism of language, in the unwillingness to recognize literature as having claims apart from philology, that the danger of the present tendency chiefly consists. The opinion seems to be gaining ground that the study of literature by itself is unprofitable, hard to disassociate from dilettanteism, and not likely to lead to much except a lavish outlay of elegant epithets of admiration. A professor of Greek in one of the Eastern colleges is reported to have said that the literary teaching of the classics would reduce itself in practice to ringing the changes on the adjective "beautiful!" It is rigorous scientific method, we are told, that needs to be painfully acquired. If a man has a certain right native instinct, his appreciation of the literature will take care of itself; and if this native instinct is lacking, it is something that no pressure from without will avail to produce. It is, then, *strengwissenschaftliche Methode* with its talismanic virtues that our every effort should be directed to impart, whereas the taste for literature is to be reckoned in with Dogberry's list of things that come by nature. It is in virtue of some such sentiment as this that the study of philology seems at present to be driving the study of literature more and more from our Eastern universities. Do not the holders of this view, we may ask, emphasize unduly the influence their method will have upon individuals, and at the same time fail to consider the effect it may have in the formation of a tendency? In the long run the gradual working of any given ideal upon the large body of average men, who simply take on the color of their environment, will produce a well-nigh irresistible movement in the direction of that ideal. If the minutiae rather than the larger aspects of the classics are insisted upon, the taste for small things will spread like a contagion among the rank and file of classical scholars, and we shall soon be threatened with an epidemic of pedantry. A particular type of scholar is as much in need of a congenial atmosphere in which to flourish as a plant is in need of a congenial soil and climate in which to flower and bring forth fruit. We cannot readily imagine a Professor Jowett appearing under existing conditions at the University of Berlin. Besides, the danger is to be taken into account that if present methods are pushed much further, the young men with the right native instinct for literature are likely to be driven out of the classics entirely. Young men of this type may not all care to be educated as though they were to be "editors, and not lovers of polite literature;" they may not feel the fascination of spending months in a classical seminary, learning how to torment the text and the meaning of a few odes of Horace, —

And torture one poor word ten thousand ways.

There is, to be sure, a very real danger in some subjects, especially in English literature, that the instruction may take too belletristic a turn. The term "culture course" has come to mean, among the undergraduates of one of our Eastern colleges, a course in which the students are not required to do any work. It is one of the main advantages of Latin and Greek over modern languages that the mere mastering of an ancient author's meaning will give to a course enough bone and sinew of solid intellectual effort to justify the teacher in adding thereto the flesh and blood of a literary interpretation. In a civilization so hard and positive in temper as our own, it is not the instinct for philology, but rather the instinct for literature and for the things of the imagination, which is likely to remain latent if left to itself. A certain dry, lexicographical habit of mind is said by Europeans to be the distinctive mark of American scholarship. Instead of fostering this habit of mind in the study of the classics by an undue insistence on philology, it should be our endeavor to counteract it by giving abundant stimulus and encouragement to the study of them as literature. In the classics more than in other subjects, the fact should never be forgotten that the aim proposed is the assimilation, and not the accumulation, of knowledge. In the classics, if nowhere else, mere erudition should be held in comparatively little account except in so far as it has been converted into culture; and culture itself should not be regarded as complete until it has so penetrated its possessor as to become a part of his character. Montaigne has said somewhere in his essays that he loved to forge his mind rather than to furnish it. The metaphor of Montaigne's phrase is somewhat mixed, but the idea it embodies is one that men born into a late age of scholarship cannot ponder too carefully. As the body of learning transmitted from the past increases in volume, it becomes constantly more difficult to maintain that exact relation between the receipt and the assimilation of knowledge which has been declared by the greatest of the Hindu sages to be the root of all wisdom. "Without knowledge," says Buddha, "there is no reflection, without reflection there is no knowledge; he who has both knowledge and reflection is close upon Nirvâna."

The risk we run nowadays is that of having our minds buried beneath a dead-weight of information which we have no inner energy, no power of reflection, to appropriate to our own uses and convert into vital nutriment. We need to be on our guard against allowing the mere collector of information to gain an undue advantage over the man who would maintain some balance between his knowledge and reflection. We are, for instance, putting a premium on pedantry, if we set up as the sole test of proficiency in the classics the degree of familiarity shown with that immense machinery of minute learning that has grown up about them. This is to exalt that mere passive intellectual feeding which is the bane of modern scholarship. It is to encourage the man who is willing to abandon all attempt at native and spontaneous thought, and become a mere register and repertory of other men's ideas in some small department of knowledge. The man who is willing to reduce his mind to a purely mechanical function may often thereby gain a mastery of facts that will enable him to intimidate the man who would make a larger use of his knowledge; for there are among scholars, as Holmes says there are in society, "fellows" who have a number of "ill-conditioned facts which they lead after them into decent company, ready to let them slip, like so many bulldogs, at every ingenious suggestion or convenient generalization or pleasant fancy." There has always existed between the man of the literal fact and the man of the general law, between the man of cold understanding and the man of thought and imagination, an instinctive aversion. We can trace the feud that has divided the two classes of minds throughout history. They were arrayed against each other in fierce debate for centuries during the Middle Ages under the name of Realists and Nominalists. The author of one of the oldest of the Hindu sacred books pronounces an anathema on two classes of people, the grammarian and the man who is over-fond of a good dinner, and debars them both from the hope of final salvation.

The remark has frequently been made that quarrels would not last long if the fault were on one side only. We may apply this truth to the debate in question, which, considered in its essence, springs from the opposition between the lovers of synthesis and the lovers of analysis. Now, Emerson has profoundly said, in his essay on Plato, that the main merit of the Greeks was to have found and occupied the right middle ground between synthesis and analysis; and this will continue to be the aim of the true scholar.

The old humanism, such as it still survives at Oxford, has in it much that is admirable; but it has become, in some respects at least, antiquated and inadequate. It would sometimes seem to lead, as it did in the case of Walter Pater, to an ultra-aesthetic and epicurean attitude toward life—to a disposition to retire into one's ivory tower, and seek in ancient literature merely a source of exquisite solace. The main fault of this English humanism, however, is that it treats the classical writers too much as isolated phenomena; it fails to relate them in a broad and vital way to modern life. It would seem, then, that new life and interest are to be infused into the classics not so much by a restoration of the old humanism as by a larger application to them of the comparative and historical methods. These methods, we hasten to add, should be informed with ideas and reinforced by a sense of absolute values. Especially in the case of a language like Latin, whose literature is so purely derivative, and which has in turn radiated its influence along so many different lines to the modern world, any mere disconnected treatment of individual authors is entirely insufficient. The works of each author, indeed, should first be considered by themselves and on their own merits, but they should also be studied as links in that unbroken chain of literary and intellectual tradition which extends from the ancient to the modern world.

It is by bringing home to the mind of the American student the continuity of this tradition that one is likely to implant in him, more effectually, perhaps, than in any other way, that right feeling and respect for the past which he so signally lacks. For if the fault of other countries and other times has been an excess of reverence for the past, the danger of this country to-day would seem rather to be an undue absorption in the present. No great monument of a former age, no Pantheon or Notre Dame, rises in the midst of our American cities to make a silent plea for the past against the cheap and noisy tendencies of the passing hour. From various elements working together obscurely in his consciousness—from the theory of human perfectibility inherited from the eighteenth century, from the more recent doctrine of evolution, above all from the object lesson of his own national life—the average American has come to have an instinctive belief that each decade is a gain over the last decade, and that each century is an improvement on its predecessor; the first step he has to take in the path of culture is to realize that movement is not necessarily progress, and that the advance in civilization cannot be measured by the increase in the number of eighteen-story buildings. The emancipation from this servitude to the present may be reckoned as one of the chief benefits to be derived from classical study. Unfortunately this superficial modernism turns many away from the study of the classics altogether, and tends to diminish, even in those who do study them, that faith and enthusiasm so necessary to overcome the initial difficulties.

The American, it is true, is often haunted, in the midst of all his surface activity, with a vague sense that, after all, his life may be deficient in depth and dignity; it is not so often, however, that he succeeds in tracing this defect in his life to its lack of background and perspective, to the absence in himself of a right feeling for the past,—that feeling which, as has been truly said, distinguishes more than any other the civilized man from the barbarian. As has already been remarked, this feeling is to be gained, in the case of the classics, not so much by treating them as isolated phenomena as by making clear the manifold ways in which they are related to the present, by leaving no chasm between ancient and modern life over which the mind is unable to pass. One of the important functions, then, of the classical teacher should be to bridge over the gap between the Greek and Roman world and the world of to-day. No preparation can be too broad, no culture too comprehensive, for the man who would fit himself for the adequate performance of such a task. His knowledge of modern life and literature needs to be almost as wide as his knowledge of the life and literature of antiquity. The ideal student of the classics should not rest satisfied until he is able to follow out in all its ramifications that Greek and Latin thought which, as Max Müller says, runs like fire in the veins of modern literature. In the case of an author like Virgil, for instance, he should be familiar not only with the classical Virgil, but also with the Virgil of after-centuries,—with Virgil the magician and enchanter who haunted the imagination of the Middle Ages, with Virgil the guide of Dante, and so on, down to the splendid ode of Tennyson. If he is dealing with Aristotle, he should be able to show the immense influence exercised by Aristotle over the mediaeval and modern European mind, both directly through the Latin tradition and indirectly through Averrhoës and the Arabs. If his author is Euripides, he should know in what way Euripides has affected modern dramatic art; he should be capable of making a comparison between the *Hippolytus* and the *Phèdre* of Racine. If he is studying Stoicism, he should be able to contrast the stoical ideal of perfection with the Christian ideal of the perfect life as elaborated by writers like St. Bonaventura and St. Thomas Aquinas. He should neglect far less than has been done heretofore the great patristic literature in Greek and Latin, as giving evidence of the process by which ancient thought passed over into thought of the mediaeval and modern types. These are only a few examples, chosen almost at random, of the wide and fruitful application that may be made of the comparative method.

How much, again, might be done to enhance the value of classical study by a freer use than has hitherto been made of the historical method! The word "historical" is intended to be taken in a large sense; what is meant is not so much a mere cataloguing of the events of ancient civilization as an investigation of the various causes that led to the greatness or decline of ancient societies. The last word on the reasons for the rise and fall of the Romans has not been spoken by Montesquieu. An investigation of the kind referred to would allow the application of many of the theories of modern science, but its results would have far more than an abstract scientific interest; they would provide us with instruction and examples to meet the problems of our own times. From the merest inattention to the teachings of the past, we are likely, in our national life, to proceed cheerfully to

Commit the oldest sins the newest kind of ways.

A sober reflection on the history of the ancient republics might put us on our guard against many of the dangers to which we ourselves are exposed. It might cure us in part of our cheap optimism. It might, in any case, make us conscious of that tendency of which Machiavelli had so clear a vision,—the tendency of a state to slip down an easy slope of prosperity into vice:—

Et in vitium fortuna labier aequa.

How much light might be shed—to give but a single illustration of what is meant—on contemporary as well as on Roman politics by a course, properly conducted, on the correspondence of Cicero!

The method just suggested of studying the classics might possibly render them less liable to the complaint now made that they are entirely remote from the interests and needs of the present. It is this feeling of the obsoleteness of the classics, joined to the utilitarian instinct so deeply imbedded in the American character, that is creating such a widespread sentiment in favor of giving the place they now hold to modern languages. The American student of the future is evidently going to have a chance to follow in the footsteps of that remarkable young woman, Miss Blanche Amory of *Pendennis,* who, it will be remembered, "improved her mind by a sedulous study of the novels of the great modern authors in the French language." It would appear, from a comparison of the catalogues of one of our Eastern universities, that its undergraduates now have an opportunity to read *La Débâcle* of Émile Zola, where twenty years ago they would have been required to read the *Antigone* of Sophocles.

We will not attempt for the present a full discussion of this important question as to the relative educational value of ancient and modern languages, but a few reasons may be given briefly in support of the view that modern languages, however valuable as a study supplementary to the classics, are quite inadequate to take their place.

M. Paul Bourget, in a recent autobiographical sketch, tells us that, as a young man, he steeped his mind in the works of

Stendhal and Baudelaire and other modern literature of the same type. He fails to explain, either to himself or others, the fact that these modern books, though written, as he says, in all truth and sincerity, should yet have given him a view of life which later led only to bitter disappointment and disillusion. M. Bourget's difficulty might have been less if he had taken into account that the authors of whom he speaks, so far from serving as a stimulus to his will and reason, merely invited him to retire into a corner and try strange experiments on his own emotional nature, and draw new and novel effects from his own capacity for sensation; that they held out to him, in short, the promise of a purely personal and sensuous satisfaction from life,—a promise which life itself may be counted upon not to keep. Now modern authors are not all, like Baudelaire, of the violently subjective type, but the intrusion of the author and his foibles into his work, the distortion of the objective reality of life by its passage through the personal medium, is much more frequent in modern than in ancient literature. Much of modern literature merely encourages to sentimental and romantic revery rather than to a resolute and manly grappling with the plain facts of existence. Romanticism may not mean the Commune, as Thiers said it did, but we may at least say that literature of the romantic type, compared with that in the classical tradition, is so deficient in certain qualities of sobriety and discipline as to make us doubt its value as a formative influence upon the minds of the young. Classical literature, at its best, does not so much tend to induce in us a certain state of feelings, much less a certain state of the nerves; it appeals rather to our higher reason and imagination—to those faculties which afford us an avenue of escape from ourselves, and enable us to become participants in the universal life. It is thus truly educative in that it leads him who studies it out and away from himself. The classical spirit, in its purest form, feels itself consecrated to the service of a high, impersonal reason. Hence its sentiment of restraint and discipline, its sense of proportion and pervading law. By bringing our acts into an ever closer conformity with this high, impersonal reason, it would lead us, although along a different path, to the same goal as religion, to a union ever more intimate with

our only true, deep-buried selves,
Being one with which we are one with the whole world.

By a complete and harmonious development of all our faculties under the guidance and control of this right reason, it would raise us above the possibility of ever again falling away

Into some bondage of the flesh or mind,
Some slough of sense, or some fantastic maze
Forged by the imperious, lonely thinking power.

This high message contained in classical literature calls for the active exercise of our own best faculties, of our intellect and imagination, in order to be understood. It may be because of this purely intellectual appeal of the classics that there is so much initial inertia to overcome in awakening an interest in them. Indeed, to transform into a Greek scholar the average young man of to-day, whose power of attention has been dissipated in the pages of the American newspaper, whose mind has been relaxed by reading the modern erotic novel,—this, to borrow one of Phillips Brooks's phrases, would sometimes seem about as promising an enterprise as to make a lancehead out of putty. The number of those who can receive the higher lessons of Greek culture is always likely to be small. The classical spirit, however, is salutary and formative wherever it occurs, and if a man is not able to appreciate it in Pindar, he may in Horace; and if not in Horace, then in Molière. French literature of the seventeenth century is, as a whole, the most brilliant manifestation of the classical spirit in modern times, and one might teach French with considerable conviction, were it not for the propensity of the American student to confine his reading in French to inferior modern authors, and often, indeed, to novels of the decadence.

Decadent novels and other fungous growths of a similar nature are not peculiar to French, but are multiplying with alarming rapidity in all the great European literatures. Modern literature has been more or less sentimental since Petrarch, and a morbidly subjective strain has existed in it since Rousseau, while of late a quality is beginning to appear which we cannot better describe than as neurotic. We may say, to paraphrase an utterance of Chamfort's, that the success of some contemporary books is due to the correspondence that exists between the state of the author's nerves and the state of the nerves of his public. Spiritual despondency, which under the name of *acedia* was accounted one of the seven deadly sins during the Middle Ages, has come in these later days to be one of the main resources of literature. Life itself has recently been defined by one of the lights of the French deliquescent school as "an epileptic fit between two nothings." It is no small resource to be able to escape from these miasmatic exhalations of contemporary literature into the bracing atmosphere of the classics; to be able to rise into that purer ether

> where those immortal shapes
> Of bright aërial spirits live insphered
> In regions mild of calm and serene air.

We can, then, by no means allow the claims of those who find in modern languages an adequate substitute for the classics. However, we agree with those who assert that if the classics are to maintain their traditional place, they should be related more largely to the needs and aspirations of modern life. With this end in view, classical study must take a new direction; we need to emulate the spirit of the great scholars of the Renaissance, but to modify their methods. As to the present excess of German tendency in American classical scholarship, it may be left to remedy itself. The German research method appeals, indeed, to certain hard, positive qualities in the American mind, but other sides of the German ideal the American will find distasteful, on closer acquaintance; above all, he will prove incapable, in the long run, of the sublime disinterestedness of the German specialist, who, so far from asking himself whether his work will ever serve any practical purpose, never stops to inquire whether it will serve any purpose at all. A reaction, then, against the exaggerations of German method and of the scientific spirit will do no harm, though the classics need to benefit by a full application of the historical and comparative methods. There is needed in the classics to-day a man who can understand the past with the result, not of loosening, but of strengthening his grasp upon the present. There is needed a type of scholar intermediary between the high school pedagogue and the university specialist, who can interpret the classics in a large and liberal spirit to American undergraduates, carrying with him into his task the consciousness that he is forming the minds and characters of the future citizens of a republic. The teaching of the classics thus understood could be made one of the best preparations for practical life, and less might be heard of the stock complaint about wasting time in the study of the dead languages. As to this last charge, we may quote from the most eloquent appeal that has been made of late years for a more liberal study of the classics,—that of Lowell in his Harvard Anniversary address. If the language of the Greeks is dead, he there says, "yet the literature it enshrines is rammed with life as perhaps no other writing, except Shakespeare's, ever was or will be. It is as contemporary with to-day as with the ears it first enraptured, for it appeals not to the man of then or now, but to the entire round of human nature itself. Men are ephemeral or evanescent, but whatever page the authentic soul of man has touched with her immortalizing finger, no matter how long ago, is still young and fair as it was to the world's gray fathers. Oblivion looks in the face of the Grecian Muse only to forget her errand. . . . We know not whither other studies will lead us, especially if dissociated from this; we do know to what summits, far above our lower region of turmoil, this has led, and what the many-sided outlook thence."

There was never greater need of the Hellenic spirit than there is to-day, and especially in this country, if that charge of lack of measure and sense of proportion which foreigners bring against Americans is founded in fact. As Matthew Arnold has admirably said, it is the Greek writers who best show the modern mind the path that it needs to take; for the modern man cannot, like the man of the Middle Ages, live by the imagination and religious faculty alone; on the other hand, he cannot live solely by the exercise of his reason and understanding. It is only by the union of these two elements of his nature that he can hope to attain a balanced growth, and this fusion of the reason and the imagination is found realized more perfectly than elsewhere in the Greek classics of the great age. Those who can receive the higher initiation into the Hellenic spirit will doubtless remain few in number, but these few will wield a potent influence for good, each in his own circle, if only from the ability they will thereby have acquired to escape from contemporary illusions. For of him who has caught the profounder teachings of Greek literature we may say, in the words of the *Imitation*, that he is released from a multitude of opinions.

PART II

THE LIFE OF LITERATURE

Babbitt asserts that the study of English with reference to its intellectual content is a serious discipline. He considers what justifies the study of English on cultural and literary rather than on sentimental and utilitarian grounds. But in the "general drift toward softness" in American education, when difficult subjects are avoided, English is jeopardized. The "old education," individualistic and humanistic, stressed ethical standards and "training for wisdom." The "new education," sociological and humanitarian, stresses "training for service and training for power." To discriminate sharply between these two approaches calls for severe intellectual discipline. Humanist educators affirm standards and insist on quality; humanitarian educators emphasize numbers. The former assert the primacy of standards; the latter, the primacy of ideals. Characteristically, Babbitt comes down hard on humanitarian education, in which he sees an absence of "a sufficiently stringent discipline of ideas" and a plethora of "equalitarian fallacies." To combat this trend and to preserve the two great traditions, classical and Christian, humanist educators, in particular teachers of English, must emphasize "the background of standard reading" and an "underlying unity of literary study." The crisis of education, Babbitt insists, imperils free institutions and the fate of civilization. (From the English Journal 9 *[February 1920]: 61-70.)*

ENGLISH AND THE DISCIPLINE OF IDEAS

I chanced recently to be glancing over a book on a subject very remote from my present topic, namely, a book on Japanese Buddhism, and I read among other things that several centuries ago there was a sect of Japanese Buddhism known as the Way of Hardships, and that shortly after there arose another sect known as the Easy Way which at once gained great popularity and tended to supplant the Way of Hardships. But the Japanese Way of Hardships is itself an easy way if one compares it with the original way of Buddha. One can follow indeed very clearly the process by which Buddhist doctrine descended gradually from the austere and almost inaccessible height on which it had been placed by its founder to the level of the prayer mill. One might read in the papers not long ago that as a final improvement some of the prayer mills in Thibet are to be operated by electricity. The tendency illustrated is not, I believe, confined to the Orient. The man who hopes to save society by turning the crank of a legislative mill may call himself a Christian, but he is probably as remote from the true spirit of Jesus as the man who hopes to perform a religious act by pressing an electric button is from the true spirit of Buddha. What stands forth plainly in both East and West is man's proneness, unless this proneness is counteracted by unceasing vigilance, to follow the lines of least, or, at all events, of lesser resistance.

How far is this human proneness manifest today in American education? As a matter of fact, the complaint is often heard at present that there is an increasing exodus from the difficult and disciplinary subjects and a rush into the soft subjects. One good sign is that those who stand for the difficult and disciplinary subjects, e.g., the professors of physics and the professors of the ancient classics, are coming more and more to see that they must co-operate and not work at cross-purposes, as they have done only too often in the past, if they are to make head against the drift toward softness. The question arises as to the position of English in this struggle between the more and the less disciplinary subjects. How far is its present popularity, as compared with Greek and Latin, a case of the supplanting of a way of hardships by an easy way? It has been my business for many years past in connection with certain courses I am giving in comparative literature to trace the great naturalistic movement that got fairly under way in the eighteenth century and has been tending more and more to displace the two great traditions, Christian and classical, that had prevailed in education, as elsewhere, up to that time. Now this naturalistic movement in the midst of which we are still living is twofold, partly utilitarian and partly sentimental, and the grounds on which not only English but other modern languages have triumphed over the ancient classics have also been to no small extent utilitarian and sentimental. English appeals to us as our mother-tongue, and at the same time some training in English is admittedly useful. We are seeing again the rapid extension of Spanish in our schools at the present time on grounds that are plainly utilitarian, grounds that have little relation to the cultural value of Spanish. The question I propose to consider is in what way one may justify the study of English on cultural and disciplinary, and not merely on sentimental or utilitarian, grounds. My own conviction is that if English is to be thus justified it must be primarily by what I am terming the discipline of ideas.

As a matter of fact one hears it commonly said nowadays that literature may be rescued from the philologist on the one hand and the mere dilettante on the other by an increase of emphasis on its intellectual content, that the teaching of literature, if it is to have virility, must be above all the teaching of ideas. This insistence on ideas, sound so far as it goes, needs, if it is to be really fruitful, to be supplemented by a careful analysis of the kind of ideas that should be taught if the humanities are to be rehabilitated. Aristotle says that the most important factor in maintaining any particular form of government is the general ethical conception or *ethos* that is given through education to the young. If the *ethos* does not coincide with the form of government, that government is doomed. A question worth asking is whether our present system of education is doing as much as it might to create an *ethos* in close accord with our existing form of government, i.e., a constitutional democracy.

Has our emancipation, in short, from the somewhat narrow traditionalism of the old American college and the attainment of encyclopedic fulness of knowledge that has marked the rise of universities been achieved without any sacrifice of the one thing needful—the sound ethical standards that the old-fashioned American college with all its limitations did do something to promote? The change that has been taking place in our education is, it should be noted, not simply a modernizing and adjusting to new conditions of the old college curriculum, but the substitution in no small degree of an entirely new spirit. The old education aimed at training for wisdom, a wisdom to be achieved in the breast of the individual. The new education aims rather, in President Eliot's phrase, at training for service and training for power. The old education was partly humanistic, partly religious; the new education is humanitarian, concerned, that is, less with making wise individuals than with improving society as a whole, and this humanitarianism is itself only an aspect of the naturalistic movement of which I have spoken, that began to triumph decisively over tradition in the middle of the eighteenth century. One cannot help harboring certain doubts as to whether this more humanitarian type of education tends as much as the old religious and humanistic type to create an *ethos* in accord with our existing institutions.

As a matter of fact, the complaint is beginning to be heard that our institutions of learning are turning out, not men with sound ethical standards, but sociological dreamers. The most marked trait of the sociological dreamer, and that from the very dawn of the humanitarian movement in the eighteenth century, has been his inordinate interest in the underdog. "All institutions," says Condorcet, for example, "ought to have for their aim the physical, intellectual, and moral amelioration of the poorest and most numerous class."

One may ask what all this has to do with the discipline of ideas. My reply is: Everything. If a teacher is humanitarian, with a predominant interest in the underdog, he will at once find himself out of touch with most of the great figures of both ancient and modern literature. I have my doubts as to whether a classical teacher will teach his subject with the fullest understanding and effectiveness if he himself—and I happen to know of a number of such classical teachers—is of socialistic or semi-Bolshevistic leanings. What has just been said applies almost as much to the modern as to the ancient classics. Milton was not an "uplifter," nor was Shakespeare; they are open rather to the charge of not having been sufficiently solicitous for the underdog. The issue that lurks in the background of the whole discussion, and which must be faced squarely, is whether our education, especially our higher education, is to be qualitative and intensive or quantitative and extensive. Those who are filled with concern for the lot of humanity as a whole, especially for the less fortunate portions of it, are wont nowadays to call themselves idealists. We should at least recognize that ideals in this sense are not the same as standards and that they are often indeed the opposite of standards. It would be easy to mention institutions of learning in this country that are at present engaged in breaking down standards in the name of ideals. It seems democratic and therefore ideal that the largest possible number should partake of the advantages of higher education, and for this and other reasons there is, as we all know, a constant temptation to let down the bars. I am just in receipt of a letter from a professor of a state institution of the Middle West mentioning an enrolment of 2,300 students in Freshman English, and at the same time raising the question how far this enrolment means the sacrifice of quality to quantity. We should not forget that in the long run our democracy will be judged by its ability to achieve high standards of quality at least as much as by its so-called ideals.

Three or four years ago a distinguished Frenchman, M. Hovelacque, published an article on America in the *Revue de Paris* in which he maintained that the essential weakness of our American civilization lay in the failure of our education to produce any equivalent of the superior man of Confucius or the καλὸς κἀγαθός of the Greeks. Later M. Hovelacque accompanied Joffre on his trip to this country and gave out to the daily press glowing interviews in which he praised us for our idealism. Now that we are big and powerful we are sure to be flattered, and it is therefore all the more important that we should not flatter ourselves. If we are told that it is not democratic to strive to produce the superior man, we should reply with Aristotle that the remedy for democracy is not more democracy, but that, on the contrary, if we wish a democracy that is to endure we should temper it with its opposite—with the idea of quality and selection. True democracy consists not in lowering the standard but in giving everybody, so far as possible, a chance of measuring up to the standard. If we are to judge by the experience of the past, the number of those who will measure up to high standards will not, even under the most favorable circumstances, be large in proportion to the mass. Sooner or later every honest teacher, no matter how inclusive in his sympathies, is forced to recognize the truth contained in the saying of Confucius that "you cannot carve rotten wood"; that comparatively few, in short, have either aptitude or inclination for wisdom.

These are the truths that we are tending to lose sight of in the present age of naturalistic and humanitarian expansion with its exaltation of quantity and numbers. We need just now to stress the qualitative and selective idea in our education if it is to produce leaders equal to the task of preserving through the present revolutionary era our birthright of liberty. The real crux of the situation, now that our traditional supports have largely failed us, is to get our humanistic quality and selection in a more positive and critical, in a word, in a more modern, fashion than heretofore.

A great many people are, as a matter of fact, setting up in these days as humanists. But it is right here that the discipline of ideas is needed if we are not to fall into confusion at the very start. When we consider carefully what many of our so-called humanists stand for, we find that they are not humanists but humanitarians. A humanism that is not sharply discriminated from humanitarianism, of which it is in many respects the exact opposite, is largely meaningless; and to discriminate properly between humanism and humanitarianism will be found to involve a severe intellectual discipline. Humanism is only one of a large class of words that call aloud at present for definition. In fact, as Socrates is reported to have said, the very beginning of genuine culture, especially in an age that has discarded traditional standards, is the scrutiny of general terms. Let us take the general term that is used to sum up our whole modern emancipation: the term liberty itself. Have we applied a scrutiny sufficiently searching as yet to this general term? In his projected *History of Liberty* Lord Acton was planning to begin with a hundred different definitions of liberty. I am not sure that any one of the hundred would have been sufficiently well grounded in the facts of human nature and at the same time in accord with what I have called the modern spirit. I can at least indicate in brief the nature of the problem. What seems to me to be driving our whole civilization toward the abyss at present is a one-sided conception of liberty, a conception that is purely centrifugal, that would get rid of all outer control and then evade or deny openly the need of achieving inner control.

I have just been reading a volume by a young instructor in government at Harvard, in which he tends to justify what the French call administrative syndicalism, recently exemplified in the policemen's strike. His final appeal is to liberty and conscience. One might suppose at first that one has to do with another Milton, but on close scrutiny one finds that Milton and this instructor mean very different things by liberty and conscience. The Miltonic liberty involves the inner obeisance of the spirit to a law that is set above the mere emancipated impulses of the natural man. Those who stand for the purely expansive and naturalistic conception of liberty are wont, as I have said, to call themselves idealists and to assert that the present evils of the body politic are due to a lack of their type of idealism. I myself hold the homely and unpopular view that these evils are due rather to a violation of the Ten Commandments. The special failing of some of our more advanced idealists would seem to be their slight regard for the commandment: Thou shalt not steal. For the Golden Age to which they invite us can be achieved only by a program of plunder and loot. Here is an extreme example from the manifesto put forth the other day by the Federation of Russian Workers of America: "Far beyond the corpses of heroes, beyond the blood-covered barricades, beyond all the terrors of civil war there already shines for us the magnificent, beautiful form of man without a God, without a master and free of authority. We declare war upon God and religious fables. We are atheists. Not to the happiness of citizenship do we call the workers, we call them to liberty—to absolute liberty." This passage puts us on the track of the violation of another commandment even more important perhaps than the commandment against stealing—the commandment, namely, against idolatry; for thus to glorify man in his natural and unmodified self is no less surely, even if less obviously, idolatry than actually to bow down before a graven image. One must include in one's definition of liberty the centripetal element, the element of control that will raise one above this humanitarian idolatry, if one is to be a true liberal. The struggle that will determine the fate of occidental civilization—and this struggle is likely to take place above all in America—is not, as is often assumed, between liberals on the one hand and mere reactionaries and traditionalists on the other, but between the true and the sham liberals. At present, in the absence of a sufficiently stringent discipline of ideas, the sham liberals are having things too much their own way.

Observe that the Bolshevist vision of man glorified by emancipation from both inner and outer control has much in common with the vision of liberty that one finds in Shelley. If this view of liberty is pestilential nonsense when put forth by the Federation of Russian Workers of America, it is pestilential nonsense when arrayed in the gorgeous lyrical iridescences of *Prometheus Unbound.* What an opportunity, in any case, for the teacher who wishes to put ideas into his teaching to compare the liberty of Milton, based on a conception of life that is partly humanistic and partly biblical, with the naturalistic and humanitarian liberty of Shelley.

Comparisons of the kind I have in mind imply background, and it is becoming more and more difficult under existing conditions to get background. The more advanced liberals of the naturalistic and humanitarian type not only spurn the past but barely tolerate the present; the true home of their spirit is that vast, windy abode, the future. Even in its less advanced stages this temper leads to what one is tempted to call a cheap contemporaneousness. Most of us are acquainted with the type of teacher who, instead of building up background in his students, is inclined to set them to studying opinions on current events in the columns of the *New Republic.* The result, so far as the tried and tested masterpieces of the past are concerned, is an increasing illiteracy. An English instructor at Harvard told me—I hope that he was exaggerating—that out of one class of 43 students only four knew anything about the Book of Job! This is a situation that seems to justify some of the most gloomy sentiments of Job—with a few from Jeremiah thrown in.

This ignorance of standard literature on the part of the younger generation is becoming so obvious that it is likely to lead to action in the near future on the part of our college faculties. In fact, I may perhaps say without any undue betrayal of academic secrets that the whole situation has recently been under discussion by the divisions of ancient and modern literature at Harvard. The conclusions that have been reached thus far may undergo modification; they have not in any case been passed on by the faculty and so are not to be regarded as official. At all events, the present intention is to require of all undergraduates who are concentrating in either ancient or modern literature a knowledge of the Bible and Shakespeare to be tested as a part of a general examination at the end of their college course. In addition, every undergraduate concentrating in modern language is to be tested as a part of the same general examination on his knowledge, to be obtained either in the original or through translation, of at least two important ancient classics; and the undergraduate concentrating in the ancient languages will be tested in like manner on two important modern classics. The students are encouraged to do this reading if possible during the summer vacation, and at all events independently of their regular courses. The ancient classics from which students may select will probably be: Homer, Sophocles, Plato, Aristotle, Cicero, Horace, and Virgil; the moderns (in addition to Shakespeare): Dante, Cervantes, Molière, Goethe, Chaucer, and Milton. Note that this scheme not only aims to give the student the background of standard reading that he now so often lacks, but emphasizes another very important point, namely, the underlying unity of literary study. The ancient and modern humanities will stand or fall together. Those who are taking advantage of present utilitarian and sentimental tendencies to promote the modern languages at the expense of the ancient are engaging in shortsighted tactics. It is naïve to suppose that utilitarians or sentimentalists who have no sense of the cultural importance of Greek and Latin will in the long run allow a serious place to what is truly liberalizing in the study of English or any other modern language.

I have said enough, I trust, to make plain what I mean by the discipline of ideas. I have expressed the belief that our most urgent problem just now is how to preserve in a positive and critical form the soul of truth in the two great traditions, classical and Christian, that are crumbling as mere dogma; and I have said that the first step in working out a positive and critical humanism in particular is to define one's general terms, above all the term liberty, and that the ideas for which the general terms stand should be studied not abstractly but concretely as reflected in main literary currents and in the works of great authors. This involves in turn the building up of background, not merely in the English and modern classics, but in those of Greece and Rome. Thus to study English with reference to its intellectual content will do more than anything to make it a serious cultural discipline. It will then be possible to refute those who look upon the present popularity of English as only an instance of the familiar human proclivity to turn from a way of hardships to an easy way. Teachers of English have, in any case, a choice to make between a humanistic conception of their subject and the current naturalistic and humanitarian conceptions. If they assume the more qualitative and selective attitude that the humanist recommends, and disregard certain equalitarian fallacies that are now being preached in the name of democracy, they can probably do more than any other body of teachers to check the present drift toward illiteracy and at the same time help to build up the complex of civilized ideas and habits, the *ethos*, as Aristotle calls it, that is necessary, especially in the leaders, if we are to be true liberals, equal to the task of preserving our present free institutions.

The need to distinguish the proper boundaries of the arts is the subject of Babbitt's second book, The New Laokoon, *from which this chapter is excerpted. Diagnosing the excesses of the arts, especially since Rousseau, he points to the craze for liberty, "eleutheromania," as leading to the corruption of creativity and of the word* beauty. *He sees the humanistic pursuit of self-discipline giving way to expansive aesthetic theories. Venerating the Dionysiac principle, romanticists and naturalists reduce beauty to impressionism, expressionism, and revery. Elimination of the law of symmetry that places limits on subjectivity, exaltation of motion over repose, emphasis on illusion and spontaneity, dismissal of selection—in these centrifugal tendencies Babbitt detects increasing decadence. Literature, in particular, has been deintellectualized and devitalized. Echoing Aristotle, whom he reveres as the greatest master of humanistic discipline, Babbitt pleads for the primacy of reason and the virtue of restraint. If the artist's, or man's, emotional nature is to be humanized, it must first acquire aim and purpose, form and proportion. (From Part II of the Conclusion of* The New Laokoon: An Essay on the Confusion of the Arts *[Boston and New York: Houghton Mifflin Co., 1910], pp. 217-52.)*

FORM AND EXPRESSION

* * * [T]he nineteenth century was a period of naturalistic excess, and therefore inclined to favor too exclusively the virtues of expansion. All the formal boundaries and limits that the past had set up were felt only as fetters to be snapped asunder in order that the human spirit might expatiate at liberty. We need to consider for a moment the effect of these expansive tendencies on the idea that must underlie more or less all creative efforts in either art or literature,—the idea of beauty. Far be it from me to attempt any abstract definition of beauty. This, to judge from the vast majority of works on aesthetics, is a temptation of the enemy. But we may draw certain interesting conclusions if we study what men have actually meant at different epochs when they spoke of a thing as beautiful; if we note the curious ways in which the word beauty has been warped to make it conform to the half-truth that happened to be in vogue at any particular time.

Thus for a certain type of neo-classicist beauty resided almost entirely in symmetry and proportion. But the symmetry and proportion, as he conceived them, were not vital but mechanical. If we took some of the theories of the Renaissance at their face value we should have to conclude that beauty in the plastic arts is something that can be constructed with a rule and compass. We have studied elsewhere this constant neo-classical tendency to confound form with formalism. As we approach the nineteenth century we find that there is a diminishing emphasis on the formal element in beauty and a growing emphasis on the element that is described by such epithets as vital, characteristic, picturesque, individual,—in short, on the element that may be summed up by the epithet expressive. In painting, color grows in favor as compared with line; in all the arts the principle of motion prevails increasingly over the principle of repose, the suggestive detail over design and composition. In brief, expression triumphs over form. Indeed, if we follow down the attempts that men have made during the past two or three centuries to define beauty, we shall find that the formal element has vanished away more and more, until nothing has been left but pure expression. (We may note in passing that this is exactly what happened to the Cheshire cat.) The ultra-romanticists go still further. Beauty is not only reduced to expression, but the expression itself is swallowed up in revery. Beauty becomes a sort of pursuit of the Chimera. Thus for Poe the highest beauty is the fugitive glance of a woman's eye, and a dream woman at that:—

> And all my days are trances,
>   And all my nightly dreams
> Are where thy gray eye glances
>   And where thy footstep gleams—
> In what ethereal dances,
>   By what eternal streams.

Beauty, as conceived by Poe and at times happily achieved in his verse, may be defined as a musical nostalgia. If we connect this conception with Poe's definition of poetry, "the rhythmical creation of Beauty," we shall have an interesting contrast with the Renaissance notion that the essence of poetry is the imitating of human actions "according to probability or necessity."

As a matter of fact the most extreme of modern aesthetic theories are merely an attempt to formulate what Poe and many other writers and artists have actually been putting in practice for the past hundred years. We may take, as an example, the aesthetic theorist who is perhaps most prominent in Germany just now,—Professor Theodor Lipps. Lipps carries to what we may hope is its ultimate exaggeration the Rousseauistic view of art,—the exaltation of motion over repose, the emphasis on trance-like illusion and pure suggestiveness. He tends to reduce beauty to a mere process of "infeeling," and virtually eliminates any over-arching law of symmetry that would set bounds to all this subjectivity. The sense of law, indeed, as something distinct either from the outer rule or individual impulse is, as I have already said, conspicuously absent from the whole modern movement. For example, the neo-classicists tended to turn the laws of verse into a set of narrow precepts, and as a result of these precepts metre became, especially in the hands of the smaller men, mechanical, inflexible, inexpressive. We are familiar in English with the "see-saw" of the couplet. In their reaction from this formalism many of the partisans of the *vers libre* have gone to the opposite extreme and fallen into sheer lawlessness. They have been unwilling to allow even the semblance of a barrier to their spacious dreams, and have made verse so flexible to all the sinuosities and windings of their revery, that they have often made it shapeless. They have succeeded in producing something that, in spite of M. Jourdain's classification, is neither verse nor prose; something that is not so much a confusion of the *genres* as the absence of any *genre;* "an indescribable something," says M. Lemaître, applying Bossuet's phrase about the human corpse after it has reached a certain degree of decomposition, "an indescribable something that no longer has a name in any language." Such is the last stage of eleutheromania. The eleutheromaniacs of poetry are in the same class as the painters who, in order that they may do justice to their "vision," are forced, as they would have us believe, to violate the most indubitable laws of design; or with the dramatists who dismiss lightly, as mere conventions, what are in reality convenient summings-up of the universal experience of mankind.

We should never have done if we tried to notice all the

ways in which the idea of beauty has been corrupted by those
who would make it purely impressionistic or expressive. One of
the most interesting attempts of this kind is that of the Neapolitan critic, Benedetto Croce, whose work on aesthetics has
gone through several editions in Italian, and has just been
translated into English. He has indeed been hailed by certain
enthusiasts as the long-awaited Messiah of aesthetics. Signor
Croce reduces beauty to pure expression, not so much by eliminating form as by giving the word form a meaning of his
own,—neither the Aristotelian and scholastic meaning, nor,
again, that of common usage. As he defines it, form is a mere
aspect, the inevitable result, as it were, of true expression. Art
has to do solely with the fresh intuitions of sense. Interference
with these intuitions on the part of the intellect is to be depre-
cated. The higher, or so-called intellectual intuitions, Signor
Croce denies. He discountenances the idea of selection in art.
The process by which the impressions one receives are trans-
muted and finally emerge as original expression, is purely
intuitive and spontaneous, and beyond the control of the will.

In short, Signor Croce is an apostle of spontaneity, but it
is the lower spontaneity,—the spontaneity of instinct and not
that of insight. His point of view is closely related to that
special form of reaction against dogmatic and mechanical
science of which I have already spoken. He shows himself one
of the keenest of intellectualists in his attacks on scientific
intellectualism. He makes many a trenchant distinction of just
the kind that we need at present. I therefore regret that I must
disagree with him so gravely in fundamentals. I regret that he
has adopted a theory of beauty that almost necessarily lays
him under the suspicion of belonging to the class of people of
whom Dryden speaks, who are ready to put the fool upon the
whole world. The conception of beauty as pure expression is
really very modern. In order to maintain it, Signor Croce has to
part company with Plato and Aristotle, and in general rule out
the Greeks as incompetent in the theory of beauty. It is only
when he gets down to comparatively recent times that he finds
the first glimmerings of the vast illumination that has dawned
upon himself. With his expansive view of beauty he looks upon
the whole attempt to set up literary and artistic *genres* as an

unwarranted meddling of the intellect with aesthetic spontaneity. All the talk that has gone on in the past about the proper boundaries of the arts, and the confusion of the arts, is, as he would have us believe, a mere logomachy.

> A tempting doctrine plausible and new!
> What fools our fathers were if this be true.

We should not fail to note an important resemblance between the pseudo-classicists and modern theorists of the kind I have been discussing. They all agree in reducing beauty to some one thing. The pseudo-classicists were for having only form, and so fell into formalism. Many of the moderns, on the other hand, discover the whole of beauty in those expressive elements that the pseudo-classicist either minimized or denied. The Abbé Batteux and Signor Croce are both aesthetic monists, the difference being that Batteux would see in all art only imitation, and Croce only expression. But let us have a wholesome distrust of aesthetic monists as well as of monists of every kind. Monism is merely a fine name that man has invented for his own indolence and one-sidedness and unwillingness to mediate between the diverse and conflicting aspects of reality. If romanticists and naturalists, no less than pseudo-classicists, have been unable to distinguish between form and formalism, and so have tried to reduce beauty to some one thing, there is no reason why we should be like them. Any sound analysis of beauty will always recognize two elements,— an element that is expansive and vital and may be summed up by the term expression, and in contrast to this an element of form that is felt rather as limiting and circumscribing law.

But though form thus limits and circumscribes, we should not therefore regard it as something inert, mechanical, external; we should not, after the pseudo-classic and romantic fashion, make concentration synonymous with narrowness and contraction, with tame acquiescence in tradition and routine. The law of human nature as distinct from the natural law is itself a law of concentration; only this law should be held flexibly and not formally, and this feat, though difficult, is not impossible with the aid of those higher intuitions at which Signor Croce sneers. Art of course cannot thrive solely, or indeed primarily, on the higher intuitions; it requires the keenest intuitions of sense. But if art is to have humane purpose, these intuitions of sense must come under the control of the higher intuitions. Otherwise art is in danger of falling into aimless expression, into what Lessing calls *der wilde Ausdruck*. With true purpose and selection, on the other hand, art may achieve form and essential symmetry. Emerson speaks of the instantaneous dependence of form upon soul, and Spenser says in a somewhat similar vein that "soul is form and doth the body make." We may agree with Emerson and Spenser if soul is taken to refer to the region of the higher intuitions; but it is evident that nowadays not only "soul" but "ideal" and other similar words have been strangely transformed, that they have come to be associated, not with the things that are above the intellect, but with the things that are below it, with what I have called the lower spontaneity. We have seen that for Lessing an ideal implied a somewhat stern process of selection and self-discipline with reference to definite standards. Since Rousseau, "soul" and "ideal" do not connotate much more than emotional expansion. A man may prove that he has "soul" by indulging in a gush of feeling, and pass as an idealist simply by letting loose his enthusiasm. In short, the words "soul" and "ideal" have already been so feminized that they can be used only with caution and may ultimately become impossible. Indeed, with their elimination of the principle of restraint the sentimental naturalists may finally discredit all the higher values of human nature and the words that describe them, until nothing is left erect but a brutal positivism.

Both Spenser and Emerson in the phrases I have just quoted are consciously Platonizing; and I myself have associated the higher intuitions with Plato. But I might just as well have associated them with Aristotle; for it is a fact that should give us pause that the master of analysis no less than the master of synthesis puts his final emphasis on these intuitions. Indeed, the form this insight assumes in Aristotle is often more to our purpose, especially in all that relates to art and literature, than the form it assumes in Plato. For example, in describing the region that is above the ordinary intellect Aristotle says that though itself motionless it is the source of life and motion, a conception practically realized one may say in Greek sculpture at its best, which perfected nearly all the arts of suggesting motion and at the same time gave to this motion a background of vital repose. Aristotle's phrase is not only admirable in itself, but it puts us on our guard against another of the main romantic and naturalistic confusions. For just as the romanticists would make concentration synonymous with narrowness and contraction, so they would see in repose only lifelessness and stagnation. Thus Herder complains that Lessing in setting such sharp bounds to expression would make "art dead and soulless; it would be lost in an inert repose that could please only a friar of the Middle Ages," etc. Now I for one should not deny that Lessing's conception of repose is in some respects too academic. Yet if art is to be complete, it must have not only expression but form that circumscribes this expression; and in direct proportion as the form is genuine, it will be suggestive of repose, of a something that without being in the least inert and soulless is nevertheless raised above the region of motion and change. This perfect union of form and expression is of course rare; but there is evidence in the art and literature of the past that it is not impossible. Mozart, for example, obeys musical law spontaneously, being in this respect at the opposite pole from some of our modern artists who, under pretext of being original and expressive, merely succeed in violating law laboriously. If true art consists in having something to say and then saying it simply, the characteristic of this modern art is to have nothing to say and then to say it in a mysterious and complicated manner.

Expression can never become form or form expression any more than expansion can become concentration or the centrifugal the centripetal. But though form and expression can never be actually merged, it is plain from all that has been said that they should stand toward one another not as clashing antinomies but as reconciled opposites. In his essay on "Beauty" Coleridge gives an abstract definition of beauty that does not especially concern us, and then adds: "In the concrete beauty is the union of the shapely and the vital"; and this is very much to our purpose. Though in one sense the shapely must also be vital, as I have tried to show, yet Coleridge's phrase remains a fair statement, perhaps the best in English, of the necessary dualism of beauty. The problem of mediating between the two terms—on the one hand, the outward push of expression, and on the other the circumscribing law—is one that may be solved in innumerable ways, but solved in some way it must be, if beauty is to be achieved that is really relevant to man. This problem has always been present to those who have thought correctly about art. For instance, Horace was thinking of some such contrast when he wrote, "It is not enough for poems to be polished, let them also have charm and lead the mind of the reader wherever they will." Nowadays, if a poem enthralled us in the way Horace describes, we should call it beautiful without any more ado; but Horace was too civilized to be guilty of any such one-sidedness. For extremes are barbarous, and if an artist lean too one-sidedly toward either the shapely or the vital, he is in danger of ceasing to be humane. There is no doubt as to the extreme toward which we are inclining to-day. One of the English reviews recently praised as the greatest work of genius of the last quarter-century Thomas Hardy's *Dynasts*,—a drama in three parts, nineteen acts, and one hundred and thirty scenes, and at the same time a medley of prose and verse (and very bad verse at that). Now *The Dynasts* is a work of genius no doubt, but of undisciplined genius surely. Though vital it is certainly not shapely. In fact, a few more such performances might reconcile us to a little Aristotelian formalism. To take an example from another field, Rodin's *Belle qui fut Heaulmière* may be vital but can scarcely be regarded as shapely. In general, Rodin and other impressionistic sculptors are straining so hard to be vital and expressive that they are in danger of overstepping the bounds of their art, of violating its special form and symmetry, and so of failing to temper their rendering of life and motion with a sufficient suggestion of repose. The whole world seems to be growing increasingly barbaric in this matter of symmetry. I have actually heard the epithet beautiful applied to sky-scrapers. Now sky-scrapers may be picturesque, or vital, or what you will, though they are usually not much more than a mixture of megalomania and commercialism. But even though they did express fully the race of industrial and financial Titans that now has us in its grip, they would still fall short of being beautiful. For Titanism is too unmeasured and unrestrained to represent at best more than one of the two terms that must be reconciled in true beauty. Contrast with lower New York the perspectives that open up from the Place de la Concorde at Paris. The Parisian symmetry is perhaps not sufficiently subtle; it is still too reminiscent of the kind that may be constructed with a rule and compass, yet by virtue of it this part of Paris makes a vastly closer approach to the beautiful than anything in lower New York.

But it is vain to talk of form and symmetry to the pure expansionist. As I have said, he tends to identify repose with inertia and concentration with narrowness. He would have us believe that art must aim exclusively at the vital and expressive, or else be fatally condemned to remain in a rut of imitation and go on repeating the same stereotyped forms. This is the fallacy at the bottom of a very celebrated piece of writing of Renan's,—his *Prayer on the Acropolis.* Renan here expresses, in language that is itself a model of form, ideas that are a denial of all the formal virtues. He begins after the romantic wont by an outburst of sympathy and comprehension for the Parthenon and the Athenians and Pallas Athene; and then enthusiasm gives way to the reflection that the followers of Athene and of classical perfection would after all confine the human spirit in the pinfold of some special form; they would neglect the infinite expressiveness and suggestiveness of other varieties of art. They would know nothing beyond reason and good sense. But the world is greater than they suppose, and so some day they will come to be regarded as the "disciples of ennui." "If thou hadst seen the snows of the pole and the mysteries of the austral sky," says Renan to Athene, "thy brow, O goddess ever calm, would not be so serene, thy head more capacious would embrace divers kinds of beauty."

One could not wish a better example of the romantic tendency to regard as an outer form what is in reality an inner discipline, in other words to confuse form with formalism. If the Parthenon has value, it is only as an adumbration of something higher than itself or any number of particular forms, of the law of unity, measure, purpose. Having got rid of the outer form, Renan would at the same time be rid of the inner discipline and of everything that opposes itself to expansion, to an infinite and indeterminate vagabondage of intellect and sensibility. He arrives, as every consistent naturalist must, at pure transformism; that is, he sees everything passing over into everything else by almost insensible gradations. There is no place in the process for the sharply drawn line of demarcation, for the firm and fast distinction. Definite standards are swallowed up in a universal relativity. "A philosophy doubtless perverse," says Renan, "has led me to believe that good and evil, pleasure and pain, beauty and ugliness, reason and madness, are transformed into one another by shades as imperceptible as those on the neck of a dove." Thus Renan's motto in dealing with ideas is like that of Verlaine in dealing with sensations, *la nuance, la nuance toujours.* Dr. Johnson says we should "neglect the minuter discriminations" and "not number the streaks of the tulip." But that is just what the whole modern school has been doing. This has meant in practice the exaltation of the feminine over the masculine powers of personality, and so the exercise of faculties in themselves necessary and legitimate has assumed the aspect of a decadence, of what M. Lasserre calls "an integral corruption of the higher parts of human nature."

Thus the *Prayer on the Acropolis,* probably the most brilliant piece of prose written during the second half of the nineteenth century, turns out, when examined from the humanistic point of view, to involve a fallacy. We may note here, as closely related to Renan's fallacy, the incalculable harm that is done to art and literature by a certain conception of progress. The doctrine of progress is often interpreted to mean that man grows by moving in one direction, whereas man actually grows by moving in different directions simultaneously; that is by mediating between various half-truths and partial glimpses of reality. For example, it is proclaimed that the music of Richard Strauss is an advance over that of Wagner, that it has still greater expressiveness and stands for a still ampler freedom. At these glad tidings the innumerable army of faddists hastens to join the procession. But there may be still a few persons who are not content merely to keep up with the procession but who would also like to know where the procession is going,—whether it is headed toward some humane goal or is simply getting farther and farther out toward the extreme tip of what Sainte-Beuve calls the romantic Kamchatka. Now our present subject is a sort of watch-tower from which we can sweep a wide horizon and so form some conjecture as to the contemporary movement and its direction. It is plain from all I have said that I myself would conclude from a survey of this kind that what we are now seeing in nearly all fields of human endeavor, in art and philosophy and education, is a violent extreme,—the extreme of scientific and sentimental naturalism. Of course the present movement may continue indefinitely. We may have theories about education still more undisciplinary than the radical forms of the elective system, a still more pathological outpouring of fiction to the exclusion of the other literary *genres*, sculpture still more impressionistic than that of Rodin and his disciples, music still more given up to the pursuit of overtones and iridescences than that of Debussy, philosophy even more careless of rationality than that of the pragmatists, ideas about art still more subversive of the element of symmetry in beauty than those of Lipps and Croce. In short, the process of dehumanizing life and literature may go on forever;—it may, but we should not count on it, especially if the French saying be true, that good sense is the genius of humanity. In the past reactions have been known to occur against extremes of this kind, and they have occasionally been sudden. Even the faddist should therefore temper his eagerness to keep up with the procession with some thought of the danger of coming in at the very end of any movement; as the Spanish proverb says, the last monkey gets drowned. For over a century now there has been an almost exclusive play of centrifugal forces; of exploration into the remote and outlying regions of nature and human nature. Some day, perhaps not remote, there may be a counter-movement toward the centre. In short, to revert to a psychological theory I have already used, the world may now be menaced by a "subliminal uprush" of common sense—however alarming this prospect may be to Mr. Bernard Shaw and his followers.

But all such prophecy is vain; everything depends on leadership, and one can never say whether the right persons will take the trouble to be born. In this sense we may agree for once with Victor Hugo, that the future belongs to God. It is of course far from certain that the world will ever see another humanistic era. For example, Sainte-Beuve, who was eminent both as a humanist and a naturalist, inclined to think that France had already had her classic age and was now on the descending slopes of decadence, where it was already difficult and might soon become impossible to have any glimpse of true beauty. Sainte-Beuve was perhaps too much haunted by this notion of the classic age,—the notion that a country like an individual has its period of childhood, and adolescence and full maturity and senile decay. This is another "biological analogy" that I for one distrust profoundly. If we must have a theory, the theory of the saving remnant might be more to our purpose than that of the classic age. Any one who makes a stand for a humane and vital concentration may perhaps, with somewhat less than the normal amount of illusion, look on himself as belonging to the saving remnant; he may at least be sure that he belongs to an infinitesimal minority. What Matthew Arnold would call the "elephantine main body" seems more convinced than ever that man, to become perfect, has only to continue indefinitely the programme of the nineteenth century,—that is, to engage in miscellaneous expansion and back it up if need be with noisy revolt against all the forms of the past. Any one who holds a different view is set down at once as a mere laggard and reactionary. But the man who is urging humane concentration may rather regard himself as a pioneer and leader of a forlorn hope, whereas the true laggard—and a dangerous laggard at that—may turn out to be the apostle of everlasting expansion, the kind of man who may be defined as the nineteenth century that is unwilling to complete itself. For this kind of man is rendering inevitable a concentration that will not be humane, but of the military and imperialistic type peculiar to epochs of decadence. When the traditional checks and inhibitions finally disappear and *élan vital* gets under way on a grand scale, with no countervailing *frein vital*, the only law that can decide which nation or which individual is to expand vitally and unrestrained is the law of cunning or the law of force. Such is the inevitable upshot of a pure naturalism.

Dark as is the outlook for the humanist, there are nevertheless some signs that the crest of the naturalistic wave has already been reached and that from now on we may expect some subsidence. On the sentimental side the naturalistic movement first found significant expression in the theory of the spontaneous and the primitive, and in one quarter, at least, the origin of the epic, romantic primitivism is plainly waning. We have seen that the neo-classic exaggeration in regard to the epic, as well as the other *genres,* was to turn it into a cold and deliberate concoction of the intellect. Buckingham, for instance, was convinced that Le Bossu, the chief neo-classic authority on the epic, had explained the "mighty magic" of Homer. The counter-exaggeration of the romanticists was to eliminate the element of conscious and deliberate art and make of the Homeric poems an almost unconscious emanation of the folk-soul. The opinion is now gaining ground that the *Iliad* and *Odyssey* are not primitive but works of consummate art, though the word art, of course, is not understood in quite the same sense as by Le Bossu. We can even see the beginnings of reaction against primitivism in the latest theories as to the origin of the mediaeval epic.

The decay of the romantic theory of the primitive and the spontaneous has important possibilities. This theory is responsible in no small measure for the mortal debility of intellect and character and will that is so evident in one whole side of the modern movement. We all know what this Rousseauistic side of romanticism has come to in its last pitiful representatives,—an Oscar Wilde or Paul Verlaine. The latest romanticists have discredited themselves, which is not perhaps a serious matter; but they have also thrown a certain discredit on art and literature, and this is far more serious. Think of the meaning that is coming to be attached in popular usage to the phrase "artistic temperament." The most urgent task just now is to react against the comparative neglect of the intellect and of what is above the intellect, which assumes so many forms in Rousseauism. The man of letters should not be so modest as to leave all the analytical keenness and intellectual virility to the scientist. Art cannot live on intellectualism, yet the pathway to the kind of creative art we need lies through the intellect. So far from fighting shy of the "false secondary power by which we multiply distinctions," we should make as many and as clear distinctions as possible and then project them like vivid sunbeams into the romantic twilight. That indeed should be the function of criticism at the present hour,—to bring once more into honor the broad, masculine, and vigorous distinction. We might then have a type of writing that is not intended primarily for women and men in their unmasculine moods,—for the tired scientist and the fagged philologist and the weary man of business.

The revival of the firm and masculine distinction can alone save us from the confusions that have crept into modern life and literature and that I have traced to two main sources,— emotional unrestraint and pseudo-science. To take an illustration almost at random, think how much of both enters into Zola's theory and practice of the novel. The pseudo-scientist sees only flux and motion, not only on the physical but also on the human plane, with no clearly defined frontiers anywhere. He thus co-operates in a way with the romantic eleuthero-maniac who wants unlimited emotional expansion. But, as I have already said, if emotion is to be humanized it must become selective, and in direct proportion as it becomes selective it ceases to be indeterminate: it acquires aim and purpose, form and proportion. The mere outward push of expression does not by itself suffice. The object on which expression expends itself must be intrinsically worth while, and this is a point that must be determined on other and higher grounds than individual feeling. We have here the truth that underlies what is apparently one of the worst of the neo-classic pedantries,—the hierarchy of the *genres*. The *genre* is to be ranked according to the intrinsic value and importance for man of the matter it treats. Because the neo-classicists turned this truth into mere conventionality there is no reason, let me repeat, why we should be like them. The essential thing, says Aristotle speaking of tragedy, is to get a good plot, and good plots are not easy to come at. According to the romanticists almost any outer incident will do if we only feel strongly enough about it. If the emotional reaction is right, we shall, as Wordsworth admonishes us, "find a tale in everything." An old man hacking vainly at a root with his mattock will then seem to us as fit a subject for poetry as

> Thebes, or Pelops' line,
> Or the tale of Troy divine.

Wordsworth's paradox, like many other paradoxes, has its own truth and usefulness, but the man who holds it is prone to fall into what M. Lasserre calls *l'emphase romantique*, romantic fustian; which may be defined as the enormous disproportion between emotion and the outer object or incident on which it expends itself. Victor Hugo abounds in fustian of this kind. A good example of musical fustian is Richard Strauss's *Domestic* Symphony. The disproportion here between expression and what is expressed is so obvious that one critic charitably hints at mental derangement. I read in one of the accounts of this composition that there are required for its performance, in addition to the usual strings, "two harps, four flutes, two oboes, one oboe d'amore, four clarinets, one bass clarinet, four bassoons, one double bassoon, four saxophones, eight horns, four trumpets, three trombones, one bass tuba, four kettle-drums, triangle, tambourine, glockenspiel, cymbals and big drum,"—and all to describe the incidents of baby's bath!

After all, there is no great mystery about this question of the *genres* and the boundaries of the arts if we consider it vitally and not formally. It reduces itself to this: a clear-cut type of person, a person who does not live in either an emotional or an intellectual muddle, will normally prefer a clear-cut type of art or literature. Thus he is not likely to care for a theatrical sermon or a play that preaches. In many historical novels he will feel that history is travestied without any corresponding gain for fiction. He will be partial to music that is first of all music and to poetry that is above all poetry. He will distrust a symphony that becomes intelligible only with reference to some picture or poem. He will not ordinarily care for a painting that is merely a symbolical transposition of a sonnet, or a sonnet that is a symbolical transposition of a painting. He will desire each art and every *genre* to be itself primarily, and to give, as Aristotle says of tragedy, its own special pleasure. This is the one serious argument against tragi-comedy, that in trying to give the special pleasure of both tragedy and comedy it may fail of the fullest unity of impression. A unified impression cannot be obtained without some degree of concentration, relevancy, purpose. This chief emphasis on the masculine elements in art need not imply any disdain for the feminine virtues, or lead to an academic excess of gray design. Right design is the first requirement, but there should also be color and movement and illusion, and, in general, expressiveness— the more the better. Each art and *genre* may be as suggestive as it can of other arts and *genres*, while remaining true to its own form and proportion. But to set color above design, illusion above informing purpose, suggestiveness above symmetry, is to encourage that predominance of the feminine over the masculine virtues that has been the main cause of the corruption of literature and the arts during the past century,— what one may in fact term the great romantic, or it might be more correct to say Rousseauistic, error.

Though the clear-cut type of person will incline toward the clear-cut type of art, the *genre tranché,*—he will be guided in deciding what is sufficiently clear-cut and what is an unjustifiable hybrid, by tact and a sense of measure and not by any rule of thumb. Matthew Arnold, commenting on the mess Wordsworth made of his attempt to classify his poetry on a new plan, remarks that the Greeks displayed an almost infallible tact in making distinctions of this kind; and we may add that they showed their tact not only in the *genres* they established, but in holding these classifications fluidly. In Greek tragedy, for example, there is a free interplay and coöperation of the different arts and *genres;* they are separated only by a slender and sinuous thread, as André Chénier says, but a thread that is never broken.

In short, the Greeks at their best had humane standards and held them flexibly. They thus effected in some degree that mediation between the One and the Many that is the highest wisdom of life. This is an achievement so difficult for the lover of half-truths, like man, that we still have to look to Greece for our chief evidence that it is possible at all. The actual forms in which the Greek embodied his mediation between extremes are relative and need not be literally revived; but though relative, as particular forms must always be, they point the way to laws that are absolute. The man of our own time who really learned the lesson of Greek life might produce work that had little outer likeness to the Parthenon or a play of Sophocles or a dialogue of Plato, but his work would resemble these Greek forms in having vital unity, vital measure, vital purpose. I am not of course urging any blind worship of the Greeks or undervaluing all that has amplified and enriched human life since classical antiquity. As a whole Greek life may serve as a warning at least as much as an example, but the warning is no less relevant to our contemporary world than the example. The critical moment of Greek life was, like the present, a period of naturalistic emancipation, when the multitude was content to live without standards, and the few were groping for inner standards to take the place of the outer standards they had lost. The Greek problems were like our own, problems of unrestraint; for what we see on every hand in our modern society, when we get beneath its veneer of scientific progress, is barbaric violation of the law of measure. Greek society perished, as our modern society may very well perish, from an excess of naturalism; but Greek art at its best is a triumph of humane restraint. Therefore both in its failures and its success, Greece, especially the Greece of Socrates and Plato and the Sophists, is rich in instruction for us,—more so, I am inclined to think, than any other period of the past whatsoever. This is the very moment that we are choosing to turn away from the study of Greek. One might suppose that before deserting the *exemplaria graeca* it would be wiser to wait until the world has another age that proves as clearly as did the great age of Greece that man may combine an exquisite measure with a perfect spontaneity, that he may be at once thoroughly disciplined and thoroughly inspired.

* * * [A]n inquiry into the nature of the *genres* and the boundaries of the arts is far-reaching and involves one's attitude not merely toward literature but toward life. To treat the question exhaustively would require a grasp of general prin-

ciples and at the same time a knowledge of each separate art and its history to which I for one make no claim. I have not even tried to be exhaustive in this sense. I have aspired at most to be a humble imitator of Lessing in his endeavor, not to achieve a complete and closed system, but to scatter the *fermenta cognitionis*.

In a chapter from Rousseau and Romanticism *Babbitt focuses on diverse forms of romantic love as these depart from the law of measure and consequently reveal a confusion or a perversion of love. Especially in Rousseauistic love does he see the incongruity between the ideal and the real. Love as an expression of the romantic discloses a lack of restraint. Babbitt condemns the use of "an unduly dalliant imagination" to enhance emotional intoxication, to pursue illusion, or to create "the romantic religion of love." Love, he argues, must be related to the quest for unity and shaped by control of impulse. Ethical civilization and a moral standard, he insists, must be fundamental considerations if the romantic imagination, and specifically its vision of love, is to be contained. If to some critics his obsessive moral concern is his chief weakness, to Babbitt it is the sustaining strength of his message, which he summarizes: "Experience after all has other uses than to supply furnishings for the tower of ivory; it should control the judgment and guide the will; it is in short the necessary basis of conduct. The greater a man's moral seriousness, the more will he be concerned with doing rather than dreaming (and I include right meditation among the forms of doing). He will also demand an art and literature that reflect this, his main preoccupation." (From* Rousseau and Romanticism *[Boston and New York: Houghton Mifflin Co., 1919], pp. 220–39.)*

ROMANTIC LOVE

What first strikes one in Rousseau's attitude towards love is the separation, even wider here perhaps than elsewhere, between the ideal and the real. He dilates in the *Confessions* on the difference of the attachment that he felt when scarcely more than a boy for two young women of Geneva, Mademoiselle Vulson and Mademoiselle Goton. His attachment for the latter was real in a sense that Zola would have understood. His attachment for Mademoiselle Vulson reminds one rather of that of a mediaeval knight for his lady. The same contrast runs through Rousseau's life. "Seamstresses, chambermaids, shop-girls," he says, "attracted me very little. I had to have fine ladies." So much for the ideal; the real was Thérèse Levasseur.

We are not to suppose that Rousseau's love even when most ideal is really exalted above the fleshly level. Byron indeed says of Rousseau that "his was not the love of living dame but of ideal beauty," and if this were strictly true Rousseau might be accounted a Platonist. But any particular beautiful object is for Plato only a symbol or adumbration of a supersensuous beauty; so that an earthly love can be at best only a stepping-stone to the Uranian Aphrodite. The terrestrial and the heavenly loves are not in short run together, whereas the essence of Rousseauistic love is this very blending. "Rousseau," says Joubert, "had a voluptuous mind. In his writings the soul is always mingled with the body and never distinct from it. No one has ever rendered more vividly the impression of the flesh touching the spirit and the delights of their marriage." I need not, however, repeat here what I have said elsewhere about this confusion of the planes of being, perhaps the most important aspect of romantic love.

Though Rousseau is not a true Platonist in his treatment of love, he does, as I have said, recall at times the cult of the mediaeval knight for his lady. One may even find in mediaeval love something that is remotely related to Rousseau's contrast between the ideal and the actual; for in its attitude towards woman as in other respects the Middle Ages tended to be extreme. Woman is either depressed below the human level as the favorite instrument of the devil in man's temptation (*mulier hominis confusio*), or else exalted above this level as the mother of God. The figure of Mary blends sense and spirit in a way that is foreign to Plato and the ancients. As Heine says very profanely, the Virgin was a sort of heavenly *dame du comptoir* whose celestial smile drew the northern barbarians into the Church. Sense was thus pressed into the service of spirit at the risk of a perilous confusion. The chivalric cult of the lady has obvious points of contact with the worship of the Madonna. The knight who is raised from one height of perfection to another by the light of his lady's eyes is also pressing sense into the service of spirit with the same risk that the process may be reversed. The reversal actually takes place in Rousseau and his followers: spirit is pressed into the service of sense in such wise as to give to sense a sort of infinitude.

Baudelaire pays his homage to a Parisian grisette in the form of a Latin canticle to the Virgin. The perversion of mediaeval love is equally though not quite so obviously present in many other Rousseauists.

I have said that the Middle Ages inclined to the extreme; mediaeval writers are, however, fond of insisting on "measure"; and this is almost inevitable in view of the large amount of classical, especially Aristotelian, survival throughout this period. But the two distinctively mediaeval types, the saint and the knight, are neither of them mediators. They stand, however, on an entirely different footing as regards the law of measure. Not even Aristotle himself would maintain that the law of measure applies to saintliness, and in general to the religious realm. The saint in so far as he is saintly has undergone conversion, has in the literal sense of the word faced around and is looking in an entirely different direction from that to which the warnings "nothing too much" and "think as a mortal" apply. Very different psychic elements may indeed appear in any particular saint. A book has been published recently on the *Romanticism of St. Francis.* The truth seems to be that though St. Francis had his romantic side, he was even more religious than romantic. One may affirm with some confidence of another mediaeval figure, Peter the Hermit, that he was, on the other hand, much more romantic than religious. For all the information we have tends to show that he was a very restless person and a man's restlessness is ordinarily in inverse ratio to his religion.

If the saint transcends in a way the law of measure, the knight on the other hand should be subject to it. For courage and the love of woman—his main interests in life—belong not to the religious but to the secular realm. But in his conception of love and measure the knight was plainly not a mediator but an extremist: he was haunted by the idea of adventure, of a love and courage that transcend the bounds not merely of the probable but of the possible. His imagination is romantic in the sense I have tried to define—it is straining, that is, beyond the confines of the real. Ruskin's violent diatribe against Cervantes for having killed "idealism" by his ridicule of these knightly exaggerations, is in itself absurd, but interesting as evidence of the quality of Ruskin's own imagination. Like other romanticists I have cited, he seems to have been not unaware of his own kinship to Don Quixote. The very truth about either the mediaeval or modern forms of romantic love—love which is on the secular level and at the same time sets itself above the law of measure—was uttered by Dr. Johnson in his comment on the heroic plays of Dryden: "By admitting the romantic omnipotence of love he has recommended as laudable and worthy of imitation that conduct which through all ages the good have censured as vicious and the bad have despised as foolish."

The man of the Middle Ages, however extravagant in his imaginings, was often no doubt terrestrial enough in his practice. The troubadour who addressed his high-flown fancies to some fair châtelaine (usually a married woman) often had relations in real life not unlike those of Rousseau with Thérèse Levasseur. Some such contrast indeed between the "ideal" and the "real" existed in the life of one of Rousseau's favorite poets, Petrarch. The lover may, however, run together the ideal and the real. He may glorify some comparatively commonplace person, crown as queen of his heart some Dulcinea del Toboso. Hazlitt employs appropriately in describing his own passion for the vulgar daughter of a London boarding-house keeper the very words of Cervantes: "He had courted a statue, hunted the wind, cried aloud to the desert." Hazlitt like other lovers of this type is in love not with a particular person but with his own dream. He is as one may say in love with love. No subject indeed illustrates like this of love the nostalgia, the infinite indeterminate desire of the romantic imagination. Something of this diffusive longing no doubt came into the world with Christianity. There is a wide gap between the sentence of St. Augustine that Shelley has taken as epigraph for his *Alastor* and the spirit of the great Greek and Roman classics. Yet such is the abiding vitality of Greek mythology that one finds in Greece perhaps the best symbol of the romantic lover. Rousseau could not fail to be attracted by the story of Pygmalion and Galatea. His lyrical "monodrama" in poetical prose, *Pygmalion,* is important not only for its literary but for its musical influence. The Germans in particular (including the youthful Goethe) were fascinated. To the mature Goethe Rousseau's account of the sculptor who became enamored of his own creation and breathed into it actual life by the sheer intensity of his desire seemed a delirious confusion of the planes of being, an attempt to drag ideal beauty down to the level of sensuous realization. But a passion thus conceived exactly satisfies the romantic requirement. For though the romanticist wishes to abandon himself to the rapture of love, he does not wish to transcend his own ego. The object with which Pygmalion is in love is after all only a projection of his own "genius." But such an object is not in any proper sense an object at all. There is in fact no object in the romantic universe—only subject. This subjective love amounts in practice to a use of the imagination to enhance emotional intoxication, or if one prefers, to the pursuit of illusion for its own sake.

This lack of definite object appears just as clearly in the German symbol of romantic love—the blue flower. The blue flower resolves itself at last, it will be remembered, into a fair feminine face—a face that cannot, however, be overtaken. The color typifies the blue distance in which it always loses itself, "the never-ending quest after the ever-fleeting object of desire." The object is thus elusive because, as I have said, it is not, properly speaking, an object at all but only a dalliance of the imagination with its own dream. Cats, says Rivarol, do not caress us, they caress themselves upon us. But though cats may suffer from what the new realist calls the egocentric predicament, they can scarcely vie in the subtle involutions of their egoism with the romantic lover. Besides creating the symbol of the blue flower, Novalis treats romantic love in his unfinished tale "The Disciples at Saïs." He contemplated two endings to this tale—in the one, when the disciple lifts the veil of the inmost sanctuary of the temple at Saïs, Rosenblütchen (the equivalent of the blue flower) falls into his arms. In the second version what he sees when he lifts the mysterious veil is—"wonder of wonders—himself." The two endings are in substance the same.

The story of Novalis's attachment for a fourteen-year-old girl, Sophie von Kühn, and of his plans on her death for a truly romantic suicide—a swooning away into the night—and then of the suddenness with which he transferred his dream to another maiden, Julie von Charpentier, is familiar. If Sophie had lived and Novalis had lived and they had wedded, he might conceivably have made her a faithful husband, but she would no longer have been the blue flower, the ideal. For one's love is for something infinitely remote; it is as Shelley says, in what is perhaps the most perfect expression of romantic longing:

> The desire of the moth for the star,
>   Of the night for the morrow,
> The devotion to something afar
>   From the sphere of our sorrow.

The sphere of Shelley's sorrow at the time he wrote these lines to Mrs. Williams was Mary Godwin. In the time of Harriet Westbrook, Mary had been the "star."

The romantic lover often feigns in explanation of his nostalgia that in some previous existence he had been enamored of a nymph—an Egeria—or a woman transcending the ordinary mould—"some Lilith or Helen or Antigone." Shelley inquires eagerly in one of his letters about the new poem by Horace Smith, " The Nympholept." In the somewhat unclassical sense that the term came to have in the romantic movement, Shelley is himself the perfect example of the nympholept. In this respect as in others, however, he merely continues Rousseau. "If it had not been for some memories of my youth and Madame d'Houdetot," says Jean-Jacques, "the loves that I have felt and described would have been only with sylphids."

Chateaubriand speaks with aristocratic disdain of Rousseau's Venetian amours, but on the "ideal" side he is not only his follower but perhaps the supreme French example of nympholepsy. He describes his lady of dreams sometimes like Rousseau as the "sylphid," sometimes as his "phantom of love." He had been haunted by this phantom almost from his childhood. "Even then I glimpsed that to love and be loved in a way that was unknown to me was destined to be my supreme felicity. . . . As a result of the ardor of my imagination, my timidity and solitude, I did not turn to the outer world, but was thrown back upon myself. In the absence of a real object, I evoked by the power of my vague desires a phantom that was never to leave me." To those who remember the closely parallel passages in Rousseau, Chateaubriand will seem to exaggerate the privilege of the original genius to look on himself as unique when he adds: "I do not know whether the history of the human heart offers another example of this nature." The pursuit of this phantom of love gives the secret key to Chateaubriand's life. He takes refuge in the American wilderness in order that he may have in this primitive Arcadia a more spacious setting for his dream.

If one wishes to see how very similar these nympholeptic experiences are not only from individual to individual, but from country to country, one has only to compare the passages I have just been quoting from Chateaubriand with Shelley's *Epipsychidion.* Shelley writes of his own youth:

> There was a Being whom my spirit oft
> Met on its visioned wanderings, far aloft,
> In the clear golden prime of my youth's dawn,
> Upon the fairy isles of sunny lawn,
> Amid the enchanted mountains, and the caves
> Of divine sleep, and on the air-like waves
> Of wonder-level dream, whose tremulous floor
> Paved her light steps; on an imagined shore,
> Under the gray beak of some promontory
> She met me, robed in such exceeding glory,
> That I beheld her not, etc.

At the time of writing *Epipsychidion* the magic vision happened to have coalesced for the moment with Emilia Viviani, though destined soon to flit elsewhere. Shelley invites his "soul's sister," the idyllic "she," who is at bottom only a projection of his own imagination, to set sail with him for Arcady. *Epipsychidion,* indeed, might be used as a manual to illustrate the difference between mere Arcadian dreaming and a true Platonism.

Chateaubriand is ordinarily and rightly compared with Byron rather than with Shelley. He is plainly, however, far more of a nympholept than Byron. Mr. Hilary, indeed, in Peacock's *Nightmare Abbey* says to Mr. Cypress (Byron): "You talk like a Rosicrucian, who will love nothing but a sylph, who does not believe in the existence of a sylph, and who yet quarrels with the whole universe for not containing a sylph." Certain distinctions would have to be made if one were attempting a complete study of love in Byron; yet after all the love of Don Juan and Haidée is one that Sappho or Catullus or Burns would have understood; and these poets were not nympholepts. They were capable of burning with love, but not, as Rousseau says of himself, "without any definite object." Where Chateaubriand has some resemblance to Byron is in his actual libertinism. He is however nearer than Byron to the libertine of the eighteenth century—to the Lovelace who pushes the pursuit of pleasure to its final exasperation where it becomes associated with the infliction of pain. Few things are stranger than the blend in Chateaubriand of this Sadic fury with the new romantic revery. Indeed almost every type of egotism that may manifest itself in the relations of the sexes and that pushed to the superlative pitch, will be found in this theoretical classicist and champion of Christianity. Perhaps no more frenzied cry has ever issued from human lips than that uttered by Atala in describing her emotions when torn between her religious vow and her love for Chactas: "What dream did not arise in this heart overwhelmed with sorrow. At times in fixing my eyes upon you, I went so far as to form desires as insensate as they were guilty; at one moment I seemed to wish that you and I were the only living creatures upon the earth; and then again, feeling a divinity that held me back in my horrible transports, I seemed to want this divinity to be annihilated provided that clasped in your arms I should roll from abyss to abyss with the ruins of God and the world." Longing is here pushed to a pitch where it passes over, as in Wagner's *Tristan and Isolde,* into the desire for annihilation.

Actual libertinism is no necessary concomitant of nympholeptic longing. There is a striking difference in this respect between Poe, for example, and his translator and disciple, Baudelaire. Nothing could be less suggestive of voluptuousness than Poe's nostalgia. "His ecstasy," says Stedman, "is that of the nympholept seeking an evasive being of whom he has glimpses by moonlight, starlight, even fenlight, but never by noonday." The embodiments of his dream that flit through his tales and poems, enhanced his popularity with the ultraromantic public in France. These strange apparitions nearly all of whom are epileptic, cataleptic, or consumptive made a natural appeal to a school that was known among its detractors as *l'école poitrinaire* [the consumptive school]. "Tender souls," says Gautier, "were specially touched by Poe's feminine figures, so vaporous, so transparent and of an almost spectral beauty." Perhaps the nympholepsy of Gérard de Nerval is almost equally vaporous and ethereal. He pursued through various earthly forms the queen of Sheba whom he had loved in a previous existence and hanged himself at last with what he believed to be her garter: an interesting example of the relation between the extreme forms of the romantic imagination and madness.

The pursuit of a phantom of love through various earthly forms led in the course of the romantic movement to certain modifications in a famous legend—that of Don Juan. What is emphasized in the older Don Juan is not merely his libertinism but his impiety—the gratification of his appetite in deliberate defiance of God. He is animated by Satanic pride, by the lust of power as well as by the lust of sensation. In Molière's treatment of the legend we can also see the beginnings of the philanthropic pose. With the progress of Rousseauism Don Juan tends to become an "idealist," to seek to satisfy in his amorous adventures not merely his senses but his "soul" and his thirst for the "infinite." Along with this idealistic Don Juan we also see appearing at a very early stage in the movement the exotic Don Juan who wishes to have a great deal of strangeness added to his beauty. In his affair with the "Floridiennes," Chateaubriand shows the way to a long series of exotic lovers.

> I said to my heart between sleeping and waking,
> Thou wild thing that always art leaping or aching,
> What black, brown or fair, in what clime, in what nation,
> By turns has not taught thee a pit-a-pat-ation?

These lines are so plainly meant for Pierre Loti that one learns with surprise that they were written about 1724 by the Earl of Peterborough.

Byron's Don Juan is at times exotic in his tastes, but, as I have said, he is not on the whole very nympholeptic—much less so than the Don Juan of Alfred de Musset, for example.

Musset indeed suggests in many respects a less masculine
Byron—Mademoiselle Byron as he has been called. In one
whole side of his art as well as his treatment of love he simply
continues like Byron the eighteenth century. But far more
than Byron he aspires to ideal and absolute passion; so that
the Musset of the *Nuits* is rightly regarded as one of the supreme embodiments, and at the same time the chief martyr, of
the romantic religion of love. The outcome of his affair with
George Sand may symbolize fitly the wrecking of thousands of
more obscure lives by this mortal chimera. Musset and George
Sand sought to come together, yet what they each sought in
love is what the original genius seeks in all things—self-expression. What Musset saw in George Sand was not the real
woman but only his own dream. But George Sand was not content thus to reflect back passively to Musset his ideal. She was
rather a Galatea whose ambition it was to create her own Pygmalion. "Your chimera is between us," Musset exclaims; but
his chimera was between them too. The more Titan and Ti-
taness try to meet, the more each is driven back into the solitude of his own ego. They were in love with love rather than
with one another: and to be thus in love with love means on the
last analysis to be in love with one's own emotions. "To love,"
says Musset, "is the great point. What matters the mistress?
What matters the flagon provided one have the intoxication?"
He then proceeds to carry a love of this quality up into the
presence of God and to present it to him as his justification for
having lived. The art of speaking in tones of religious consecra-
tion of what is in its essence egoistic has never been carried further than by the Rousseauistic romanticist. God is always
appearing at the most unexpected moments. The highest of
which man is capable apparently is to put an uncurbed imagination into the service of an emancipated temperament. The
credo that Perdican recites at the end of the second act of *On
ne badine pas avec l'Amour* throws light on this point. Men
and women according to this credo are filled with every
manner of vileness, yet there is something "sacred and sublime," and that is the union of two of these despicable beings.

The confusion of ethical values here is so palpable as
scarcely to call for comment. It is precisely when men and

women set out to love with this degree of imaginative and emotional unrestraint that they come to deserve all the opprobrious epithets Musset heaps upon them. This radiant apotheosis of love and the quagmire in which it actually lands one is, as I have said, the whole subject of *Madame Bovary* * * * *

The romantic lover who identifies the ideal with the superlative thrill is turning the ideal into something very transitory. If the *summum bonum* is as Browning avers the "kiss of one girl," the *summum bonum* is lost almost as soon as found. The beautiful moment may however be prolonged in revery. The romanticist may brood over it in the tower of ivory, and when thus enriched by being steeped in his temperament it may become more truly his own than it was in reality. "Objects make less impression upon me than my memory of them," says Rousseau. He is indeed the great master of what has been termed the art of impassioned recollection. This art is far from being confined in its application to love, though it may perhaps be studied here to the best advantage. Rousseau, one should note, had very little intellectual memory, but an extraordinarily keen memory of images and sensations. He could not, as he tells us in the *Confessions,* learn anything by heart, but he could recall with perfect distinctness what he had eaten for breakfast about thirty years before. In general he recalls his past feelings with a clearness and detail that are perhaps more feminine than masculine. "He seems," says Hazlitt, one of his chief disciples in the art of impassioned recollection, "to gather up the past moments of his being like drops of honey-dew to distil a precious liquor from them; his alternate pleasures and pains are the bead-roll that he tells over and piously worships; he makes a rosary of the flowers of hope and fancy that strewed his earliest years." This highly developed emotional memory is closely associated with the special quality of the romantic imagination—its cult of Arcadian illusion and the wistful backward glance to the vanished paradise of childhood and youth when illusion was most spontaneous. "Let me still recall [these memories]," says Hazlitt, "that they may breathe fresh life into me, and that I may live that birthday of thought and romantic pleasure over again! Talk of the ideal! This is the only true ideal—the heavenly tints of Fancy reflected in the bubbles that float upon the spring-tide of human life." Hazlitt converts criticism itself into an art of impassioned recollection. He loves to linger over the beautiful moments of his own literary life. The passing years have increased the richness of their temperamental refraction and bestowed upon them the "pathos of distance." A good example is his account of the two years of his youth he spent in reading the *Confessions* and the *Nouvelle Héloïse*, and in shedding tears over them. "They were the happiest years of our life. We may well say of them, sweet is the dew of their memory and pleasant the balm of their recollection."

Rousseau's own Arcadian memories are usually not of reading, like Hazlitt's, but of actual incidents, though he does not hesitate to alter these incidents freely, as in his account of his stay at Les Charmettes, and to accommodate them to his dream. He neglected the real Madame de Warens at the very time that he cherished his recollection of her because this recollection was the idealized image of his own youth. The yearning that he expresses at the beginning of his fragmentary *Tenth Promenade*, written only a few weeks before his death, is for this idyllic period rather than for an actual woman. A happy memory, says Musset, repeating Rousseau, is perhaps more genuine than happiness itself. Possibly the three best known love poems of Lamartine, Musset, and Hugo respectively—*Le Lac, Souvenir*, and *La Tristesse d'Olympio*, all hinge upon impassioned recollection and derive very directly from Rousseau. Lamartine in particular has caught in the *Le Lac* the very cadence of Rousseau's reveries.

Impassioned recollection may evidently be an abundant source of genuine poetry, though not, it must be insisted, of the highest poetry. The predominant rôle that it plays in Rousseau and many of his followers is simply a sign of an unduly dalliant imagination. Experience after all has other uses than to supply furnishings for the tower of ivory; it should control the judgment and guide the will; it is in short the necessary basis of conduct. The greater a man's moral seriousness, the more he will be concerned with doing rather than dreaming (and I include right meditation among the forms of doing). He will also demand an art and literature that reflect this, his main preoccupation. Between Wordsworth's definition of poetry as "emotion recollected in tranquillity," and Aristotle's definition of poetry as the imitation of human action according to probability or necessity, a wide gap plainly opens. One may prefer Aristotle's definition to that of Wordsworth and yet do justice to the merits of Wordsworth's actual poetical performance. Nevertheless the tendency to put prime emphasis on feeling instead of action shown in the definition is closely related to Wordsworth's failure not only in dramatic but in epic poetry, in all poetry in short that depends for its success on an element of plot and sustained narrative.

A curious extension of the art of impassioned recollection should receive at least passing mention. It has been so extended as to lead to what one may term an unethical use of literature and history. What men have done in the past and the consequences of this doing should surely serve to throw some light on what men should do under similar circumstances in the present. But the man who turns his own personal experience into mere dalliance may very well assume a like dalliant attitude towards the larger experience of the race. This experience may merely provide him with pretexts for revery. This narcotic use of literature and history, this art of creating for one's self an alibi as Taine calls it, is nearly as old as the romantic movement. The record of the past becomes a gorgeous pageant that lures one to endless imaginative exploration and lulls one to oblivion of everything except its variety and picturesqueness. It becomes everything in fact except a school of judgment. One may note in connection with this use of history the usual interplay between scientific and emotional naturalism. Both forms of naturalism tend to turn man into the mere product and plaything of physical forces—climate, heredity, and the like, over which his will has no control. Since literature and history have no meaning from the point of view of moral choice they may at least be made to yield the maximum of aesthetic satisfaction. Oscar Wilde argues in this wise for example in his dialogue *The Critic as Artist*, and concludes that since man has no moral freedom or responsibility, and cannot therefore be guided in his conduct by the past experience of the race, he may at least turn this experience into an incomparable "bower of dreams." "The pain of Leopardi crying out against life becomes our pain. Theocritus blows on his pipe and we laugh with the lips of nymph and shepherd. In the wolfskin of Pierre Vidal we flee before the hounds, and in the armor of Lancelot we ride from the bower of the queen. We have whispered the secret of our love beneath the cowl of Abelard, and in the stained raiment of Villon have put our shame into song," etc.

The assumption that runs through this passage that the mere aesthetic contemplation of past experience gives the equivalent of actual experience is found in writers of far higher standing than Wilde—in Renan, for instance. The aesthete would look on his dream as a substitute for the actual, and at the same time convert the actual into a dream. (*Die Welt wird Traum, der Traum wird Welt.*) It is not easy to take such a programme of universal dreaming seriously. In the long run the dreamer himself does not find it easy to take it seriously. For his attempts to live his chimera result, as we have seen in the case of romantic love, in more or less disastrous defeat and disillusion. The disillusioned romanticist continues to cling to his dream, but intellectually, at least, he often comes at the same time to stand aloof from it * * *

*Babbitt praises Arnold as a positive and critical humanist. He cites Arnold's awareness of man's "permanent self that is felt in its relation to his ordinary self as a power of control." In this "permanent self," thus, Arnold discloses his opposition to the relative spirit and to man's ordinary self of passing desire, which result in anarchy. Though Babbitt perceives in Arnold a "dubious side"—for example, a fear of precise analysis and a tendency to set up poetry as a substitute for philosophy and religion—he salutes his instinctive good sense. That Arnold saw the importance of the role that the humanistic idea should play in a qualitative and selective democracy emphasizes his modernism. Babbitt praises the completeness of Arnold's critical positivism: his perception of the importance of man's inner self as opposed to the Philistine belief that material organization can serve as a remedy for moral anarchy. In Arnold he recognizes inspiration, austerity, seriousness, in short, the requirements of the humanist progra*i.*. The maxim that Arnold often repeated, "Semper aliquid certi propendum est" ("Always some certain end must be kept in view"), could have been one of Babbitt's own favorites. (From* Spanish Character and Other Essays, *ed. Frederick Manchester, Rachel Giese, and William F. Giese [Boston and New York: Houghton Mifflin Co., 1940], pp. 48–65; originally published as a review of* Matthew Arnold: How to Know Him, *by Stuart Pratt Sherman, in the* Nation *105 [1917]: 117–21.)*

MATTHEW ARNOLD

Two or three good articles on Matthew Arnold have been written, notably that by Mr. W. C. Brownell in his *Victorian Prose Masters,* but Professor Sherman has the distinction of writing the first good book. Without being blindly partisan, Professor Sherman is himself a convinced Arnoldian, and so his interpretation has something of that "indispensable personal gusto" of which he speaks* * * *

I

Now that Arnold and his message have been put thus persuasively before Americans, one is naturally tempted to inquire what value this message is likely to have for them. In answering this question, it is well to insist with Professor Sherman on a point that is often missed—on Arnold's essential modernity. What is more, one may affirm that Arnold was misunderstood by his contemporaries, not because he was less modern, but because he was more modern than they, and that he is still misunderstood for the same reason. One needs, however, to protect this statement by a definition of the word modern. This word is often used, and no doubt inevitably used, to describe the latest thing; but it is not in this sense merely that men like Goethe, Sainte-Beuve, and Renan use it—Renan, for example, when he speaks of Petrarch as the "founder of the modern spirit." It is not in the sense of the latest thing that Arnold uses the word in his address on *The Modern Element in Literature*. According to all these men, the modern spirit is synonymous with the positive and critical spirit, the refusal to take things on authority. The Greeks of the great period are, according to Arnold, modern in this sense and therefore much nearer to us than the men of the Middle Ages. Practically this positive and critical temper has been fostered by physical science and the type of progress that is due to science. This positivism has been more or less inimical to tradition ever since the Renaissance, but the decisive collapse of outer authority took place in the course of the eighteenth century. What supervened in many individuals upon the discrediting of all the forms of the past was a great spiritual isolation, a feeling of vacancy and forlornness; life no longer seemed to them to have any center or meaning. The old order had lost its hold on their intellect, but still retained its hold on their imagination. Perhaps no Englishman has expressed more perfectly than Arnold in his poetry this particular form of nostalgia. Arnold, it is true, did not continue to wander disconsolate "between two worlds, one dead, the other powerless to be born"; but if he finally threw in his lot with the modern spirit and the future, it was only after a severe struggle. He had, as Professor Sherman says, a "somewhat unhappily divided personality." He was later to praise the Greeks, not only for being positive and critical, but also for achieving what we too must achieve if we are to carry through our modern experiment successfully— the union of imagination and reason. This union is far from perfect in Arnold himself. His dominant note when he is most himself imaginatively is elegiac. He even seems at times, as someone has complained, to reduce the Muse to the rôle of hospital nurse. His reason so disapproved of this use of poetry that he actually withdrew for a time his *Empedocles* from circulation. On the other hand, when he set out to write poetry that would satisfy his reason, his imaginative fire seemed to desert him. Professor Sherman remarks of the very austere *Merope* that it will seem to some "a melancholy illustration of the disaster in store for a poet who sets out on his progress attended by an inspector of schools, a professor, and a critic."

II

It was not unusual toward the middle of the nineteenth century for a man to adopt like Arnold a positive and realistic attitude and at the same time to cast many a lingering look behind, to feel, so far as the struggle between the old order and the modern spirit was concerned, that his heart and his head did not belong to the same individual. Wherein Arnold differed from the ordinary man of this type as well as from his contemporaries in general was in the completeness of his positivism. Those who prided themselves most on their modernity were positive only according to the natural law; as for the human law they were simply for getting rid of it along with the traditional forms in which it had got itself embedded. But man, Arnold insisted, is the creature of two laws. In addition to his ordinary self of passing impulse and desires he has a permanent self that is felt in its relation to his ordinary self as a power of control. As a matter of experience, man can find happiness only in so far as he exercises this control. To deny such a conflict in man between a law of the spirit and a law of the members is simply to avert one's face from the facts and so to fall short of being completely positive and critical. The result of such an evasion is moral anarchy, all the more dangerous, one may add, when combined with an increasing grip on the natural law, or what amounts to the same thing, an increasing mechanical and material efficiency.

To be an active and militant humanist along these modern lines was an extremely rare achievement during the last century not merely in England, but on the Continent. One can scarcely find any equivalent among the Frenchmen who were in so many respects Arnold's masters. Sainte-Beuve, for example, was active and militant, but as a servant of the natural law. His humanism was on the whole epicurean, something that resided less in his character than in his sensibility. Anatole France is as a matter of fact nearer to Sainte-Beuve in the quality of his humanism than is Matthew Arnold.

Arnold's remedy for anarchy—the failure to rise sufficiently above the level of one's ordinary self—is, it is hardly necessary to say, culture. The warfare that Arnold waged on the Philistine in the name of culture is not to be confused with the romantic revolt from convention. To the respectability of the Philistine, Heine opposed, Arnold complains, positive disrespectability. So far from favoring Bohemianism, Arnold was not willing to pardon any outer irregularity even in a Dante. What the romanticist attacked first of all in the Philistine was his lack of aesthetic refinement; what Arnold attacked first of all was his lack of wholeness. The opposite of the man who is aiming at totality is the man who suffers from a stunted growth, who has partial and provincial views. "I hate all overpreponderance of single elements." This sentence more perhaps than any other that could be cited gives the key to Arnold's prose writings. In working out his model of a rounded human nature that he sets up for imitation he turns to the past; for if the positivist is not willing that the past should be imposed on him as a dogma he admits its validity as experience. The human law is not susceptible of final abstract formulation. It is many-sided and elusive. For this or that aspect of it we need to go to this or that country or individual or period. Greece can supply certain elements, Judea certain other elements, to the man who seeks to live proportionately. Arnold always assumes a core of normal experience, a permanent self in man, and rates a writer according to the degree of his insight into this something that abides through all the flux of circumstance, or, as he himself would say, according to the depth and soundness of this writer's criticism of life. It was inevitable, as Professor Sherman points out, that Arnold should be comparatively indifferent to that great fetish of modern scholarship, the historical method, which tends to deny the enduring scale of values, and to see everything relatively, to account for everything in terms of time and place.

The few writers, chiefly poets, who seem to Arnold to tend to imaginative wholeness, to combine ethical insight in an eminent degree with excellence of form, or, as he would say, high seriousness of substance with the grand style, he puts in a class apart; they differ from other writers not merely in degree but in kind. This general distinction, which goes back to Aristotle, is surely sound, and those who have sought to discard high seriousness in favor of intensity or some other criterion are simply compromising poetry and literature; they are playing into the hands of the utilitarian, who would relegate literature to the recreative side of life, who has no place in his scheme of things for the literature of wisdom, literature that ministers to leisure in the Aristotelian sense. It must be granted, however, that Arnold is not always as clear or consistent as he might be in the working out of his main distinction. When we ask him for a definition of the grand style in poetry and of the special quality of imagination, the ethical imagination, as one may say, that underlies it, he supplies us instead with brief passages from the great poets that we are to use as touchstones, a method not always easy to reconcile with his previous assertion that the worth of a poem is determined, not by separate passages, but by its architectonics, its total structure. He fights shy of theory because "the critical perception of poetic truth is," he feels, "of all things the most volatile, elusive, and evanescent." So far as he means by theory the merely metaphysical, every type of positivist will sympathize with him. But there seems to be something more than this in his avoidance of theory—some survival, namely, of the romantic fear of precise analysis. I have already mentioned Aristotle, and as a matter of fact Aristotle is almost necessarily the master of those who, like Arnold, seek to put humanistic and religious truth on a critical basis. Now two things are needed to make the complete Aristotelian: in the first place, hard consecutive thinking in working out principles, and in the second place, the utmost flexibility in the application of them. For, though fixed principles exist, one must grant Bergson that life in the concrete is "a perpetual gushing forth of novelties." If one is to bridge correctly the gap between the general law and the particular instance, one cannot be too finely perceptive, too "undulating and diverse." Unfortunately, Arnold seems at times to carry over into the realm of principle, where hard consecutive thinking is the prime requisite, the fluidity that is only permissible in the realm of practice.

Inasmuch as high seriousness of substance and the grand style coexist only in the best poets, Arnold is led to set up the best poetry as a substitute for philosophy and religion; to proclaim that what is best in philosophy and religion themselves is their unconscious poetry. Various correctives to statements of this kind may be supplied from Arnold himself, yet, even so, this remains his dubious side. One may affirm that the man of today will be more aided in his struggle toward standards by the study of Aristotle (perhaps the most modern of the ancients), especially of the *Ethics* and *Politics,* than by reading Homer, the chief of poets; and one may at the same time refuse to go to the opposite extreme with Plato and indict Homer for his lack of religious seriousness. Yet Aristotle's excellence of substance, so far from being associated with the grand style, is associated with something that at times comes perilously near jargon.

In the *Ethics* the most uncompromising analysis kindles at last into religious insight. Arnold got from Christianity much that Aristotle did not have. His attempt to bring this Christian truth into line with the modern spirit in the form of culture has in it much that is admirable, but seems to fall somewhat short in both the keenness of analysis and the insight. Of much of the opposition that Arnold aroused he himself has given the correct explanation: "More than half the world can never accept the person of whom they learn, but kick at the same time they learn." We can nevertheless understand the uneasiness of those who felt that he did not perceive the full gravity of the situation that has been created by the weakening of the traditional beliefs. Nor is it certain that he has rescued the full soul of truth from these beliefs in his definition of religion as morality touched by emotion. Jonathan Edwards, who combined genuine religious insight with the most unacceptable form of theology, insists in one of his sermons that religion is more than mere intellect or morality or emotion; it is above and beyond all these; it is a "pure supernatural light." The early Buddhists, who carried into this question an almost more than Aristotelian thoroughness of analysis, recognized a stage in meditation when religion is still mingled with emotion, but as the meditation deepens, the emotion disappears and gives way to unalloyed peace—*alta rerum quies.* The problem at bottom is whether in his dealings with religion Arnold rises far enough above the naturalistic level, which in his case means the stoical level. Professor Sherman suggests this problem very happily when he detects the autobiographical note in Arnold's comment on the final inadequacy of the philosophy of Marcus Aurelius. The point might be further elucidated by contrasting Arnold with Tennyson. Arnold did not, like Tennyson, accept the Victorian compromise; intellectually he is more firmly knit than Tennyson, superior to him, as he himself says, in being in "the main movement of mind" of his epoch. But there has passed into some of Tennyson's poems, into *Crossing the Bar,* for example, or the *Ode to Virgil,* a something that is simply not found in Arnold, a suggestion, at least, of the pure supernatural light.

III

If Arnold did not quite succeed in bringing religion into accord with the modern spirit without any sacrifice of its essence, he was surely on the right track even here. On the other hand, he not only worked out a positive and critical humanism that is very sound in itself, but he saw with admirable clearness the rôle that the humanistic idea should play in a democracy. In this respect he was ahead not only of his own time, but of ours. The England of his time still felt the reaction that had followed the struggle against revolutionary radicalism and Napoleon. So far as "the main movement of mind" interfered with the stock notions of the middle class which was succeeding in power to the aristocracy, it was simply for getting rid of mind. Arnold bent his chief efforts against this intellectual imperviousness, but he did not therefore wish to go back to the sheer expansiveness of the revolutionary period— its throwing off not only of outer but of inner checks. But what has actually been coming about both in England and in America has been just that—a resumption of the main expansive movement, a resurgent radicalism, attended more and more by the advent to power of what Arnold terms the populace. A writer like H. G. Wells harks back over the heads of the Victorians, as Professor Sherman pointed out in the *Nation*, to revolutionary Utopists like Shelley.

To say that most of us today are purely expansive is only another way of saying that most of us continue to be more concerned with the quantity than with the quality of our democracy. But this attitude raises very grave questions. Democracy is now going forth on a crusade against imperialism. The whole teaching of history is that the upshot of a certain type of democracy—and there are signs that this is the very type that is being developed—is imperialism. The only way to avert this danger may be to recognize the aristocratic principle, the need of standards and discipline. In that case Arnold, in working for a qualitative and selective democracy, showed himself more hard-headed and realistic, more modern, in short, than most of us. Anyone who should succeed today like Arnold at his best in being completely modern, positive, that is, according to both the natural and the human law, would make our eager progressives, the editors of the *New Republic,* let us say, seem almost archaic. Even an editor of the *New Republic* may, it is true, be modern enough to see that democracy needs discipline. In that case he looks for this discipline to some form or other of "efficiency," an excellent thing in its place, but when thus lifted out of its place, leading straight to that Philistinism or worship of mere machinery against which Arnold waged lifelong warfare. Not to get beyond the idea of material organization as a remedy for moral anarchy is still to linger in the zones of illusion peculiar to the nineteenth century.

Arnold looked, so far as he looked to any outer agency for securing a qualitative democracy, to an education that was to be held up to high standards by the state and was in turn to supply the state with thoroughly trained leaders. The contrast between the man who is positive according to both the human and the natural law and the man who is positive only according to the natural law comes out in his debate with Huxley on the rival claims of science and literature. Huxley, however, was comparatively moderate in his naturalism. The full peril of trying to bring the whole of human nature under a single law is seen rather in Herbert Spencer, who believed in man's descent from the anthropoid ape and worked out a scheme of education which puts an undue emphasis on this connection. In maintaining that Arnold's solution of the all-important problem of getting a sound leadership for democracy is a sort of compromise between Carlyle and J. S. Mill, Professor Sherman is ingenious but not always convincing. It seems hardly possible to secure a humanist by mediating between a romanticist and a utilitarian. One hesitates to grant Professor Sherman that Carlyle's temper was "soundly conservative" or that his psychology, even in his old age, was that of the true Tory. A full discussion of this point is not here possible. Let us simply ask ourselves what Dr. Johnson, perhaps the last of the great Tories, would have thought of anything so eruptive and irrational as Carlyle's notion of the "hero"; whether he would, like Carlyle, have seen in the French Revolution "a Truth clad in hellfire" and rejoiced in its "bursting through formulas and customs." The securing of a high quality of leadership through the interplay of education and government is as a matter of fact the central idea of Aristotle, an idea that Arnold completes from Christianity. Professor Sherman himself suggests as much when he writes: "By taking thought Arnold had become ardently progressive. . . . He aimed at something like the democracy of Athens—without the slaves. He aspired toward a society in the grand style for everybody. . . . That remote ideal he had in mind when he called himself a Liberal of the future." Arnold, if not quite so sanguine as this passage implies, wished at least a society in which the failure of anyone to measure up to the best standards should be due to inner, not outer, hindrances.

IV

Arnold, then, wished to go with democracy, but on condition—

and in this he showed the true modern spirit—that it should be a qualitative and selective democracy. He held that a democracy of this type might in forming its standards derive much aid from criticism. For an example of what he meant by criticism one may turn to his comments on our American democracy. It is interesting to read after the lapse of more than thirty years his address on *Numbers* and his essay on *Civilization in the United States,* and ask ourselves whether we have corrected what he perceived to be our main peril—the drift toward commonness, the lack in our national life of "depth and savor." In many respects this drift toward commonness, some might maintain, instead of being checked has been accelerated. "The Americans are an excellent people," Arnold wrote from Boston in 1883, "but their press seems to me at present an awful symptom." This symptom has become still more awful. We have witnessed since then the rise of the scarehead and the comic supplement. It was said of the people of ancient Miletus that, though they were not fools, they did just the things that fools would do. A glance at a current display of our newspapers and popular magazines suggests that, though we are not fools, we are reading just the things that fools would read. An American of the present day reading his Sunday newspaper in a state of lazy collapse is one of the most perfect symbols of the triumph of quantity over quality that the world has yet seen. Various views have been put forth as to the essence of democracy. If a man went simply by what he saw, he might be tempted to affirm that the essence of democracy is melodrama. It is the eagerness for the melodramatic thrill to which our newspapers and our "movies" cater. It is melodrama that attracts the five million or more readers of the novels of Harold Bell Wright.

Charlie Chaplin, it was recently announced "officially," is to receive $1,075,000 for appearing in eight films. This and similar facts would seem to throw some light on the passion we are developing for "whatsoever things are elevated." Goethe's warning against the bondage of the commonplace that Arnold was so fond of quoting (*Was uns alle bändigt, das Gemeine*) [what binds us all, the common] needs to be supplemented by another sentence of Goethe's as to the source of this bondage:

"The pursuit of pleasure makes common" (*Geniessen macht gemein*). Our old Puritan standards, Arnold notes, inculcated reverence, and in so far were a corrective of commonness. But from the point of view of the moral realist the main movement in this country would seem to have been from Puritanism toward epicureanism. We are, to be sure, very "idealistic"; but our "idealism" resolves itself largely on analysis into the very thing to which Arnold objected—into having an almost religious regard for the average man and deferring unduly to his opinions as expressed in shifting majorities. If the various symptoms of commonness I have been citing show anything, they show that the average man we have thus idealized is increasingly epicurean; he is for making the most of the passing moment with scant regard for any abiding scale of values. "Good time" are the magic words that many Americans of today seem to see written in great blazing letters on the very face of the firmament. If this drift continues, we may, in spite of our "progressiveness" and "idealism," develop a psychology not unlike that of the Roman decadence. It is not sure that the optimistic temper that Arnold admired in Americans and singled out for special praise in Emerson is entirely unconnected with our religion of the average man and the absence of standards it presupposes. It is easier to be buoyant if one thinks with the Ohio lady of whom Arnold tells, that excellence is common and abundant, than if one holds with Arnold himself that "excellence dwells among rocks hardly accessible, and a man must almost wear his heart out before he can reach her." Yet a buoyancy that is won at the expense of standards may turn out to have its drawbacks.

The majority, says Arnold, following the sages, is unsound. If we are to get quality in our democracy, it will not be so much through endless schemes for uplifting the average man as through increasing the size of our "remnant." This doctrine of the saving remnant has been denounced as priggish. It is the exact opposite. A man to belong to the remnant must be humble, must feel the need of looking to some standard set above his ordinary self. Anyone who thus looks up has some chance of becoming worthy to be looked up to in turn. If a considerable group of individuals thus take on the yoke of a

common standard, it will tend by its concerted effort and the
force of its example to leaven the whole social lump. Part of our
failure to achieve a sufficiently large remnant with high standards Arnold connected with our education. He was "more than
doubtful about our pullulating colleges and universities." The
changes in our education since his visit can scarcely be said to
have met his objections. Those who have been shaping our educational destinies during the past generation or two have in
point of fact been even nearer in spirit to Herbert Spencer than
to Huxley. Our reformers said with truth that the old college
curriculum needed broadening. What they have actually done
is not to broaden this curriculum, but to change its essence.
The main trend has been away from an education that was, in
intention at least, partly humanistic, partly religious, to an
education that is partly sentimental, partly utilitarian. Our
latest exponents of "this brisk and flourishing movement," as
Arnold calls it, are working with a veritable gusto to get rid of
what vestiges of humane standards we still have. Here again
the proper procedure is not to attempt a mere return to tradition, but like Arnold to oppose to a one-sided positivism a
thoroughgoing positivism, to insist on the facts in human nature that our Abraham Flexners simply fail to grasp.

I have perhaps been overstating the case that might be
made out against us from a strictly Arnoldian point of view.
Arnold's main contention, however, can scarcely be said to
have lost its force: that we are too much taken up with the
quantity and not enough with the quality of our democracy. If
we let our ordinary selves run riot, it may be well to reflect, the
resulting harm will not be confined to the aesthetic sensi-
bilities of a few "highbrows." Our only choice, as I have said,
may prove to be not between a qualitative and a quantitative
democracy, but between a qualitative democracy and imperialism. The great foe of democracy, a foe that has repeatedly been
fatal to it in the past, is anarchy, and the corrective of anarchy,
we cannot repeat too often, is not efficiency (as the term is now
understood efficiency moves on the merely naturalistic level of
man's being), but humanistic or religious discipline. If we are
to have such a discipline we must have standards, and to get
our standards under existing conditions we must have criti-

cism. "What the Americans most urgently require," says Arnold, "is a steady exhibition of cool and sane criticism." So far from having solved this problem, the "human problem," as Arnold terms it, we have not as yet even faced it fairly. We have no end of clever people, but clever people without standards. Professor Sherman not only joins to unmistakable brilliancy a concern for standards, but he is getting at his standards in a thoroughly modern and positive way. We may hope that in this respect he is a precursor, one of those sharpshooters of whom Arnold speaks who go in advance of "the elephantine main body" and prepare the future.

Babbitt counts the French moralist Joseph Joubert (1754-1824), no less than Matthew Arnold, among the "keen-sighted few." Joubert's writings on ethics, politics, theology, and literature reveal the dignity of criticism. He may be called "the critics' critic much as Spenser . . . the poets' poet." This high estimation appears in Babbitt's third major book, The Masters of Modern French Criticism, *which analyzes the confusion of standards in criticism corresponding to the confusion of genres in literature, examined in* The New Laokoon. *To be sure, Joubert has certain limitations, and one must not "accord him privileges too far beyond our common humanity." He is, for example, "too resolutely traditional" in politics and religion. But ultimately he is a distinguished critic who did not, like other moderns, "go mad over the powers of suggestion" and resisted the glorification of "unchecked spontaneity." Shrewd and practical, Joubert was a master of style, which Alfred North Whitehead has defined as "the ultimate morality of mind." Joubert disclosed both control of language and courage of judgment in this sentence: "Revolutions are times when the poor man is not sure of his probity, the rich man of his fortune and the innocent man of his life." (From* The Masters of Modern French Criticism *[Boston and New York: Houghton Mifflin Co., 1912], pp. 34–59.)*

JOUBERT

If Madame de Staël is the best type of the Rousseauistic enthusiast at the beginning of the nineteenth century we have in Joubert the representative of a very different kind of enthusiasm, the enthusiasm that may be associated with Plato rather than with Rousseau. The sharpness of the contrast between the Platonist and the Rousseauist may be inferred from Joubert's very severe judgment on Madame de Staël ＊ ＊ ＊ ＊ He writes in one of his letters that he had "avoided seeing her a thousand times and looked on her as a fatal and pernicious being." Yet when she died and the news of her death had been received with general silence and indifference, in strange contrast to the tumult in which she had lived, one of those most sincerely moved was Joubert. "The clouding over of such a reputation," he writes, "really afflicted me, and when I saw that no one was willing to think of this poor woman, I began to think of her all by myself and to regret with inconsolable bitterness the misuse she had made of so much intellect, energy and goodness."

So far as the general public was concerned Joubert himself lived in entire obscurity, more "enamored," in his own phrase, "of perfection than of glory." Yet he was singularly fortunate both in the friendships he enjoyed during his lifetime and the kind of reputation he has had since his death. His *Pensées* were presented to French readers by Chateaubriand and Sainte-Beuve, and to English readers by Matthew Arnold in one of the best critical essays ever written in English. The literary *Pensées* show such a fine quality of critical insight that Joubert has come to be regarded as the critics' critic much as Spenser has been called the poets' poet. He has that gift of ornate conciseness which he himself declared to be the supreme beauty of style. It is not, however, his phrase that he polishes, he says, but his idea; "I wait until the drop of light that I need is formed and falls from my pen." His ambition was so to express the exquisite as to give it general currency. Now it is not easy to imagine a continuous discourse made up entirely of the exquisite and we are not surprised when Joubert says he is unfitted for continuous discourse. "I lack intermediary ideas." His saying that sages do not compose reminds one of Emerson's description of the sentences in his own essays as infinitely repellent particles.

The danger for a critic who aims solely at the exquisite or in his own phrase at "expressing the inexpressible" and who lacks intermediary ideas, is that he may become affected and obscure, and Joubert does not altogether avoid these penalties of oversubtlety. "To reach the regions of light," he says, "one must pass through the clouds." Unfortunately Joubert does not always disengage himself from the clouds. But personally, I should not agree with those critics who prefer his *Letters* to the *Thoughts* because of their greater simplicity and naturalness. The *Letters*, however, do reveal one essential side of Joubert far more completely than the *Thoughts*. They are pervaded by a fine vein of whimsical humor, an habitual sportiveness, that suggests to Sainte-Beuve a comparison with Charles Lamb. It seemed to Joubert an important part of wisdom to distinguish the very few things that are to be taken seriously and then to take all other things playfully. *En tout il me faut quelque jeu.* He is at the opposite pole from those "serious and gloomy spirits who have very futile doctrines"; a sentence that inevitably calls to mind many modern reformers.

Possibly the danger of a sort of transcendental *préciosité* in Joubert appears most clearly in some of his thoughts on religion. He recognizes the existence of matter only by courtesy. If the Creator withdrew his breath from the world, he says, it would "become what it was before time, a grain of flattened metal, an atom in the void, even less than this; a mere nothing." Another sage of whom Joubert frequently reminds one, does not feel that he can dispose of matter quite so lightly. "I can reason down or deny everything," says Emerson, "except this perpetual Belly: feed he must and will, and I cannot make him respectable." One is tempted to say that in both the literal and figurative sense, Joubert lacked body. He himself admitted the justness of Madame de Châtenay's remark that he seemed a pure spirit who had stumbled on a body by chance and made the best he could of it.

Though we can detect in Joubert something of the shrinking of the valetudinarian from the rough and tumble of life, we cannot insist too strongly that his spirituality is true spirituality and not the Rousseauistic imitation. The words that he traced almost with his dying hand really sum up the effort of his whole life: "22 March, 1824. The true, the beautiful, the just, the holy!" He is far removed from a man like Coleridge who retired from his actual obligations into a cloud of opium and German metaphysics. The contrast between Coleridge's speculations and his daily practice recalls Joubert's thought, "Religion is neither a theology nor a theosophy; it is more than all that: a discipline, a law, a yoke, an indissoluble engagement." Though one of the frailest of invalids, Joubert never failed to meet the demands of life. He was justified in saying of himself, "Behind the strength of many men there is weakness, whereas behind my weakness there is strength; the weakness is in the instrument." His fellow-citizens in the little town of Montignac where he was born elected him justice of the peace and long preserved, we are told, the memory of his efficiency.

Sainte-Beuve does not seem to me to strike quite the right note of praise when he says that "once to have known one of these divine spirits (like Joubert) who seem the living definition of the phrase of the poet: *divinae particulam aurae* [particle of divine breath], is to be forever disgusted with all that is not fine, delicate, delectable; with all that is not perfume and pure essence; it is to prepare for oneself assuredly many annoyances and misfortunes." This passage suggests too strongly that Joubert was too good for human nature's daily food, whereas he was one of the shrewdest and most practical of men. He even pushed too far his horror of the merely speculative when he said you can learn more of the art of government from a single page of Machiavelli's *Prince* than from the whole of Montesquieu's *Spirit of Laws.*

The danger of Joubert's avowed dislike for mere reality, *l'affreuse réalité* [frightful reality], as he calls it, is not so much a romantic retreat into the tower of ivory as an undue sympathy for certain conceptions of the noble style and the grand manner. He says in defending Corneille that we should rise above the trivialities of earth even if we have to mount on stilts. His attitude towards the opposite school of art appears in his remark that the novels of Lesage "seem to have been written in a coffee-house by a player of dominoes just after leaving the theatre."

Joubert's shrinking from *l'affreuse réalité* is also to be connected with the fact that he had lived through the Reign of Terror. "The Revolution," he says, "drove my spirit from the real world by making it too horrible for me." "Revolutions are times when the poor man is not sure of his probity, the rich man of his fortune and the innocent man of his life."

Joubert as a young man had come into contact with Diderot and had got the initiation into the new critical spirit that such a contact implies. But even without the Revolution Joubert would never have been a thorough-going modern. The ancients, he says, were appealed to by the magic of the past and not like the moderns by the magic of the future, and he was in this respect a true ancient. The French are wont, rightly for the most part, to call their reactionaries "haters of things new" (*misonéismes*); but the epithet that should be applied to

Joubert is the more gracious Greek,—"lover of things old" (φιλάρχαιος). "The great drawback of the new books," he says, "is that they keep us from reading the old ones."

What the eighteenth century wanted, according to Joubert, was not religious liberty, but irreligious liberty. It was for discarding as mere prejudice everything that did not make itself immediately intelligible either to reason or feeling. "My discoveries, and every one has his own," he says, "have brought me back to prejudices." "Our reformers have said to experience: thou art a dotard, and to the past: thou art a child." The other extreme towards which Joubert himself inclines is to impose the past too despotically on the present. Though he vivifies tradition with insight, more perhaps than any other French reactionary, he is nevertheless too resolutely traditional. Such has been the revolutionary stress of the past hundred years that it has rarely failed to disturb the poise even of the most finely tempered spirits. Joubert tends to see only the benefits of order just as Emerson tends to see only the benefits of emancipation.

In the name of what he conceives to be order, he would be too ready to deliver society over to the Jesuits and fix it in a sort of hieratic immobility. He sees our main modern misfortune in what Emerson regards as our main modern gain. "Unhappy epochs," he exclaims, "when every man weighs everything by his own weight, and walks, as the Bible says, by the light of his own lamp"; when the broad communications that formerly existed with heaven are broken and every one has to build his private ladder. Indeed the more leading-strings the better, if it be true, as he asserts, that "few are worthy of experience, most allow themselves to be corrupted by it."

Joubert is of course consistent in his severe handling of the two great leaders of eighteenth century thought, Voltaire and Rousseau. He can, to be sure, imagine good coming from a reformed Rousseau, but can conceive of no circumstances in which a Voltaire would be of any profit. "Voltaire," he says, "would have read patiently thirty or forty folio volumes to find in them one little irreligious jest. That was his passion, his ambition, his mania." Yet in the final analysis the irreligion of Voltaire is a less insidious danger than the pseudo-religion of

Rousseau. "I speak to tender, to ardent, to lofty spirits, to spirits born with one of these distinctive characteristics of religion, and I say to them: Only J. J. Rousseau can detach you from religion and nothing but religion can cure you of J. J. Rousseau."

If Joubert leans too much to the side of reaction in his politics and religion he preserves in the main a remarkable poise in his literary opinions. He was placed between an age that had been rational in a way to discredit the reason and an age that was going to be imaginative in a way to discredit the imagination. He protests against the excess of the past and utters a warning against the excess that was to come. Yet nothing would give a falser notion of Joubert's work than to look on it primarily as a warning or a protest, or upon his rôle as only negative and restrictive. For the French he is not merely the author of the *Pensées,* but, along with Fontanes, the literary mentor of Chateaubriand. Now of these two "guardian angels" of Chateaubriand, as Sainte-Beuve calls them, Joubert was the one who inspired and encouraged, whereas Fontanes was rather inclined to caution and hold back. In his attacks on formalism, in his plea for hospitality of mind and feeling, Joubert had his face turned towards the future. *Ayons le coeur et l'esprit hospitaliers* [Let us have a hospitable heart and spirit]—this one phrase sums up about all that is legitimate in the new criticism.

The eighteenth century had wrought harm to poetry, partly by imposing a mechanical imitation, partly by the abuse of rationalism. Joubert is constantly vindicating the claims of the imagination against both the formalists and the rationalists. "Nothing that does not enrapture is poetry; the lyre is so to speak a winged instrument." No view of life is sound that lacks imaginative wholeness. "Whatever we think, we must think with our whole selves, soul and body," and above all avoid one-sidedness. "Man is an immense being in some sort, who may exist partially but whose existence is delectable in proportion as it becomes full and complete." It would not be easy to find an utterance more satisfying than this from the point of view of the humanist. Above all Joubert is severe upon the one-sided intellectualists (and here again his animus against the eighteenth century appears). Philosophers fall into unreality from "confounding what is spiritual with what is abstract." He warns us to distrust words in philosophical books that "have not become generally current and are fit only to form a special dialect." "How many people become abstract in order to appear profound! Most abstract terms are shadows concealing voids." Philosophy should "have a Muse and not be a mere reasoning shop."

Joubert, it should be added, was himself a man of wide philosophical reading. He was one of the first Frenchmen to make a thorough study of Kant, whom he read in the Latin translation—"a German Latin," he writes Madame de Beaumont, "as hard as pebbles." Getting at Kant's ideas is like cracking ostrich eggs with one's head and then most often finding nothing in them. "A man," Joubert remarks, "may sprain his mind as well as his body," and he seems to have suffered a sort of intellectual sprain from reading this Latin translation of Kant. His final judgment on Kant is that he was intellectual where he should have been intuitive and so "missed the true measure of all things."

Joubert, according to Chateaubriand, wanted his philosophy to be at the same time painting and poetry. A philosophical thought, as Joubert believed, when it got thoroughly matured lost its abstract rawness, as it were, and took on atmosphere, form, sound, light, color. Possibly his unwillingness to speak abstractly, even when abstraction is plainly indicated, is responsible for the somewhat over-luxuriant metaphor, the effect of *préciosité,* that I have already noted in some of the *Thoughts.* He seems very modern in his insistence that words should not be treated as mere algebraic signs after the fashion of the eighteenth century, that they should not be robbed, so to speak, of their aura of suggestiveness. He felt and encouraged the subtle emotional interplay and blending of the different arts that was to figure so largely in the romantic movement. "Beautiful verses," to quote one of his many utterances on this subject, "are exhaled like sounds and perfumes," and this should seem good doctrine to a follower of Verlaine. "We should not portray objects," to cite another advanced saying, "but our feelings about objects"; and this should satisfy even a post-impressionist.

But Joubert was careful to follow his own rule and never utter a truth without at the same time putting forth its complementary truth. He did not, like so many moderns, go mad over the powers of suggestiveness. After speaking of *nous qui chantons avec des pensées et peignons avec des paroles* [we who sing with thoughts and paint with words], after saying that when "you understand a word perfectly, it becomes, as it were, transparent, you see its color and form, you feel its weight," etc., he admits that the main thing in a word is not its color or its music, but its meaning; and that when words are so chosen and arranged as to express the meaning most clearly, they are likely also to seem the most harmonious. "What is wanted," he says, "is not merely the poetry of images but the poetry of ideas." "When the image masks the object, and you make of the shadow a body, when expression gives such pleasure that you no longer tend to pass beyond, to penetrate to the meaning, when the figure in fine absorbs the whole of your attention, you are held up on the way and the road is taken for the goal, because a bad guide is conducting you." This hits severely many of the French romanticists, Gautier certainly, and I should not hesitate to add, Hugo.

Unfortunately the French romanticists could scarcely have agreed with Joubert about the goal of poetry, for their enthusiasm was not like his, Platonic, but Rousseauistic, that is, they sought to escape from abstraction, not by rising above the ordinary intellectual level, but by sinking beneath it; and so the romantic movement turned in the main not to the legitimate revival of the imagination that Joubert desired, but to the glorification of an unchecked spontaneity. Joubert's actual use of the word enthusiasm might be made the subject of an interesting study. To what often goes by that name he applies some other word—*passion, verve, entrailles,* or the like. True enthusiasm in his sense is not associated with heat and movement as in Madame de Staël, but with light and serenity, and might best be defined, says Sainte-Beuve, as "exalted peace." And so Joubert reserves the word for the great poets, the saints and the sages. He speaks, for example, of the enthusiasm of Virgil.

Perhaps the difference between the two types of enthusiasts, the Platonist and the Rousseauist, comes out most clearly in the use they would make of imaginative illusion. Joubert is nowhere more original than in his ideas about the rôle of illusion in life and art. Here if anywhere he justifies his boast that he is more Platonic than Plato (*Platone platonior*). He defends art and literature against Plato by arguments that are themselves highly Platonic. The artist should not be satisfied with copying the objects of sense, for in that case his works would fall under Plato's censure of being at two removes from reality, mere "shadows of a shadow world." He should, on the contrary, so use the objects of sense as to adumbrate a higher reality; so as to produce a cast, a hollow cast as it were, of a heavenly archetype. Now this adumbration of a higher reality can only be achieved by the medium of imaginative illusion. By imaginative illusion communication may be established between the reality of sense and the reality of spirit. We may be made to "imagine souls by the means of bodies." "Heaven, seeing that there were many truths which by our nature we could not know, and which it was to our interest, nevertheless, not to be ignorant of, took pity on us and granted us the faculty of imagining them." We can perceive the truth in this sense only through a veil of illusion, and it is the grace of the truth to be thus veiled. This intimate blending of illusion and wisdom is the charm of life and of art. "God deceives us perpetually and wishes us to be deceived; and when I say that he deceives us," Joubert adds, "I mean by illusions and not by frauds." Illusion thus conceived becomes an integral part of reality, and we must not strive to see anything in its nakedness;—*il ne faut rien voir tout nu.*

There are evidently two extremes, that of Dean Swift, for example, who would tear all the veils from human nature and look on it without illusion, and that of Rousseau who would take the illusion and leave the reality (at least as Joubert would understand this word). In both cases the end was misanthropy. A comparison might indeed be made between Swift and Rousseau so as to illustrate in a curious way the maxim that extremes meet.

Joubert has remarks of extraordinary penetration not only on the right use of imaginative illusion, but on its misuse by the Rousseauists, on what one may call the false illusion of decadence. If Rousseau did not relate illusion to the reality of spirit, he did relate it in a way to the reality of sense; he used it to throw a sort of glamour over earthly impulse, especially the master impulse of sex. In his attitude towards this master impulse, Joubert not only departs from Rousseau, but is one of the least Gallic of Frenchmen. "By chastity," he says, "the soul breathes a pure air in the most corrupt places, by continence it is strong whatever may be the state of the body; it is royal by its empire over the senses; it is fair by its light and peace." Reason may suffice for ordinary virtues, according to Joubert, but religion alone can make us chaste.

Bernardin de Saint-Pierre not only exalted passion à la Rousseau, says Joubert, but threw a pseudo-idealistic glamour over the whole of nature. The result is a sort of "ecstatic epicureanism, a gravely Anacreontic morality." "There is in the style of Bernardin de Saint-Pierre a prism that wearies the eyes; when you have read him a long time you are charmed to see that verdure and trees are less highly colored in the country than in his writings. His harmonies make us love the dissonances that he banished from the world and that you find in it at every step. Nature, it is true, has its music; but luckily it is rare. If reality offered the melodies that these gentlemen find everywhere you would live in an ecstatic languor and die in a swoon."

A question of some delicacy presents itself,—how did Joubert deal with the Rousseauism of Chateaubriand? "When my friends have only one eye," says Joubert, "I look at them in profile." But it is plain that criticism did not lose its rights even in the case of his friends. "Chateaubriand," he says, "has given to the passions an innocence they do not have, or that they have only once. In *Atala* the passions are covered with long white veils." The letter that he wrote to Molé about the character of Chateaubriand is a masterpiece of psychological analysis. In this letter Joubert anticipates some of the severest judgments of Sainte-Beuve, and at the same time contrives to seem not only amiable but affectionate. Joubert is not in the least a "beautiful soul" in the romantic sense with all the flabbiness that the phrase implies. We are asked to accept about everything nowadays on the ground that otherwise we shall show ourselves narrow and unsympathetic. "I love few pictures," Joubert replies, "few operas, few statues, few poems, and yet I am a great lover of the arts."

In other words, sympathy must be ideally combined with selection, which means in practice that expansion must be tempered by concentration, that vital impulse must be submitted to vital control. When Joubert was told that a great many passions are required in literature, "Yes," he replied, "a great many *restrained* passions." I have already quoted his charge that Rousseau ruined morality by turning the conscience itself into a passion, by making it not a bridle but a spur; and Joubert adds that "taste is the literary conscience of the soul." Now taste, like most other desirable things, is dualistic in its nature, is a mediation between extremes; but the selective and restrictive aspect of taste that Joubert emphasizes is not only the most important in itself, but it is the aspect which the moderns from Rousseau to Signor Croce have most persistently neglected and denied. We have seen that Madame de Staël tended to identify genius with taste, and to make both purely expansive. Joubert inclines rather to the extreme of concentration. "If there is a man," he writes, "tormented by the accursed ambition to put a whole book in a page, a whole page in a phrase, and that phrase in a word, it is I." "The ancient critics said: *Plus offendit nimium quam parum* [Excess is more offensive than too little]. We have almost inverted this maxim by bestowing praise on every form of abundance." Joubert attacks repeatedly another closely related naturalistic vice, the worship of mere force or energy, the literary Napoleonism of which Sainte-Beuve accused Balzac. "Without delicacy," says Joubert, "there is no literature." "To write well a man should have a natural facility and an acquired difficulty." We are more familiar with perhaps the exact opposite, with the man who had little natural facility, but who has at least succeeded in acquiring the sterile abundance of the journalist. Joubert has not a trace of our modern megalomania. "What is exquisite is better than what is ample. Merchants revere big books, but readers love little ones," etc. *Heureux est l'écrivain qui peut faire un beau petit livre* [Happy is the author who can write a beautiful little book].

Though Joubert was in a high degree judicial and selective, the standards by which he judged and selected were not
formal, but intuitive. "Professional critics," he says, expressing his disdain for the formalists, "can distinguish and appreciate neither uncut diamonds nor gold in the bar. They are
merchants and know in literature only the coins which have
currency. Their criticism has balances and scales but neither
crucible nor touchstone." That was the difficulty with La
Harpe; he knew the rules, but not the reason which is the rule
of the rules, and which determines at once their limit and their
extent. He knew the trade but not the art of criticism.

Though he possessed the critical touchstone of which he
speaks I am not setting up Joubert himself as infallible—that
would be to accord him privileges too far beyond our common
humanity. That he could be insufficiently on his guard against
formalism even in poetry where he is usually most at home, is
shown by his comparison of Milton with the Abbé Delille,
which is not only bad but almost monumental in its badness.
Perhaps his blindness here is an instance of the potency of the
Zeitgeist which he was one of the first to define adequately.

Still his critical intuition puts him on his guard as a rule
even against the *Zeitgeist.* Perhaps indeed Joubert may be
most adequately defined in contradistinction to the formalist,
as the intuitive critic. But in that case we shall need to define
with some care the word intuition. The intellect is evidently dependent on intuition, as was pointed out long ago by Aristotle,
for its knowledge both of what is below and what is above
itself. We may therefore distinguish two main orders of intuitions corresponding closely to the two main types of enthusiasm we have already defined: on the one hand, the sensuous
or aesthetic, and on the other, the spiritual, or as they are
sometimes termed the intellectual, intuitions. Intuitions of the
Many and intuitions of the One, we may also call them, making
themselves felt respectively, to repeat a contrast I have
already used, as vital impulse and vital control. We may speak,
for instance, of the intuition of an Emerson; we may also apply
the word to the aesthetic sensitiveness, the fine literary perception of a Charles Lamb. M. Lemaître says that Joubert was
a *singulière et délicieuse créature,* but he does not make espe-

cially clear why Joubert was "singular" and "delicious." The reason, as it seems to me, is that he was intuitive in both of the main senses I have defined. Like Emerson he possessed "the gift of vision, the eye of the spirit, the instinct of penetration, prompt discernment; in fine, natural sagacity in discovering all that is spiritual." Hazlitt says that Lamb tried old authors on his palate as epicures taste olives. So did Joubert. It would be almost needless to multiply examples of his literary perceptiveness.

Moreover he never confuses, like so many mere aesthetes, the planes of being corresponding to the different orders of intuitions. Men have always been conscious of the contrast between the rational and the intuitive sides of human nature, a contrast that pervades the literature of the world as that between the head and the heart. But the word heart is evidently subject to the same ambiguity as the word intuition itself. When Pascal, for example, says that the "heart has reasons of which the reason knows nothing," he evidently refers to the super-sensuous or spiritual intuitions. When La Rochefoucauld, on the other hand, says that the "head is always the dupe of the heart," he evidently refers to the desires and impulses that rise like a cloud about the intellect from the sub-rational region of human nature. A comparative study might be made between Rousseau and Pascal in such a way as to show that, though both writers make everything hinge upon the heart, they attach to the word heart entirely different meanings because they use it to describe different orders of intuition.

These distinctions seem especially needed at present when the thinkers who have the attention of the world, thinkers like James and M. Bergson and Signor Croce, are all agreed at least in appealing from intellect to intuition. If Joubert has so little in common with these thinkers, it is plainly because they are intuitive only in the Rousseauistic sense, and not like him in the Platonic sense as well. James and M. Bergson do not, like Joubert, look on the One as a living intuition, but as an inert intellectual concept; and they would have us believe that we can escape from this intellectualism only by diving into the

flux,—in other words by cultivating our intuitions of the
Many. It is to be feared that Joubert would have said of this
modern philosophy what he said of the philosophy of change in
the form it had assumed in his own time: "I detest these horrible maxims as the ancient sages would have done." He
looked with suspicion on philosophies which, so far from
throwing light on previous philosophies, simply contradict
them; and from this point of view, he would have looked with
special suspicion on M. Bergson. For if M. Bergson's conception of reality be correct, most of the great philosophers of
the past, beginning with Plato and Aristotle, have had, not
merely a mistaken, but an absolutely inverted view of reality.

To say that Joubert is spiritually intuitive is to put him in
the class of sages; a class, the representatives of which are
recognizable through the infinitely diverse accidents of time
and space by their agreement on essentials. It would, for
example, be easy to collect a list of parallel passages from Joubert and Emerson. "When there is born in a nation," says Joubert, "an individual capable of producing a great thought, another one is born capable of understanding it and admiring it."
Here is Emerson's favorite doctrine that "the hearing ear is
always found close to the speaking tongue." The following
thought, the equivalent of which might also be found in Emerson, we should be justified in calling Buddhistic, especially if
we remember that the very name Buddha means the Awakened: "How many people eat, drink and get married; buy, sell
and build; make contracts and attend to their fortune; have
friends and enemies, pleasures and pains; are born, grow up,
live and die,—but asleep!" Men tend to come together in proportion to their intuitions of the One; in other words the true
unifying principle of mankind is found in the insight of its
sages. We *ascend* to meet.

Possibly the contrast between the intuitiveness of Joubert
and the sages and that of M. Bergson may be brought out
most clearly by comparing their attitude towards time. Reality
is a pure process of flux and change according to M. Bergson,
and this change takes place in time; so that "time is the very
stuff of which our lives are made." We should strive to see

things not *sub specie aeternitatis,* but *sub specie durationis.*
Under how many forms, under what diverse conditions of time
and space, would it be possible to find the opposite assertion!
"The sage is delivered from time," says Buddha. "Happy is
the soul in which time no longer courses!" says Michael
Angelo. "Time," says Joubert, "measured here below by the
succession of beings which are constantly changing and being
renewed, is seen and felt, and reckoned and exists. Higher up
there is no change or succession, or new or old, or yesterday or
to-morrow." (Elsewhere Joubert adds that there is time even in
eternity, though not a terrestrial and earthly time which is
counted by the movement and succession of bodies.) Emerson
affirms in somewhat similar fashion of "the core of God's
abysm":—

> There Past, Present, Future shoot
> Triple blossoms from one root.

And so we might lengthen indefinitely the list of those who
have found their supreme reality, not like M. Bergson in time,
but in transcending time.

If a man becomes a sage only by being spiritually intuitive, it is highly desirable, and indeed necessary, if he is to be a
critic or creator of art and literature, that he should also be
intuitive in the sense M. Bergson recommends. Perhaps, indeed, the wisest man is he who has both orders of intuitions
and then mediates between them; who joins to his sense of
unity a fine perception of the local, the individual, the transitory. Joubert's quality as a critic is revealed especially by the
fact that he not only had standards but held them fluidly. His
insistence on the fixed and the permanent is nearly always
tempered by the sense of change and instability. "A man must
provide himself," he says, in his highly metaphorical fashion,
"with anchors and ballast, that is, with fixed and constant
opinions, and then he should allow the banners to float free and
the sails to swell; the mast alone should remain unshaken."
Again: "Truth in one's style is an indispensable virtue and sufficient to recommend a writer. If on every manner of subject
we wished to write nowadays as people wrote in the time of
Louis XIV we should have no truth in our style, for we no
longer have the same humors, the same opinions, the same

manners. . . . The more the *genre* in which you write is related
to your character, to the manners of the age, the more your
style should depart from that of writers who have been models
only because they excelled in expressing in their works either
the manners of their epoch or their own character. Good taste
itself in this case allows you to depart from the best taste, for
taste changes with manners, even good taste." Yet Joubert
adds (and here, perhaps, the reactionary note appears), that
there are *genres* that do not change. "I think that the sacred
orator would always do well to write and think as Bossuet
would have thought and written." "The vogue of books," he
writes in another passage, "depends on the taste of different
centuries; even what is old is exposed to variations of fashion.
Corneille and Racine, Virgil and Lucan, Seneca and Cicero,
Tacitus and Livy, Aristotle and Plato, have had the palm only
in turn. Nay more: in the same life, according to the ages, in the
same year according to the seasons, and sometimes in the
same day according to the hours, we prefer one book to another
book, one style to another style, one intellect to another intellect." "In literature and in established judgments on authors,"
says Joubert, in language that anticipates Anatole France,
"there is more conventional opinion than truth. How many
books, whose reputation is made, would fail to achieve this
reputation if it had to be won again!"

Though Joubert is thus willing to concede a great deal to
the element of relativity he is not ready to go to the point of
seeing in literature merely an expression of society. "It is a
hundred times better," he said, "to suit a work to the nature of
the human spirit than to what is called the state of society.
There is something unchanging in man; and that is why there
are unchanging rules in the arts and in works of art, beauties
which will always please or modes of expression that will give
pleasure only for a short time." *Il y a quelque chose d'immu-
able dans l'homme!* [There is something unchanging in man!]
The writers who are themselves likely to endure are those who,
like Joubert, really perceived this enduring something in man
and aimed at it. "Heaven," as he says, "is for those who think
about it." It is equally appropriate that the work of Madame
de Staël, whose main interest was not in this essential aspect

of literature, but in literature as the expression of society, that is, as the reflection of changing circumstances, should itself count less intrinsically than relatively and historically.

Joubert must of course rank below those who were truly creative, those who have left a definitive monument, who have had not only ideas but also, in his own phrase, the house in which to lodge them. He spent so much time in meditating his own monument and in making sure of the materials that were to enter into it that when he had at last made sure, as he tells us, that he had found what he wanted, it was too late, it was time to die. Yet in his own words, "a few memorable utterances are enough to make a great spirit illustrious. There are thoughts that contain the essence of a whole book." His own reputation is likely to rest securely on a number of thoughts and utterances of this kind. The world cannot afford to forget him, unless indeed the gift of intuition, as I have tried to define it, should prove more common among critics in the future than it has been in the past.

PART III

IDEAS AND THE WORLD

In the last chapter of Democracy and Leadership, *which examines democracy as the political expression of naturalism, Babbitt speaks as a conservative prophet who detects a disintegration in American culture and society. Democracy, he insists, must be judged by its leaders and by standards of leadership. For the most part, he concludes, both are lacking, and the pernicious results include a weakening of the inner life, sham spirituality, quantitative habits of mind, "sheer restlessness of spirit... and intemperate commercialism." Yet, as has been remarked, Babbitt is not a pessimist, but rather an observer who, closely scrutinizing the limitations of American democracy, sees the seamy side of political life and does not hesitate to call a seam a seam. His observations, that democracy has become a "standardized and commercialized melodrama" and that "we are moving through an orgy of humanitarian legalism towards a decadent imperialism," hardly make him popular. Although for some he appeared "on sleepless guard duty," lest we ignore that modern American civilization is "an immense and glittering superstructure on insecure foundations," for others his pronouncements merely reflected "New England, Republican prejudices." In the light of present-day conditions, "Democracy and Standards," like* Democracy and Leadership, *needs to be pondered both for its style and for its defense of the human soul. (From* Democracy and Leadership *[Boston and New York: Houghton Mifflin Co., 1924], pp. 239–317.)*

DEMOCRACY AND STANDARDS

Judged by any quantitative test, the American achievement is impressive. We have ninety per cent of the motors of the world and control seventy-five per cent of its oil; we produce sixty per cent of the world's steel, seventy per cent of its copper, and eighty per cent of its telephones and typewriters. This and similar statistical proof of our material preëminence, which would have made a Greek apprehensive of Nemesis, seems to inspire in many Americans an almost lyrical complacency. They are not only quantitative in their estimates of our present accomplishment, but even more so if possible in what they anticipate for the future. Now that we have fifteen million

135

automobiles they feel, with Mr. Henry Ford, that we can have no higher ambition than to expand this number to thirty million. Our present output of fifty million tons of steel a year is, according to Mr. Schwab, a mere trifle compared with our probable output of twenty years hence. In short, an age that is already immersed in things to an unexampled degree is merely to prepare the way for an age still more material in its preoccupations and still more subservient to machinery. This, we are told, is progress. To a person with a proportionate view of life it might seem rather to be full-blown commercial insolence.

The reasons for the quantitative view of life that prevails in America are far from being purely political. This view has resulted in a large measure from the coming together of scientific discovery with the opening up of a new continent. It has been possible with the aid of science to accomplish in a hundred years what even the optimistic Thomas Jefferson thought might take a thousand. The explanation, it has been said, of much that is obscure to us in the Chinese may be summed up in the words "lack of elbow-room." We in this country, on the other hand, have received a peculiar psychic twist from the fact that we have had endless elbow-room. A chief danger both to ourselves and others is that we shall continue to have a frontier psychology long after we have ceased to have a frontier. For a frontier psychology is expansive, and expansiveness, I have tried to show, is, at least in its political manifestations, always imperialistic.

If quantitatively the American achievement is impressive, qualitatively it is somewhat less satisfying. What must one think of a country, asks one of our foreign critics, whose most popular orator is W. J. Bryan, whose favorite actor is Charlie Chaplin, whose most widely read novelist is Harold Bell Wright, whose best-known evangelist is Billy Sunday, and whose representative journalist is William Randolph Hearst? What one must evidently think of such a country, even after allowing liberally for overstatement, is that it lacks standards. Furthermore, America suffers not only from a lack of standards, but also not infrequently from a confusion or an inversion of standards. As an example of the inversion of standards we may take the bricklayer who, being able to lay two thousand bricks a day, is reduced by union rules to laying five hundred. There is confusion of standards, again, when we are so impressed by Mr. Henry Ford's abilities as organizer and master mechanic that we listen seriously to his views on money; or when, simply because Mr. Edison has shown inventive genius along certain lines, we receive him as an authority on education. One is reminded of the story of the French butcher who, having need of legal aid, finally, after looking over a number of lawyers, selected the fattest one.

The problem of standards, though not identical with the problem of democracy, touches it at many points and is not therefore the problem of any one country. Europeans, indeed, like to look upon the crudity and chaotic impressionism of people who are no longer guided by standards as something specifically American. "America," says the *Saturday Review* [of London], "is the country of unbalanced minds, of provincial policies and of hysterical Utopias." The deference for standards has, however, been diminished by a certain type of democracy in many other countries besides America. The resulting vulgarity and triviality are more or less visible in all of these countries;—for example, if we are to believe Lord Bryce, in New Zealand. If we in America are perhaps preëminent in lack of distinction, it is because of the very completeness of our emancipation from the past. Goethe's warning as to the retarding effect of the commonplace is well known (*Was uns alle bändigt, das Gemeine* [what binds us all, the common]). His explanation of what makes for the commonplace is less familiar: "Enjoyment," he says, "makes common." (*Geniessen macht gemein.*) Since every man desires happiness, it is evidently no small matter whether he conceives of happiness in terms of work or of enjoyment. If he work in the full ethical sense that I have attempted to define, he is pulling back and disciplining his temperamental self with reference to some standard. In short, his temperamental self is, in an almost literal sense, undergoing conversion. The whole of life may, indeed, be summed up in the words diversion and conversion. Along which of these two main paths are most of us seeking the happiness to the pursuit of which we are dedicated by our Declaration of Independence? The author of this phrase, Thomas

Jefferson, remarks of himself: "I am an Epicurean." It cannot be gainsaid that an increasing number of our young people are, in this respect at least, good Jeffersonians. The phrase that reflects most clearly their philosophy of life is perhaps "good time." One might suppose that many of them see this phrase written in great blazing letters on the very face of the firmament. As *Punch* remarked, the United States is not a country, but a picnic. When the element of conversion with reference to a standard is eliminated from life, what remains is the irresponsible quest of thrills. The utilitarian and industrial side of the modern movement comes into play at this point. Commercialism is laying its great greasy paw upon everything (including the irresponsible quest of thrills); so that, whatever democracy may be theoretically, one is sometimes tempted to define it practically as standardized and commercialized melodrama. This definition will be found to fit many aspects of our national life besides the moving-picture industry. The tendency to steep and saturate ourselves in the impression of the moment without reference to any permanent pattern of human experience is even more marked, perhaps, in our newspapers and magazines. It was said of the inhabitants of a certain ancient Greek city that, though they were not fools, they did just the things that fools would do. It is hard to take a glance at one of our news-stands without reflecting that, though we may not be fools, we are reading just the things that fools would read. Our daily press in particular is given over to the most childish sensationalism. "The Americans are an excellent people," Matthew Arnold wrote from Boston in 1883, "but their press seems to me an awful symptom." This symptom was not so awful then as now; for that was before the day of the scarehead and the comic supplement. The American reading his Sunday paper in a state of lazy collapse is perhaps the most perfect symbol of the triumph of quantity over quality that the world has yet seen. Whole forests are being ground into pulp daily to minister to our triviality.

One is inclined, indeed, to ask, in certain moods, whether the net result of the movement that has been sweeping the Occident for several generations may not be a huge mass of standardized mediocrity; and whether in this country in particular we are not in danger of producing in the name of democracy one of the most trifling brands of the human species that the world has yet seen. To be sure, it may be urged that, though we may suffer loss of distinction as a result of the democratic drift, by way of compensation a great many average people will, in the Jeffersonian sense at least, be made "happy." If we are to judge by history, however, what supervenes upon the decline of standards and the disappearance of leaders who embody them is not some equalitarian paradise, but inferior types of leadership. We have already been reminded by certain developments in this country of Byron's definition of democracy as an "aristocracy of blackguards." At the very moment when we were most vociferous about making the world safe for democracy the citizens of New York refused to reëlect an honest man as their mayor and put in his place a tool of Tammany, an action followed in due course by a "crime wave"; whereupon they returned the tool of Tammany by an increased majority. The industrial revolution has tended to produce everywhere great urban masses that seem to be increasingly careless of ethical standards. In the case of our American cities, the problem of securing some degree of moral cohesion is further complicated by the presence of numerous aliens of widely divergent racial stocks and cultural backgrounds. In addition our population is not only about half urban, but we cannot be said, like most other countries, to have any peasantry or yeomanry. Those Americans who actually dwell in the country are more and more urban in their psychology. The whole situation is so unusual as to suggest doubts even from a purely biological point of view. "As I watch the American nation speeding gaily, with invincible optimism down the road to destruction," says Professor William McDougall, an observer of the biological type, "I seem to be contemplating the greatest tragedy in the history of mankind."

We are assured, indeed, that the highly heterogeneous elements that enter into our population will, like various instruments in an orchestra, merely result in a richer harmony; they will, one may reply, provided that, like an orchestra, they be properly led. Otherwise the outcome may be an unexampled

cacophony. This question of leadership is not primarily biological, but moral. Leaders may vary in quality from the man
who is so loyal to sound standards that he inspires right conduct in others by the sheer rightness of his example, to the
man who stands for nothing higher than the law of cunning
and the law of force, and so is, in the sense I have sought to
define, imperialistic. If democracy means simply the attempt
to eliminate the qualitative and selective principle in favor of
some general will, based in turn on a theory of natural rights, it
may prove to be only a form of the vertigo of the abyss. As I
have tried to show in dealing with the influence of Rousseau on
the French Revolution, it will result practically, not in equality, but in a sort of inverted aristocracy. One's choice may be,
not between a democracy that is properly led and a democracy
that hopes to find the equivalent of standards and leadership
in the appeal to a numerical majority, that indulges in other
words in a sort of quantitative impressionism, but between a
democracy that is properly led and a decadent imperialism.
One should, therefore, in the interests of democracy itself seek
to substitute the doctrine of the right man for the doctrine of
the rights of man.

The opposition between traditional standards and an
equalitarian democracy based on the supposed rights of man
has played an important part in our own political history, and
has meant practically the opposition between two types of
leadership. The "quality" in the older sense of the word suffered its first decisive defeat in 1829 when Washington was
invaded by the hungry hordes of Andrew Jackson. The imperialism latent in this type of democracy appears in the Jack-
sonian maxim: "To the victors belong the spoils." In his
theory of democracy Jackson had, of course, much in common
with Thomas Jefferson. If we go back, indeed, to the beginnings of our institutions, we find that America stood from the
start for two different views of government that have their
origin in different views of liberty and ultimately of human
nature. The view that is set forth in the Declaration of Independence assumes that man has certain abstract rights; it has
therefore important points of contact with the French revolutionary "idealism." The view that inspired our Constitution,

on the other hand, has much in common with that of Burke. If the first of these political philosophies is properly associated with Jefferson, the second has its most distinguished representative in Washington. The Jeffersonian liberal has faith in the goodness of the natural man, and so tends to overlook the need of a veto power either in the individual or in the State. The liberals of whom I have taken Washington to be the type are less expansive in their attitude towards the natural man. Just as man has a higher self that acts restrictively on his ordinary self, so, they hold, the State should have a higher or permanent self, appropriately embodied in institutions, that should set bounds to its ordinary self as expressed by the popular will at any particular moment. The contrast that I am establishing is, of course, that between a constitutional and a direct democracy. There is an opposition of first principles between those who maintain that the popular will should prevail, but only after it has been purified of what is merely impulsive and ephemeral, and those who maintain that this will should prevail immediately and unrestrictedly. The American experiment in democracy has, therefore, from the outset been ambiguous, and will remain so until the irrepressible conflict between a Washingtonian and a Jeffersonian liberty has been fought to a conclusion. The liberal of the type of Washington has always been very much concerned with what one may term the unionist aspect of liberty. This central preoccupation is summed up in the phrase of Webster: Union and liberty, one and inseparable. The liberty of the Jeffersonian, on the other hand, makes against ethical union like every liberty that rests on the assertion of abstract rights. Jefferson himself proclaimed not only human rights, but also state rights. Later the doctrine of state rights was developed with logical rigor by Calhoun, whereas the doctrine of human rights was carried through no less uncompromisingly by the abolitionists. The result was two opposing camps of extremists and fire-eaters; so that the whole question of union, instead of being settled on ethical lines, had to be submitted to the arbitrament of force.

The man who has grasped the full import of the conflict between the liberty of the unionist and that of the Jeffersonian has been put in possession of the key that unlocks American history. The conflict between the two conceptions is not, indeed, always clear-cut in particular individuals. There is much in Jefferson himself that contradicts what I have been saying about Jefferson. A chief business of criticism, however, is to distinguish, in spite of peripheral overlappings, between things that are at the centre different. For example, to link together in a common admiration Jefferson and John Marshall, our most eminent unionist after Washington himself, is proof of lack of critical discrimination rather than of piety towards the fathers. Jefferson and Marshall knew perfectly that they stood for incompatible things, and it is important that we should know it also. "Marshall," says John Quincy Adams in his Diary, "has cemented the Union which the crafty and quixotic democracy of Jefferson had a perpetual tendency to dissolve."

By his preoccupation with the question of the union, Lincoln became the true successor of Washington and Marshall. In making of Lincoln the great emancipator instead of the great unionist, in spite of his own most specific declarations on this point, we are simply creating a Lincoln myth, as we have already created a Washington myth. We are sometimes told that the good democrat needs merely to be like Lincoln. But to be like Lincoln one must know what Lincoln was like. This is not only a task for the critic, but, in view of the Lincoln myth, a more difficult task than is commonly supposed. It is especially easy to sentimentalize Lincoln because he had a strongly marked vein of sentimentalism. Nevertheless, in spite of the peripheral overlappings between the democracy of Lincoln and that of Jefferson or even between that of Lincoln and Walt Whitman, one should insist on the central difference. One has only to read, for example, the Second Inaugural along with the *Song of Myself* if one wishes to become aware of the gap that separates religious humility from romantic egotism. We should be careful again, in spite of peripheral overlappings, not to confound the democracy of Lincoln with that of [Theodore] Roosevelt. What we feel at the very centre in Roosevelt is the dynamic rush of an imperialistic personality. What we feel at the very centre in Lincoln, on the other hand, is an element of judicial control; and in close relation to this control a profound conception of the rôle of the courts in maintaining free institutions. The man who has studied the real Lincoln does not find it easy to imagine him advocating the recall of judicial decisions.

The Jeffersonian liberal is, as a rule, much more ostentatiously fraternal than the liberal in the other tradition. Yet he is usually inferior in human warmth and geniality to the unionist. Washington and Marshall and Lincoln at their best combined practical sagacity with a central benignity and unselfishness. Jefferson, on the other hand, though perhaps our most accomplished politician, did not show himself especially sagacious in dealing with specific emergencies. Furthermore, it is hard to read his *Anas* and reflect on the circumstances of its composition without concluding that what was central in his personality was not benignity and unselfishness but vindictiveness.

Statesmen who deserve the praise I have bestowed on our unionist leaders are, as every student of history knows, extremely rare. The type of constitutional liberty that we owe to these men before all others is one of the greatest blessings that has ever been vouchsafed to any people. And yet we are in danger of losing it. The Eighteenth Amendment is striking proof of our loss of grasp, not only on the principles that underlie our own Constitution, but that must underlie any constitution, as such, in opposition to mere legislative enactment.

Our present drift away from constitutional freedom can be understood only with reference to the progressive crumbling of traditional standards and the rise of a naturalistic philosophy that, in its treatment of specifically human problems, has been either sentimental or utilitarian. The significant changes in our own national temper in particular are finally due to the fact that Protestant Christianity, especially in the Puritanic form, has been giving way to humanitarianism. The point is worth making because the persons who have favored prohibition and other similar "reforms" have been attacked as Puritans. Genuine Puritanism was, however, a religion of the inner life. Our unionist leaders, Washington, Marshall, and Lincoln, though not narrowly orthodox, were still religious in the traditional sense. The struggle between good and evil, as they saw it, was still primarily not in society, but in the individual. Their conscious dependence on a higher or divine will could not fail to be reflected in their notion of liberty. Jefferson, on the contrary, associated his liberty, not with God, but with "nature." He admired, as is well known, the liberty of the American Indian. He was for diminishing to the utmost the rôle of government, but not for increasing the inner control that must, according to Burke, be in strict ratio to the relaxation of outer control. When evil actually appears, the Jeffersonian cannot appeal to the principle of inner control; he is not willing again to admit that the sole alternative to this type of control is force; and so he is led into what seems at first sight a paradoxical denial of his own principles: he has recourse to legislation. It should be clear at all events that our present attempt to substitute social control for self-control is Jeffersonian rather than Puritanical. So far as we are true children of the Puritans, we may accept the contrast established by Professor Stuart P. Sherman between our own point of view and that of the German: "The ideal of the German is external control and 'inner freedom'; the Government looks after his conduct and he looks after his liberty. The ideal of the American is external freedom and inner control; the individual looks after his conduct and the Government looks after his liberty. Thus *Verboten* in Germany is pronounced by the Government and enforced by the police. In America *Verboten* is pronounced by public opinion and enforced by the individual conscience. In this light it should appear that Puritanism, our national principle of concentration, is the indispensable check on democracy, our national principle of expansion. I use the word Puritanism in the sense given to it by German and German-American critics: *the inner check upon the expansion of natural impulse.*"

Professor Sherman's contrast has been true in the past and still has some truth—at least enough for the purposes of war-time propaganda. But what about our main drift at present? It is plainly away from the point of view that Professor Sherman ascribes to the Puritan and towards the point of view that he ascribes to the German. "The inner check upon the expansion of natural impulse" is precisely the missing element in the Jeffersonian philosophy. The Jeffersonian has therefore been led to deal with the problem of evil, not vitally and in terms of the inner life, but mechanically. Like the Jesuit he has fallen from law into legalism. It has been estimated that for one *Verboten* sign in Germany we already have a dozen in this country; only, having set up our *Verboten* sign, we get even by not observing it. Thus prohibition is pronounced by the Government, largely repudiated by the individual conscience, and enforced (very imperfectly) by the police. The multitude of laws we are passing is one of many proofs that we are growing increasingly lawless.

There are, to be sure, peripheral overlappings between the point of view of the Puritan and that of the humanitarian legalist. The Puritan inclined from the start to be meddlesome, as any one who has studied the activities of Calvin at Geneva will testify. But even here one may ask whether the decisive arguments by which we have been induced to submit to the meddling of the prohibitionist were not utilitarian rather than puritanical. "Booze," says Mr. Henry Ford, "had to go out when modern industry and the motor car came in." The truth may be that we are prepared to make any sacrifice to the Moloch of efficiency, including, apparently, that of our federal Constitution.

The persons who have been carrying on of late a campaign against the Puritans like to look on themselves as "intellectuals." But if the primary function of the intellect is to make accurate distinctions, it is plain that they do not deserve the title. For in dealing with this whole subject they have fallen into a twofold confusion. So far as they identify with Puritanism the defence of the principle of control in human nature, they are simply attacking under that name the wisdom of the ages and all its authentic representatives in both East and West. To bestow, on the other hand, the name of Puritans on the humanitarian legalists who are now sapping our spiritual virility is to pay them an extravagant and undeserved compliment. Let us take as an example of the attacks on the Puritans that of Mr. Theodore Dreiser, culminating in the grotesque assertion regarding the United States: "No country has such a peculiar, such a seemingly fierce determination to make the Ten Commandments work." We are murdering one another at the rate of about ten thousand a year (with very few capital convictions) and are in general showing ourselves more criminally inclined than any other nation that is reputed to be civilized. The explanation is that we are trying to make, not the Ten Commandments, but humanitarianism work—and it is not working. If our courts are so ineffective in punishing crime, a chief reason is that they do not have the support of public opinion, and this is because the public is so largely composed of people who have set up sympathy for the underdog as a substitute for all the other virtues, or else of people who hold that the criminal is the product of his environment and so is not morally responsible. Here as elsewhere there is a coöperation between those who mechanize life and those who sentimentalize it.

The belief in moral responsibility must be based on a belief in the possibility of an inner working of some kind with reference to standards. The utilitarian, as I have sought to show, has put his main emphasis on outer working. The consequence of this emphasis, coinciding as it has with the multiplication of machines, has been the substitution of standardization for standards. The type of efficiency that our master commercialists pursue requires that a multitude of men should be deprived of their specifically human attributes, and become mere cogs in some vast machine. At the present rate even the grocer in a remote country town will soon not be left as much initiative as is needed to fix the price of a pound of butter.

Standardization is, however, a less serious menace to standards than what are currently known as "ideals." The person who breaks down standards in the name of ideals does not seem to be impelled by base commercial motives, but to be animated, on the contrary, by the purest commiseration for the lowly and the oppressed. We must have the courage to submit this humanitarian zeal to a close scrutiny. We may perhaps best start with the familiar dictum that America is only another name for opportunity. Opportunity to do what? To engage in a scramble for money and material success, until the multimillionaire emerges as the characteristic product of a country dedicated to the proposition that all men are created equal? According to Napoleon, the French Revolution was also only another name for opportunity (*la carrière ouverte aux talents* [the career open to talents]). Some of our commercial supermen have evidently been making use of their opportunity in a very Napoleonic fashion. In any case, opportunity has meaning only with reference to some true standard. The sentimentalist, instead of setting up some such standard by way of protest against the wrong type of superiority, inclines rather to bestow an unselective sympathy on those who have been left behind in the race for economic advantage. Even when less materialistic in his outlook, he is prone to dodge the question of justice. He does not ask whether a man is an underdog because he has already had his opportunity and failed to use it, whether, in short, the man that he takes to be a victim of the social order is not rather a victim of his own misconduct or at least of his own indolence and inattention. He thus exposes himself to the penalties visited on those who set out to be kinder than the moral law.

At bottom the point of view of the "uplifter" is so popular because it nourishes spiritual complacency; it enables a man to look on himself as "up" and on some one else as "down." But there is psychological if not theological truth in the assertion of Jonathan Edwards that complacent people are a "particular smoke" in God's nostrils. A man needs to look, not down, but up to standards set so much above his ordinary self as to make him feel that he is himself spiritually the underdog. The man who thus looks up is becoming worthy to be looked up to in turn, and, to this extent, qualifying for leadership. Leadership of this type, one may add, may prove to be, in the long run, the only effectual counterpoise to that of the imperialistic superman.

No amount of devotion to society and its supposed interests can take the place of this inner obeisance of the spirit to standards. The humanitarian would seem to be caught here in a vicious circle. If he turns from the inner life to serve his fellow men, he becomes a busybody. If he sets out again to become exemplary primarily with a view to the benefit of others, he becomes a prig. Nothing will avail short of humility. Humility, as Burke saw, is the ultimate root of the justice that should prevail in the secular order, as well as of the virtues

that are specifically religious. The modern problem, I have
been insisting, is to secure leaders with an allegiance to standards, now that the traditional order with which Burke associated his standards and leadership has been so seriously
shaken. Those who have broken with the traditional beliefs
have thus far shown themselves singularly ineffective in dealing with this problem of leadership, even when they have admitted the need of leaders at all. The persons who have piqued
themselves especially on being positive have looked for leadership to the exponents of physical science. Auguste Comte, for
example, not only regarded men of science as the true modern
priesthood, but actually disparaged moral effort on the part of
the individual. I scarcely need to repeat here what I have said
elsewhere—that the net result of a merely scientific "progress"
is to produce efficient megalomaniacs. Physical science, excellent in its proper place, is, when exalted out of this place, the
ugliest and most maleficent idol before which man has as yet
consented to prostrate himself. If the essence of genuine
science is to face loyally all the facts as they present themselves without dogmatic prepossessions, one is justified in
asking whether the man who forgets that physical science is, in
Tennyson's phrase, the second, not the first, is genuinely scientific; whether the very sharpest discrimination does not need
to be established between science and utilitarianism. Aristotle,
for example, was a true man of science; he was not a utilitarian.
Francis Bacon, on the other hand, is the prophet of the whole
utilitarian movement, but one may doubt his eminence as a
man of science. Quite apart from the fact that he failed to make
important scientific discoveries, one may question the validity
of the Baconian method. His failure to do justice to deduction
as part of a sound scientific method has often been noted. A
more serious defect is his failure to recognize the rôle of the
imagination, or, what amounts to the same thing, the rôle of
exceptional genius in the making of scientific discoveries.

One cannot grant that an aristocracy of scientific intellectuals or indeed any aristocracy of intellect is what we need.
This would mean practically to encourage the *libido sciendi*
and so to put pride in the place of humility. Still less accept-
able would be an aristocracy of artists; as the word art has

come to be understood in recent times, this would mean an aristocracy of aesthetes who would attempt to base their selection on the *libido sentiendi.* The Nietzschean attempt, again, to found the aristocratic and selective principle on the sheer expansion of the will to power (*libido dominandi*) would lead in practice to horrible violence and finally to the death of civilization. The attempts that were made during the past century to establish a scale of values with reference to the three main lusts of the human heart often took on a mystical coloring. Man likes to think that he has God as an ally of his expansive conceit, whatever this conceit may chance to be. When, indeed, one has passed in review the various mysticisms of the modern movement, as they are set forth, for example, in the volumes of M. Seillière, one is reminded of the saying of Bossuet: "True mysticism is so rare and unessential and false mysticism is so common and dangerous that one cannot oppose it too firmly."

If one discovers frequently a pseudo-mystical element in the claims to leadership of the aesthetes, the supermen and the scientific intellectuals, this element is even more visible in those who would, in the name of democracy, dispense with leadership altogether. Thus Walt Whitman, as we have seen, would put no check on his "spontaneous me"; he would have every one else indulge his "idiocrasy" to the same degree, be a "genius," in short, in the full romantic sense of the term. A liberty thus anarchical is to lead to equality and fraternity. If one tells the democrat of this type that his programme is contrary to common sense and the facts of experience, he is wont to take refuge in mystical "vision." One needs in effect to be very mystical to suppose that men can come together by flying off each on his temperamental tangent. Whitman does not admit the need of the leader who looks up humbly to some standard and so becomes worthy to be looked up to in turn. The only leadership he contemplates apparently is that of the ideal democratic bard who flatters the people's pride and chants the divine average. He represents in an extreme form the substitution for vital control of expansive emotion under the name of love. Pride and self-assertion, when tempered by love, will not, he holds, endanger the principle of union. The Union, though "always swarming with blatherers, is yet," he says, "always

sure and impregnable." The records of the past are not reas-
suring as to the maintenance of ethical union in a community
that is swarming with "blatherers." At all events, the offset to
the blatherers will be found, not in any divine average, but in
the true leader—the "still strong man in a blatant land." We
come here to another opposition that is one of first principles
and is not therefore subject to mediation or compromise—the
opposition, namely, between the doctrine of the saving remnant and that of the divine average. If one deals with human
nature realistically one may find here and there a person who is
worthy of respect and occasionally one who is worthy of reverence. Any one, on the other hand, who puts his faith in the
divinity of the average is destined, if we are to trust the
records of history, to pass through disillusion to a final
despair. We are reaching the stage of disillusion in this country
at the present moment. According to the author of *Main
Street*, the average is not divine but trivial; according to the
author of the *Spoon River Anthology*, it is positively hideous.
It can scarcely be gainsaid that contemporary America offers
an opening for satire. A great many people are gradually
drifting into materialism and often cherishing the conceit at
the same time that they are radiant idealists. But satire, to be
worth while, must be constructive. The opposite of the trivial
is the distinguished; and one can determine what is distinguished only with reference to standards. To see Main
Street on a background of standards would be decidedly
helpful; but standards are precisely what our so-called realists
lack. They are themselves a part of the disease that they are attempting to define.

The democratic idealist is prone to make light of the whole
question of standards and leadership because of his unbounded
faith in the plain people. How far is this appeal to the plain
people justified and how far is it merely demagogic? There is
undoubted truth in the saying that there is somebody who
knows more than anybody, and that is everybody. Only one
must allow everybody sufficient time to sift the evidence and
add that, even so, everybody does not know very much. Burke
told the electors of Bristol that he was not flattering their
opinions of the moment, but uttering the views that both they

and he must have five years thence. Even in this triumph of the sober judgment of the people over its passing impression, the rôle of the true leader should not be underestimated. Thus in the year 1795 the plain people of America were eager to give the fraternal accolade to the French Jacobins. The great and wise Washington opposed an alliance that would almost certainly have been disastrous, and as a result he had heaped upon him by journals like the *Aurora*, the forerunner of our modern "journals of opinion," epithets that, as he himself complained, would not have been deserved by a common pickpocket. In a comparatively short time Washington and his group were seen to be right, and those who seemed to be the spokesmen of the plain people were seen to be wrong. It is not clear that one can have much faith even in the sober second thought of a community that has no enlightened minority. A Haytian statesman, for example, might not gain much in appealing from Haytian opinion of to-day to Haytian opinion of five years hence. The democratic idealist does not, however, mean as a rule by an appeal to the plain people an appeal to its sober second thought. He means rather the immediate putting into effect of the will of a numerical majority. Like the man in the comic song the people is supposed to "want what it wants when it wants it." Our American drift for a number of years has unquestionably been towards a democracy of this radical type, as is evident from the increasing vogue of the initiative, referendum, and recall (whether of judges or judicial decisions) as well as from popular primaries and the direct election of Senators. The feeling that the people should act directly on all measures has led to the appearance in certain States of ballots thirty feet long! Yet the notion that wisdom resides in a popular majority at any particular moment should be the most completely exploded of all fallacies. If the plain people at Jerusalem had registered their will with the aid of the most improved type of ballot box, there is no evidence that they would have preferred Christ to Barabbas. In view of the size of the jury that condemned Socrates, one may affirm confidently that he was the victim of a "great and solemn referendum." On the other hand, the plain people can be shown to have taken a special delight in Nero. But the plain people, it will be replied, has been educated and enlightened. The intelligence tests applied in connection with the selective draft indicate that the average mental age of our male voters is about fourteen. The intelligence testers are, to be sure, under some suspicion as to the quality of their own intelligence. A more convincing proof of the low mentality of our population is found, perhaps, in the fact that the Hearst publications have twenty-five million readers.

"There is nothing," says Goethe, "more odious than the majority; for it consists of a few powerful leaders, a certain number of accommodating scoundrels and subservient weaklings, and a mass of men who trudge after them without in the least knowing their own minds." If there is any truth in this analysis the majority in a radical democracy often rules only in name. No movement, indeed, illustrates more clearly than the supposedly democratic movement the way in which the will of highly organized and resolute minorities may prevail over the will of the inert and unorganized mass. Even though the mass does not consent to "trudge" after the minority, it is at an increasing disadvantage in its attempts to resist it. Physical science is on the side of the tyrannical minority. The ordinary citizen cannot have a machine gun by his fireside or a "tank" in his back yard. The most recent type of revolutionary idealist, though his chief concern is still to bestow benefit on the people, does not, to do him justice, hope to achieve this benefit through the majority, but rather through the direct action of organized minorities. He feels that he is justified in cramming his nostrum down the throat of the people, if necessary by force.

The radical of this type is coming round to the doctrine of the saving remnant and recognizing in his own way that everything finally hinges on the quality of the leadership. His views, however, as to this quality differ strangely from the traditional views. One must admit that, whatever theories of leadership may have been held traditionally, actual leadership has never been any too good. One scarcely suspects, as John Selden remarked, "what a little foolery governs the world." Moreover, the folly which has prevailed at the top of society, and that from the time of the Trojan War, has ever been faithfully reflected in the rank and file (*Quidquid delirant reges [plec-tuntur Achivi]* [Whatever follies their kings commit, the Achaians are punished]). One who surveys the past is at times tempted to acquiesce in the gloomy judgment of Dryden: "No government has ever been or ever can be wherein time-servers and blockheads will not be uppermost. The persons are only changed, but the same juggling in state, the same hypocrisy in religion, the same self-interest and mismanagement will remain forever. Blood and money will be lavished in all ages only for the preferment of new faces with old consciences." One should note, however, a difference between the bad leader-ship of the past and that of the modern revolutionary era. The leaders of the past have most frequently been bad in violation of the principles they professed, whereas it is when a Robes-pierre or a Lenin sets out to apply his principles that the man who is interested in the survival of civilization has reason to tremble.

Dryden's passage seems to suggest that what is really needed is not new faces with old consciences, but a transforma-tion of conscience itself. It is precisely such a transformation that a revolutionary idealist like Robespierre hopes to effect. For the corrupt conscience of the old type of aristocratic leader he would substitute a social conscience. The popular will that is inspired by this conscience is so immaculate, as we have seen, that it may safely be put in the place not merely of the royal but of the divine will. I have already tried to show that a leader who sets out to be only the organ of a "general will" or "divine average," that is conceived at times as essentially reasonable and at other times as essentially fraternal, will actually become imperialistic. It may be well at this point to submit this democratic idealism to still further analysis with special reference to its probable effect on our own international relations. The tendency for some time past has been to treat international law, not theoretically as an embodiment of reason, but positively as an embodiment of will. In that case, if international law is to reflect any improvement in the relations between states, it must be shown that the substitution of the popular will for the divine will has actually tended to promote ethical union among men even across national frontiers. If we analyze realistically the popular will, we find that it means the will of a multitude of men who are more and more emancipated from traditional standards and more and more given over to what I have termed the irresponsible quest of thrills. These thrills are, as we all know, supplied by sensational newspapers and in international affairs involve transitions, often disconcertingly sudden, from pacifism to jingoism. Any one who can recollect the period immediately preceding our conflict with Spain will be sufficiently aware of the rôle that this type of journalism may play in precipitating war. Let us ask ourselves again whether the chances of a clash between America and Japan are likely to diminish if Japan becomes more democratic, if, in other words, the popular will is substituted for the will of a small group of "elder statesmen." Any one who knows what the Japanese sensational press has already done to foment suspicion against America is justified in harboring doubts on this point.

A democracy, the realistic observer is forced to conclude, is likely to be idealistic in its feelings about itself, but imperialistic in its practice. The idealism and the imperialism, indeed, are in pretty direct ratio to one another. For example, to be fraternal in Walt Whitman's sense is to be boundlessly expansive, and a boundless expansiveness, is, in a world like this, incompatible with peace. Whitman imagines the United States as expanding until it absorbs Canada and Mexico and dominates both the Atlantic and the Pacific—a programme that would almost certainly involve us in war with the whole world. If we go, not by what Americans feel about themselves, but by what they have actually done, one must conclude that we have shown ourselves thus far a consistently expansive, in other words, a consistently imperialistic, people. We have merely been expanding, it may be replied, to our natural frontiers; but we are already in the Philippines, and manifestly in danger of becoming involved in Asiatic adventures. Japan, a country with fifty-seven million inhabitants (increasing at the rate of about six hundred thousand a year), on a group of islands not as large as the State of California, only seventeen per cent of which is arable, has at least a plausible pretext for reaching out beyond her natural frontiers. But for us, with our almost limit-

less and still largely undeveloped resources, to risk the horrors
of war under modern conditions for anything we are likely to
gain from expanding eastward, would be an extreme example
of sheer restlessness of spirit and of an intemperate commercialism. It is a part of our psychology that each main incident
in our national history should take on a highly idealistic coloring. For example, we were on the verge of a conflict with
Mexico a few years ago as the result of an unwarranted
meddling with her sovereignty. President Wilson at once described the incipient struggle as a war of "service." Cicero
says that Rome gained the mastery of the world by coming to
the aid of her allies. In the same way it may be said some day
of us that, as the result of a series of outbursts of idealism, we
changed from a federal republic to a highly centralized and
bureaucratic empire. We are willing to admit that all other
nations are self-seeking, but as for ourselves, we hold that we
act only on the most disinterested motives. We have not as yet
set up, like revolutionary France, as the Christ of Nations, but
during the late war we liked to look on ourselves as at least the
Sir Galahad of Nations. If the American thus regards himself
as an idealist at the same time that the foreigner looks on him
as a dollar-chaser, the explanation may be due partly to the
fact that the American judges himself by the way he feels,
whereas the foreigner judges him by what he does.

This is not, of course, the whole truth. Besides our tradition of idealism there is our unionist tradition based on a sane
moral realism. "It is a maxim," says Washington, "founded on
the universal experience of mankind, that no nation is to be
trusted further than it is bound by its interests; and no president, statesman or politician will venture to depart from it."
All realistic observation confirms Washington. Those who are
inspired by his spirit believe that we should be nationally prepared, and then that we should mind our own business. The
tendency of our idealists, on the other hand, is to be unpre-
pared and then to engage in more or less general meddling. A
third attitude may be distinguished that may properly be associated with Roosevelt. The follower of Roosevelt wants pre-
paredness, only he cannot, like the follower of Washington, be
counted on to mind his own business. The humanitarian would,

of course, have us meddle in foreign affairs as part of his programme of world service. Unfortunately, it is more difficult than he supposes to engage in such a programme without getting involved in a programme of world empire. The term sentimental imperialism may be applied to certain incidents in ancient Roman history. Some of the motives that we professed for entering the Great War remind one curiously of the motives that men like Flamininus professed for going to the rescue of Greece. Cicero, writing over a century later and only a few months before his assassination by the emissaries of the Triumvirs, said that he himself had once thought that Rome stood for world service rather than for world empire, but that he had been bitterly disillusioned. He proceeds to denounce Julius Caesar, the imperialistic leader *par excellence,* as a demon in human form who did evil for its own sake. But Caesar had at least the merit of seeing that the Roman ethos was changing, that as the result of the breakdown of religious restraint (for which Stoical "service" was not an adequate substitute), the Romans were rapidly becoming unfit for republican institutions.

Some persons, indeed, are inclined to go beyond particular comparisons of this kind and develop a general parallel between decadent Rome and modern America. Such a parallel is always very incomplete and must be used with great caution. We need, in the first place, to define with some precision what we mean by decadence. The term is often used vaguely by persons who are suffering from what one may call the illusion of the "good old times." Livy is surely a bit idyllic when he exclaims: "Where will you now find in one man this modesty and uprightness and loftiness of spirit that then belonged to a whole people?" Yet if one compares the Rome of the Republic with the Rome of the Empire one is conscious of a real decline. The Senate that had seemed to Cineas, the adviser of Pyrrhus, an assembly of demigods, had become by the time of Tiberius a gathering rather of cringing sycophants. Horace was uttering only the sober truth when he proclaimed the progressive degeneracy of the Romans of his time. The most significant symptom of this degeneracy seemed to Horace and other shrewd observers to be the relaxation of the bonds of the family.

Are we witnessing a similar moral deliquescence in this country, and, if so, how far has it gone? One of our foreign critics asserts that we have already reached the "Heliogabalus stage"—which is absurd. But at the same time it is not to be denied that the naturalistic notion of liberty has undermined in no small measure the two chief unifying influences of the past—the Church and the family. The decline in the discipline of the family has been fairly recent. Persons are still living who can remember the conditions that prevailed in the Puritan household. The process of emancipation from the older restraint has not usually presented itself as a lapse into mere materialism. Idealism in the current sense of that term has tended to take the place of traditional religion. The descendants of the Puritans have gone in for commercialism, to be sure, especially since the Civil War, but it has been commercialism tempered by humanitarian crusading. As I have pointed out, the humanitarian does not, like the genuine Puritan, seek to get at evil in the heart of the individual, so that he is finally forced to resort to outer regulation. The egoistic impulses that are not controlled at their source tend to prevail over an ineffectual altruism in the relations of man with man and class with class. The special mark of materialism, which is to regard property, not as a means to an end, but as an end in itself, is more and more visible. The conservative nowadays is interested in conserving property for its own sake and not, like Burke, in conserving it because it is an almost indispensable support of personal liberty, a genuinely spiritual thing. As for the progressive, his preoccupation with property and what he conceives to be its just distribution amounts to a morbid obsession. Orderly party government will become increasingly difficult if we continue to move in this direction, and we shall finally be menaced by class war, if, indeed, we are not menaced by it already. Every student of history is aware of the significance of this particular symptom in a democracy. One may sum up what appears to be our total trend at present by saying that we are moving through an orgy of humanitarian legalism towards a decadent imperialism.

The important offsetting influence is our great unionist tradition. One should not, however, underestimate the difficulties in the way of maintaining this tradition. The idea that the State should have a permanent or higher self that is felt as a veto power upon its ordinary self rests ultimately upon the assertion of a similar dualism in the individual. We have seen that this assertion has in the Occident been inextricably bound up with certain Christian beliefs that have been weakened by the naturalistic movement. We are brought back here to the problem with which we have been confronted so often in the course of the present argument, how, namely, to get modern equivalents for the traditional beliefs, above all some fresh basis for the affirmation of a *frein vital* or centripetal element in liberty. What the men of the French Revolution wanted, according to Joubert, was not religious liberty, but irreligious liberty. In that case, the French modernist retorts bitterly, you would have us give up revolutionary liberty and become Jesuits. Similarly, if one points out to an American modernist the inanity of his idealism as a substitute for the traditional controls, he will at once accuse you of wishing to revert to Puritanism. Strictly speaking, however, one does not need to revert to anything. It is a part of my own method to put Confucius behind Aristotle and Buddha behind Christ. The best, however, that even these great teachers can do for us is to help us to discover what is already present in ourselves. From this point of view they are well-nigh indispensable.

Let us begin, therefore, by ridding our minds of unreal alternatives. If we in America are not content with a stodgy commercialism, it does not follow that we need, on the one hand, to return to Puritanism, or, on the other, to become "liberals" in the style of *The New Republic*; nor, again, need we evolve under the guidance of Mr. H. L. Mencken into second-rate Nietzscheans. We do need, however, if we are to gain any hold on the present situation, to develop a little moral gravity and intellectual seriousness. We shall then see that the strength of the traditional doctrines, as compared with the modernist position, is the comparative honesty with which they face the fact of evil. We shall see that we need to restore to human nature in some critical and experimental fashion the "old Adam" that the idealists have been so busy eliminating. A restoration of this kind ought not to lead merely to a lapse from naturalistic optimism into naturalistic pessimism;

nothing is easier than such a lapse and nothing at bottom is more futile. Both attitudes are about equally fatalistic and so undermine moral responsibility. A survey of the facts would suggest that man is morally responsible, but that he is always trying to dodge this responsibility; that what he suffers from, in short, is not fate in any sense of the word, but spiritual supineness. There may be truth in the saying that the devil's other name is inertia. Nothing is more curious than to trace historically the way in which some great teaching like that of Christ or Buddha has been gradually twisted until man has adjusted it more or less completely to his ancient indolence. Several centuries ago there was a sect of Japanese Buddhism known as the Way of Hardships; shortly after there arose another sect known as the Easy Way which at once gained great popularity and tended to supplant the Way of Hardships. But the Japanese Way of Hardships is itself an easy way if one compares it with the original way of Buddha. One can follow, indeed, very clearly the process by which Buddhist doctrine descended gradually from the austere and almost inaccessible height on which it had been placed by its founder to the level of the prayer mill. It was announced in the press not long ago that as a final improvement some of the prayer mills in Thibet are to be operated by electricity. The man who hopes to save society by turning the crank of a legislative mill or who sets up as a "socio-religious engineer" may call himself a Christian, but he is probably as remote from the true spirit of Jesus as some Eastern votary of the Easy Way is from the true spirit of Buddha.

The essence of man's spiritual indolence, as I have already pointed out, is that he does not wish to look up to standards and discipline himself with reference to them. He wishes rather to expand freely along the lines of his dominant desire. He grasps eagerly at everything that seems to favor this desire and so tends, as the saying is, to keep him in good conceit with himself. Disraeli discovered, we are told, that the best way to get on with Queen Victoria was to flatter her and not to be afraid of overdoing the flattery, but to "lay it on with a trowel." Demos, as was pointed out long ago, craves flattery like any other monarch, and in his theory of popular sovereignty Rousseau has, it must be admitted, laid this flattery on with a trowel. In general, his notion that evil is not in man himself, but in his institutions, has enjoyed immense popularity, not because it is true, but because it is flattering.

Observations of the kind I have been making are likely to lay one open to the charge of cynicism. One needs, however, to cultivate a wholesome cynicism as the only way of avoiding the unwholesome kind—that of the disillusioned sentimentalist. When I speak of a wholesome cynicism, I mean that of Aristotle who says that "most men do evil when they have an opportunity," or that of Bossuet, expressing the moderate Christian view, when he speaks of "the prodigious malignity of the human heart always inclined to do evil." There is no harm in cynicism provided the cynic does not think of himself as viewing human nature from the outside and from some superior pinnacle. In the sense I have just defined, cynicism, indeed, has many points in common with religious humility.

Let us pursue then our realistic analysis without fear of the charge of cynicism. Man would not succumb so easily to flattery if he did not begin by flattering himself; his self-flattery is closely related in turn to his moral indolence. I have said that the whole of life may be summed up in the words diversion and conversion. But man does not want conversion, the adjustment in other words of his natural will to some higher will, because of the moral effort it implies. In this sense he is the everlasting trifler. But, though he wishes diversion, he is loath at the same time to admit that he is missing the fruits of conversion. He wills the ends, because they are plainly desirable, but he does not will the means because they are difficult and disciplinary. In short, he harbors incompatible desires and so listens eagerly to those who encourage him to think that it is possible to have the good thing without paying the appointed price.

Two main modes in which men are thus flattered may be distinguished. First, in an age of authority and accepted standards, they are induced to substitute for the reality of spiritual discipline some ingenious art of going through the motions. An extreme example is that of the fashionable lady described by

Boileau who (with the aid of her spiritual director) had convinced herself that she could enjoy all the pleasures of hell on the way to paradise. What concerns us now, however, is not the mode of flattery that is based on exaggerated respect for outer authority, but the other main mode that flourishes in an age of individualism. The cushions that, according to Bossuet, the Jesuits put under the sinner's elbows are as nothing compared to the cushions that the sinner puts under his own elbows when left to himself. In a period like the present every man is his own Jesuit. Rousseau's sycophancy of human nature proved to be particularly suited to the requirements of the individualistic era. By his sophistry of feeling he satisfied in a new and fetching fashion man's permanent desire, especially in the realm of moral values, to have his cake and eat it too. The self-flattery that encourages the huddling together of incompatible desires has never been pushed further than in this movement. When one considers, for instance, the multitude of those who have hoped to combine peace and brotherhood with a return to nature, one is forced to conclude that an outstanding human trait is a prodigious and pathetic gullibility.

The chief corrective of gullibility is, in an age of individualistic emancipation, a full and free play of the critical spirit. The more critical one becomes at such a time, the more likely one is to achieve standards and avoid empty conceits. Now to criticize is literally to discriminate. The student of both the natural and the human law needs to be very discriminating; one should note, however, an important difference between them. The discrimination of the man of science is exercised primarily upon physical phenomena, that of the humanist primarily upon words. "The beginning of genuine culture," Socrates is reported to have said, "is the scrutiny of general terms." Socrates himself was so accomplished in this type of scrutiny that he still deserves to be the master of those who are aiming at criticism. I have said that the hope of civilization lies not in the divine average, but in the saving remnant. It is plain that in an age like the present, which is critical in every sense of the word, the remnant must be highly Socratic.

Discrimination of the humanistic type is especially needed in the field of political theory and practice. Confucius, when asked what would be his first concern if the reins of government were put into his hands, replied that his first concern would be to define his terms and make words correspond with things. If our modern revolutionaries have suffered disillusions of almost unparalleled severity, it is too often because they have given their imagination to words, without making sure that these words corresponded with things; and so they have felt that they were bound for the promised land when they were in reality only swimming in a sea of conceit. "The fruit of dreamy hoping is, waking, blank despair." The disenchantment of Hazlitt with the French Revolution is typical of that of innumerable other "idealists." "The French Revolution," he says, "was the only match that ever took place between philosophy and experience; and, waking from the trance of theory to the sense of reality, we hear the words *truth, reason, virtue, liberty* with the same indifference or contempt that the cynic, who has married a jilt or a termagant, listens to the rhapsodies of lovers."

The reason that the Rousseauist often alleges for his attacks on the analytical intellect, the necessary instrument of a Socratic dialectic, is that it destroys unity. His disparagement of analysis may be due, however, even less to his love of unity than to his dislike of effort. It may be that, like Rousseau himself, he is seeking to give to indolence the dignity of a philosophical occupation. If it is a strenuous thing to concentrate imaginatively on the facts of the natural order, the concentration on the facts of the human order that enables one to use one's terms correctly is even more strenuous. What a monstrous inequality, said Lincoln, to pay an honest laborer seventy cents a day for digging coal and a President seventy dollars a day for digging abstractions! The argument that Lincoln thus puts forth ironically, a follower of Karl Marx would be capable of employing seriously. But if the President does honest work, if he digs his abstractions properly, instead of substituting some art of going through the motions, he must display the utmost contention of spirit. There have been moments in recent years when a President of this kind would have been worth to the country many times seventy dollars a day. Did the idealistic abstractions, one must make bold to ask, that Mr. Woodrow Wilson poured forth so profusely when President, satisfy the Socratic and Confucian test—did they correspond with things? The late Mr. Walter H. Page concluded, after unusual opportunities of observation, that Mr. Wilson was *"not* a leader, but rather a stubborn phrasemaker." Fine words, according to the homely adage, butter no parsnips. They may, however, it would seem, put a man in the White House. Mr. Wilson, it should be remembered, was not only an ex-college president himself, but in his main policies he had the eager support of practically the whole corporation of college presidents. If Mr. Page's estimate of Mr. Wilson should prove to be correct, it would follow that our American remnant—and college presidents should surely belong to the remnant—is not sufficiently critical. The question is one of some gravity, if it be true, as I said at the outset, that democracy will in the long run have to be judged, like any other form of government, by the quality of its leadership, and if it be true, furthermore, that under existing conditions we must get our standards and our leadership along Socratic rather than traditional lines. "What the Americans most urgently require," said Matthew Arnold, "is a steady exhibition of cool and sane criticism." That is precisely what they require and what they have never had.

If we had a Socratic remnant one of its chief concerns would be to give a civilized content to the catch-words that finally govern the popular imagination. The sophist and the demagogue flourish in an atmosphere of vague and inaccurate definition. With the aid of the Socratic critic, on the other hand, Demos might have some chance of distinguishing between its friends and its flatterers—something that Demos has hitherto been singularly unable to do. Let one consider those who have posed with some success as the people's friends from Cleon of Athens to Marat; and from Marat to William Randolph Hearst. It would sometimes seem, indeed, that the people might do very well were it not for its "friends." The demagogue has been justified only too often in his assumption that men may be led, not by their noses, but by their ears as

tenderly as asses are. The records of the past reveal that the
multitude has frequently been persuaded by a mirage of words
that the ship of state was steering a straight course for Eldo-
rado, when it was in reality drifting on a lee-shore; and the
multitude has not been apprized of the peril until it was within
the very sound of the breakers.

It is only too evident that we are not coping adequately
with this special problem of democracy; that we are, on the
contrary, in danger of combining the strength of giants with
the critical intelligence of children. Millions of Americans were
ready not so very long ago to hail William Jennings Bryan as a
"peerless leader." Other millions are ready apparently to
bestow a similar salute on Henry Ford—in spite of the almost
incredible exhibition he made of himself with his "Peace Ship."
If our Socratic critics were sufficiently numerous, the followers
of such leaders would finally become conscious of something in
the air that was keen, crisp, and dangerous; they might finally
be forced to ask themselves whether the ideals with which they
were being beguiled really mean anything, or at all events anything more than the masking in fine phrases of the desire to
get one's hand into the other citizen's pocket. The devil, as is
well known, is a comparatively harmless person unless he is allowed to disguise himself as an angel of light. An unvarnished
materialism is in short less to be feared than sham spirituality.
Sham spirituality is especially promoted by the blurring of distinctions, which is itself promoted by a tampering with general
terms. A dialectical scrutiny of such terms is therefore indispensable if one is to determine whether what a man takes to be
his idealism is merely some windy inflation of the spirit, or
whether it has support in the facts of human experience.

I have already made some application of the Socratic
method to idealism, a term that has come to be almost synonymous with humanitarianism. I have pointed out, for instance,
how the utilitarian has corrupted the word comfort and the
sentimentalist the word virtue. The idealist may, indeed, retort
that I have myself admitted that certain elements essential to
salvation are omitted in the Socratic scheme of things, and
that for these elements we need to turn from Socrates to
Christ; and he will proceed to identify the gospel of Christ with

his own gospel of sympathy and service. Humanitarian idealism unquestionably owes much of its prestige, perhaps its main prestige, to the fact that it has thus associated itself with Christianity. I have sought to show, however, on strictly psychological grounds, that humanitarian service does not involve, in either its utilitarian or its sentimental form, the truths of the inner life and that it cannot therefore be properly derived from Christ. The transformation, indeed, of this great master of the inner life into a master of "uplift" must seem to austere Christians, if there are any left, a sort of second crucifixion. In substituting the love of man for the love of God the humanitarian is working in a vicious circle, for unless man has in him the equivalent of the love of God he is not lovely. Furthermore, it is important that man should not only love but fear the right things. The question was recently raised at Paris why medical men were tending to usurp the influence that formerly belonged to the clergy. The obvious reply is that men once lived in the fear of God, whereas now they live in the fear of microbes. It is difficult to see how one can get on humanitarian lines the equivalent of the truth that the fear of the Lord is the beginning of wisdom.

Perhaps there is no better way of dealing with the humanitarian movement than to take one's point of departure in certain sayings of Jesus and at the same time so to protect them by a Socratic dialectic as to bring out their true meaning. For the present desideratum, it may be, is not to renounce Socrates in favor of Christ, but rather to bring Socrates to the support of Christ.

Three sayings of Jesus would seem especially relevant, if we wish to bring out the contrast between his inspired and imaginative good sense and humanitarianism: (1) "Render unto Caesar the things that are Caesar's and unto God the things that are God's." (2) "By their fruits ye shall know them." (3) One should build one's house upon the rock.

I have already glanced at a violation of the first of these maxims—that, namely, which has taken place in connection with the humanitarian attempt to abolish war even at the expense of justice, and the closely related attempt to convert the prince of peace into a prince of pacifism. Americans often fear that the Roman Catholic Church may use the machinery of democracy to its own ends; and in parts of the country where Catholic voters are in the majority such apprehensions—for example, the apprehension regarding the Catholic domination of the schools—may not be entirely without foundation. It was not, however, a Catholic but a Protestant who recently felt it necessary to recall to his fellow believers that the kingdom of heaven is within us and not at Washington. The Protestant churches seem to be turning more and more to social service, which means that they have been substituting for the truths of the inner life various causes and movements and reforms and crusades. If W. J. Bryan had been born fifty years earlier he would very likely have been a religious revivalist; the religion of the revivalist was still in a fashion a religion of the inner life. Bryan's protest, however, in connection with his crusade for free silver, against the crucifixion of the people on a cross of gold, not only involves an unusually mawkish mixture of the things of God and the things of Caesar, but might have led to political action that, so far from being religious, would have been subversive of common honesty.

One should face frankly the question whether the crusading spirit is in any of its manifestations genuinely Christian. The missionary spirit, the purely spiritual appeal from man to man, is unquestionably Christian. By the crusading spirit I mean, on the other hand, the attempt to achieve spiritual ends collectively through the machinery of the secular order. If one takes a long-range view, the question is one that should be of special interest to Frenchmen, for France has been more than any other country the crusading nation. It has been said that the religious crusading of the Middle Ages in which France played the leading part showed that Europe was already sloughing off genuine Christianity. The contrast is striking in any case between the Christianity of this period and that of the first centuries. The more or less legendary account of the Theban Legion that was ready to fight bravely for the Emperor when he kept within the temporal domain, but allowed itself to be martyred to the last man unresistingly rather than worship him as a God, reflects accurately enough the attitude of the early Christian. The ruthless massacre that marked the first entrance of the crusaders into Jerusalem (15 July, 1099) is sufficient proof that they did not maintain any such distinction between the spiritual and the temporal order. It seems hardly necessary to ask which of the two, the crusader or the member of the Theban Legion, was nearer in spirit to the Founder. By his confusion of the things of God with the things of Caesar the crusader was in danger of substituting a will to power for the will to peace that is at the heart of genuine Christianity. The emergence of the will to power is even more obvious in the humanitarian crusader, as I attempted to show in my study of the Rousseauistic side of the French Revolution. The revolutionary formula, "liberty, equality, fraternity," is in itself only a portentous patter of words. These words may, no doubt, be so defined both separately and in their relation to one another as to have a genuinely religious meaning. Understood in the fashion of Rousseau, that is, as summing up the supposed results of a return to "nature," they encouraged one of the most virulent forms of imperialism. The French themselves are growing more and more doubtful about the "idealistic" side of their Revolution (it goes without saying that the Revolution had other sides). They are growing more realistic in temper. The great problem for them as for all of us is, that, on being disillusioned regarding this type of idealism, they should not become merely Machiavellian realists.

At all events, France can no longer be looked upon as the crusading nation. It is becoming the dangerous privilege of the United States to display more of the crusading temper than any other country in both its domestic and its foreign policies. Yet if one may properly question the religious crusading of which the French were once so fond (*Gesta Dei per Francos*), how much more properly may one question the activities of our "uplifters" (*Gesta humanitatis per Americanos*). We are being deprived gradually of our liberties on the ground that the sacrifice is necessary to the good of society. If we attend carefully to the psychology of the persons who manifest such an eagerness to serve us, we shall find that they are even more eager to control us. What one discovers, for example, under the altruistic professions of the leaders of a typical organization for humanitarian crusading, like the Anti-Saloon League, is a growing will to power and even an incipient terrorism. Let one consider again Mr. Woodrow Wilson, who, more than any other recent American, sought to extend our idealism beyond our national frontiers. In the pursuit of his scheme for world service, he was led to make light of the constitutional checks on his authority and to reach out almost automatically for unlimited power. If we refused to take his humanitarian crusading seriously we were warned that we should "break the heart of the world." If the tough old world had ever had a heart in the Wilsonian sense, it would have been broken long ago. The truth is that this language, at once abstract and sentimental, reveals a temper at the opposite pole from that of the genuine statesman. He was inflexible and uncompromising in the defence of his "ideal," the League of Nations, which, as a corrective of the push for power on the national scale, is under the suspicion of being only a humanitarian chimera. At the same time he was only too ready to yield to the push for power of the labor unions (Adamson Act), a form of the instinct of domination so full of menace to free institutions that, rather than submit to it, a genuine statesman would have died in his tracks. One may contrast profitably the way in which Mr. Wilson faced this issue with the way in which Grover Cleveland, perhaps the last of our Presidents who was unmistakably in our great tradition, faced the issue of free silver.

The particular confusion of the things of God and the things of Caesar promoted by Mr. Wilson and the other "idealists" needs to have brought to bear on it the second of the sayings of Jesus that I have cited ("By their fruits ye shall know them"). The idealists so plainly fail to meet the test of fruits that they are taking refuge more and more, especially since the war, in their good intentions. We can no more grant that good intentions are enough in dealing with men than we can grant that they suffice a chemist who is handling high explosives. Under certain conditions, human nature itself may become one of the highest of high explosives. Above all, no person in a position of political responsibility can afford to let any "ideal" come between him and a keen inspection of the facts. It is only too evident that this true vision was found before the war in imperialists of the type of Lord Roberts rather than in liberals of the type of Asquith and Grey. It does not follow that the realism that one should oppose to the "idealists" need be of a merely imperialistic type; it may be a complete moral realism. The moral realist will not allow himself to be whisked off into any cloud-cuckoo-land in the name of the ideal. He will pay no more attention to the fine phrases in which an ideal of this kind is clothed than he would to the whistling of the wind around a corner. The idealist will, therefore, denounce him as "hard." His hardness is in any case quite unlike that of the Machiavellian realist. If the moral realist seems hard to the idealist, this is because of his refusal to shift, in the name of sympathy or social justice or on any other ground, the struggle between good and evil from the individual to society. If we restore the moral struggle to the individual, we are brought back at once to the assertion in some form or other of the truths of the inner life. The question that may properly be raised at present is not whether this or that cause or movement or reform is breaking down, but whether humanitarian crusading in general as a substitute for the inner life is not breaking down. The failure of humanitarianism might be even more manifest than it is were it not for the survival—and that even in the humanitarians themselves—of habits that derive from an entirely different view of life. The ethos of a community does not disappear in a day, even when the convictions that sustain it have been undermined. This slow decline of an ethos adds to the difficulty of judging any particular doctrine by its fruits. These fruits are often slow to appear. For example, no one has been more successful in breaking down American educational tradition in favor of humanitarian conceptions than President Eliot, who is himself an unusually fine product of the Puritan discipline. He has owed his great influence largely to the fact that many men are sensitive to a dignified and impressive personality, whereas very few men are capable of weighing the ultimate tendencies of ideas. One might have more confidence in the elective system if it could be counted on to produce President Eliots.

Though the traditional habits survive the traditional beliefs, they do not survive them indefinitely. With the progressive weakening, not merely of the Puritan ethos, but of the Christian ethos of the Occident in general, it may become harder and harder to justify humanitarianism experimentally. This movement has from Bacon's time stood for fruits and, in all that concerns man's power and material comfort and utility, it has as a matter of fact been superlatively fruitful. But it has also professed to give the fruits of the spirit—for example, peace and brotherhood—and here its failure is so conspicuous as to lead one to suspect some basic unsoundness.

At this point the third saying of Jesus that I have quoted comes into play—the saying as to the importance of building on the rock. The storm has come and it is not clear that our modern house is thus firmly established. The impression one has is rather that of an immense and glittering superstructure on insecure foundations.

The basis on which the whole structure of the new ethics has been reared is, as we have seen, the assumption that the significant struggle between good and evil is not in the individual but in society. If we wish once more to build securely, we may have to recover in some form the idea of "the civil war in the cave." If one admits this "war," one may admit at the same time the need of the work of the spirit, if one is to bring forth the fruits of the spirit. If one denies this war, one transfers the work to the outer world or substitutes for it a sympathy that involves neither an inner nor an outer working. A main problem of ethics, according to Cicero, is to prevent a divorce between the honorable (*honestum*) and the useful (*utile*). If these terms are not sophisticated, he says, the honorable and the useful will be found to be identical. But such a sophistication has taken place as a result of the emphasis on an outer rather than on an inner working * * * The fruitful has thus come to be identified with the useful and finally (in a narrow and doctrinal sense) with the utilitarian. The whole problem has assumed a gravity that it did not have in the time of Cicero because of the way in which we have got ourselves implicated, by our one-sided pursuit of utility, in an immense mass of interlocking machinery.

One needs, however, if one is to recover a firm basis for the spiritual life, to get behind even the word work. The sophistication of this word would not have been possible had it not been for the previous sophistication of the word nature. This word should receive the first attention of any one who is seeking to defend on Socratic lines either humanistic or religious truth. Apply a sufficiently penetrating dialectic to the word nature, one is sometimes tempted to think, and the sophist will be put out of action at the start. The juggling with this word can be traced from the ancient Greek who said that the distinction between the honorable and the shameful has no root in nature, but is merely a matter of convention, to Renan who said that "nature does not care for chastity." This juggling has always been the main source of an unsound individualism. The contrast between the natural and the artificial that has flourished since the eighteenth century and underlies the romantic movement is especially inadmissible. "Art," as Burke says, "is man's nature." I have already referred to Diderot's dismissal of the opposition between a law of the spirit and a law of the members as "artificial," and have said that the proper reply to such sophistry is not to take refuge in theology, but to insist upon this opposition as one of the "immediate data of consciousness"; that we shall thus get experimentally the basis we require if we are to do the work of the spirit and bring forth its fruits. A confusion like that of Diderot is so serious that the defining of the one word "nature" would justify a dialectical battle along Socratic lines the like of which has never been seen in the history of the world. When it was over, the field of conflict would be covered thick with dead and dying reputations; for there can be no doubt that many of the leaders of the present time have fallen into the naturalistic error.

On one's definition of work, which itself depends on one's definition of nature, will depend in turn one's definition of liberty. One is free to work and not to idle. Only when liberty is properly defined according not merely to the degree, but to the quality of one's working, is it possible to achieve a sound definition of justice (To every man according to his works). One's definition of justice again will be found to involve one's definition of peace in the secular order: for men can live at peace with one another only in so far as they are just. As for religious peace, it is not subject to definition. In the scriptural phrase, it passeth understanding.

Above all, if one is to achieve a sound philosophy of will, there must be no blurring of the distinction between the spiritually inert and the spiritually energetic. The point is one that should be of special interest to Americans. The European has tended in his typical moments, and that from the time of the Greeks, to be an intellectual. There are signs, on the other hand, that if America ever achieves a philosophy of its own, it will be rather a philosophy of will. We have been called the "people of action." Under the circumstances it is a matter of some moment both for ourselves and for the rest of the world whether we are to be strenuous in a completely human or in a merely Rooseveltian sense.

One may grant, indeed, that in a world like this the Rooseveltian imperialist is a safer guide than the Jeffersonian or Wilsonian "idealist." But there is no reason why one should accept either horn of this dilemma. The most effective way of dealing with the Jeffersonian idealism is to submit to a Socratic dialectic the theory of natural rights that underlies it. This theory rests on the sophistical contrast between the natural and the artificial of which I have just spoken, a contrast that encourages a total or partial suppression of the true dualism of the spirit and of the special quality of working it involves. With this weakening of the inner life it becomes possible to assert a lazy or, what amounts to the same thing, an anarchical liberty. For true liberty is not liberty to do as one likes, but liberty to adjust oneself, in some sense of that word, to law. "The Abbé Coigniard," says Anatole France, "would not have signed a line of the declaration of the rights of man because of the excessive and unjust discrimination it establishes between man and the gorilla." The true objection to the declaration of the rights of man is the exact opposite of the one stated by M. France: it does not establish a sufficiently wide gap between man and the gorilla. This gap can be maintained only if one insists that genuine liberty is the reward of ethical effort; it tends to disappear if one presents liberty as a free gift of "nature."

It may, indeed, be urged that the theory of natural rights, though false, may yet be justified as a "useful fiction," that it has often shown itself an effective weapon of attack on the iniquities of the existing social order. One may doubt, however, the utility of the fiction, for what it tends to oppose to the existing order is not a better order but anarchy. No doubt the established order of any particular time and place that the partisan of "rights" would dismiss as conventional and artificial is, compared with true and perfect order, only a shadow; but such as it is, it cannot be lightly abandoned in favor of some "ideal" that, when critically examined, may turn out to be only a mirage on the brink of a precipice. The "unwritten laws of heaven" of which the great humanist Sophocles speaks are felt in their relation to the written law, not as a right, but as a stricter obligation.

The tendency of the doctrine of natural rights to weaken the sense of obligation, and so to undermine genuine liberty, may be studied in connection with its influence on the common law which has prevailed among the English-speaking peoples. The spirit of this law at its best is that of a wholesome moral realism. Under the influence of the school of rights the equity that is often in conflict with strict law was more or less identified with a supposed law of "nature." This identification encouraged an unsound individualism. The proper remedy for an unsound individualism is a sound individualism, an individualism that starts, not from rights, but from duties. The actual reply to the unrestraint of the individual has been another doctrine of rights, the rights of society, which are sometimes conceived almost as metaphysically as the older doctrine of the rights of man. The representatives of this school of legal thinking tend to identify equity with the principle of social utility. Judges have already appeared who have so solicited the strict letter of the law in favor of what they deemed to be socially expedient as to fall into a veritable confusion of the legislative and judicial functions. Unfortunately those who represent society at any particular moment and who are supposed to overflow with a will to service will be found by the realistic observer (in so far at least as they are mere humanitarian crusaders in whom there is no survival of the traditional controls) to be developing, under cover of their altruism, a will to power. On the pretext of social utility they are ready to deprive the individual of every last scrap and vestige of his freedom and finally to subject him to despotic outer control. No one, as Americans of the present day are only too well aware, is more reckless in his attacks on personal liberty than the apostle of "service." He is prone in his furtherance of his schemes of "uplift" not only to ascribe unlimited sovereignty to society as against the individual, but to look on himself as endowed with a major portion of it, to develop a temper, in short, that is plainly tyrannical.

We seem, indeed, to be witnessing in a different form the emergency faced by the early Christians. The time may come again, if indeed it has not come already, when men will be justified in asserting true freedom, even, it may be, at the cost of their lives, against the monstrous encroachments of the materialistic state. The collectivistic ideal suffers, often in an exaggerated form, from the underlying error of *laisser faire* against which it is so largely a protest. It does not reveal an adequate sense of the nature of obligation and of the special type of effort it imposes. As a result of its shallowness in dealing with the idea of work, it is in danger of substituting for real justice the phantasmagoria of social justice. Some of the inequalities that the collectivist attacks are no doubt the result of the unethical competition promoted by *laisser faire.* But the remedy for these inequalities is surely not the pursuit of such chimeras as social or economic equality, at the risk of sacrificing the one form of equality that is valuable—equality before the law.

Equality as it is currently pursued is incompatible with true liberty; for liberty involves an inner working with reference to standards, the right subordination, in other words, of man's ordinary will to a higher will. There is an inevitable clash, in short, between equality and humility. Historically humility has been secured more or less at the expense of the intellect. I have myself been trying to show that it is possible to defend humility, and in general the truths of the inner life, by a critical method and in this sense to put Socrates in the service of Christ. The question of method is, in any case, allimportant if one is to heal the feud between the head and the heart that has subsisted in the Occident in various forms from

Graeco-Roman times. Intellect, though finally subordinate to will, is indispensable in direct ratio to the completeness of one's break with traditional standards. It is then needed to test from the point of view of reality the unity achieved by the imagination and so to supply new standards with reference to which the higher will may exercise its power of veto on the impulses and expansive desires. When will and intellect and imagination have been brought into right relation with one another, one arrives at last at the problem of the emotions, to which the Rousseauist, in his misplaced thirst of immediacy, gives the first place. To have standards means practically to select and reject; and this again means that one must discipline one's feelings or affections, to use the older word, to some ethical centre. If the discipline is to be effective, so that a man will like and dislike the right things, it is as a rule necessary that it should become a matter of habit, and that almost from infancy. One cannot wait until the child has reached the so-called age of reason, until, in short, he is in a position to do his own selecting, for in the meanwhile he may have become the victim of bad habits. This is the true prison house that is in danger of closing on the growing boy. Habit must, therefore, as Aristotle says, precede reason. Certain other ideas closely connected with the idea of habit, need to receive attention at this point. The ethos of a community is derived in fact, as it is etymologically, from habit. If a community is to transmit certain habits to its young, it must normally come to some kind of agreement as to what habits are desirable; it must in the literal meaning of that word achieve a convention. Here is a chief difference between the true and the false liberal. It has been said of our modernists that they have only one convention and that is that there shall be no more conventions. An individualism that is thus purely temperamental is incompatible with the survival of civilization. What is civilized in most people is precisely that part of them which is conventional. It is, to be sure, difficult to have a convention without falling into mere conventionalism, two things that the modernist confounds; but then everything that is worthwhile is difficult.

The combining of convention with a due respect for the liberty of the individual involves, it must be admitted, adjustments of the utmost delicacy. Two extremes are about equally undesirable: first, the convention may be so rigid and minute as to leave little scope for the initiative of the individual. This formalistic extreme was reached, if Occidental opinion be correct, in the China of the past, and also in the older French convention that Rousseau attacked. At the opposite pole is the person who is spontaneous after the fashion encouraged by Rousseau and who, in getting rid of conventions, has also got rid of standards and abandoned himself to the mere flux of his impressions. The problem of standards would be simple if all we had to do was to oppose to this anarchical "liberty" a sound set of general principles. But so far as actual conduct is concerned, life resolves itself into a series of particular emergencies, and it is not always easy to bridge the gap between these emergencies or concrete cases and the general principle. It has been held in the Occident, at least from the time of Aristotle, and in the Orient, at least from the time of Confucius, that one should be guided in one's application of the general principle by the law of measure. The person who thus mediates successfully seems, in the phrase of Pascal, to combine in himself opposite virtues and to occupy all the space between them. As a general principle, for example, courage is excellent, but unless it be tempered in the concrete instance by prudence, it will degenerate into rashness. According to Bossuet, "Good maxims pushed to an extreme are utterly ruinous." (*Les bonnes maximes outrées perdent tout.*) But who is to decide what is the moderate and what the extreme application of a good maxim? The casuist or legalist would not only lay down the general principle, but try to deal exhaustively with all the cases that may arise in the application of it, in such wise as to deprive the individual, so far as possible, of his autonomy. The cases are, however, inexhaustible, inasmuch as life is, in Bergson's phrase, a perpetual gushing forth of novelties. A Jesuitical casebook or the equivalent is after all a clumsy substitute for the living intuition of the individual in determining the right balance to strike between the abiding principle and the novel emergency. While insisting, therefore, on the need of a convention, one should strive to hold this convention flexibly, imaginatively, and, as it were, progressively. Without a convention of some kind it is hard to see how the experience of the past can be brought to bear on the present. The unconventional person is assuming that either he or his age is so unique that all this past experience has become obsolete. This very illusion has, to be sure, been fostered in many by the rapid advance of the physical sciences.

So much experience has accumulated in both the East and the West that it should seem possible for those who are seeking to maintain standards and to fight an anarchical impressionism, to come together, not only as to their general principles, but as to the main cases that arise in the application of them. This convention, if it is to be effective, must, as I have already suggested, be transmitted in the form of habits to the young. This is only another way of saying that the civilization of a community and ultimately the government of which it is capable is closely related to the type of education on which it has agreed. (One should include in education the discipline that children receive in the family.) "The best laws," says Aristotle, "will be of no avail unless the young are trained by habit and education in the spirit of the constitution." Aristotle complains that this great principle was being violated in his time. Is it being observed in ours? It will be interesting in any case to make a specific application of the Aristotelian dictum to our American education in its relation to American government. Assuming that what we wish to preserve is a federal and constitutional democracy, are we training up a class of leaders whose ethos is in intimate accord with this type of government? The older type of American college reflected faithfully enough the convention of its time. The classical element in its curriculum was appropriately subordinated to the religious element, inasmuch as the leadership at which it aimed was to be lodged primarily in the clergy. It would have been possible to interpret more vitally our older educational convention, to give it the broadening it certainly needed and to adapt it to changed conditions. The new education (I am speaking, of course, of the main trend) can scarcely be said to have developed in this fashion from the old. It suggests rather a radical break with our traditional ethos. The old education was, in intention at least, a training for wisdom and character. The new education has been summed up by President Eliot in the phrase: training for service and power. We are all coming together more and more in this idea of service. But, though service is supplying us in a way with a convention, it is not, in either the humanistic or the religious sense, supplying us with standards. In the current sense of the word it tends rather to undermine standards, if it be true, as I have tried to show, that it involves an assumption hard to justify on strictly psychological grounds—the assumption that men can come together expansively and on the level of their ordinary selves. The older education was based on the belief that men need to be disciplined to some ethical centre. The sentimental humanitarian opposes to a definite curriculum which aims at some such humanistic or religious discipline the right of the individual to develop freely his bent or temperamental proclivity. The standard or common measure is compromised by the assertion of this supposed right, and in about the same measure the effort and spirit of emulation that the standard stimulates disappears. The very word curriculum implies a running together. Under the new educational dispensation, students, instead of running together, tend to lounge separately. Interest is transferred from the classroom to the athletic field, where there is a standard of a kind and, with reference to this standard, something that human nature craves—real victory or real defeat. The sentimentalist also plays into the hands of the utilitarian, who likewise sets up a standard with reference to which one may strive and achieve success or failure. Anything that thus has a definite aim tends to prevail over anything that, like a college of liberal arts under the elective system, is comparatively aimless. One cannot admit the argument sometimes heard that, because the older education had a definite end, it was therefore vocational in the same sense as the schools of business administration, for example, that have been developing so portentously of late in our educational centres. The older education aimed to produce leaders and, as it perceived, the basis of leadership is not commercial or industrial efficiency, but wisdom. Those who have been substituting the cult of efficiency for the older liberal training are, of course, profuse in their professions of service either to country or to mankind at large. The question I have been raising * * *, however, is whether anything so purely expansive as service, in the humanitarian sense, can supply an adequate counterpoise to the pursuit of unethical power, whether the proper counterpoise is not to be sought rather in the cultivation of the principle of vital control, first of all in the individual and finally in the State.

I have said that one's attitude towards the principle of control will determine one's definition of liberty, and that the Jeffersonians inclining, as they did, to the new myth of man's natural goodness, looked askance, not merely at the traditional restraints, but at everything that interfered with a purely expansive freedom. Jefferson himself saw to some extent the implications of his general position for education in particular. He is, for example, one of the authentic precursors of the elective system. The education that the Jeffersonian liberty has tended to supplant set up a standard that limited the supposed right of the individual to self-expression as well as the inbreeding of special aptitudes in the interests of efficiency; it was not, in short, either sentimental or utilitarian. There is a real relation between the older educational standard that thus acted restrictively on the mere temperament of the individual and the older political standard embodied in institutions like the Constitution, Senate, and Supreme Court, that serve as a check on the ordinary or impulsive will of the people. It follows from all I have said that the new education does not meet the Aristotelian requirement: it is not in intimate correspondence with our form of government. If the veto power disappears from our education there is no reason to anticipate that it will long survive in the State. The spirit of the leaders will not be that which should preside over a constitutional democracy.

The best of our elder statesmen, though they opposed a standard to the mere flux of popular impulse and made sure that the standard was appropriately embodied in institutions, did not associate their standard with any theory of the absolute. Herein they showed their sagacity. One cannot separate too carefully the cause of standards from that of the absolute. Standards are a matter of observation and common sense, the absolute is only a metaphysical conceit. In political thinking this conceit has led to various theories of unlimited sovereignty. Judged by their fruits all these theories are, according to John Adams, "equally arbitrary, cruel, bloody, and in every respect diabolical." They can be shown, at all events, to be hard to reconcile with a proper respect for personal liberty. It is a fortunate circumstance that the very word sovereignty does not occur in our Constitution. The men who made this Constitution were for granting a certain limited power here and another limited power somewhere else, and absolute power nowhere. The best scheme of government they conceived to be a system of checks and balances. They did not, however, look on the partial powers they bestowed as being on the same level. They were aware that true liberty requires a hierarchy and a subordination, that there must be something central in a state to which final appeal may be made in case of conflict. The complaint has, indeed, been made that they left certain ambiguities in the articles of union that had finally to be clarified on the battle-field. If they had been more explicit, however, it is not probable that they would have been able to establish a union at all. They were confronted with the difficult task of gaining recognition for the centripetal element in government in the face of the most centrifugal doctrine the world has ever known—the doctrine that encourages men to put their rights before their duties.

John Marshall deserves special praise for the clearness with which he saw that the final centre of control in the type of government that was being founded, if control was to have an ethical basis and not be another name for force, must be vested in the judiciary, particularly in the Supreme Court. This court, especially in its most important function, that of interpreting the Constitution, must, he perceived, embody more than any other institution the higher or permanent self of the State. With a sound and independent judiciary, above all with a sound and independent supreme bench, liberty and democracy may after all be able to coexist. Many people are aware that personal liberty and the security of private property, which is almost inseparable from it, are closely bound up with the fortunes of the Supreme Court. Their ideas are, however, often vague as to the nature of the menace that overhangs our highest tribunal. We are familiar with the rant of Gompers and his kind against the courts; we also know what to expect from the radical press. We are not surprised, for example, when a social-istic periodical, published at Girard, Kansas, devotes a special issue of five million copies to an assault on the federal judi-ciary. A menace that is perhaps more serious than this open hostility may be defined as a sort of "boring from within." This phrase seems to fit the professors in our law schools who are departing from the traditional standards of the law in favor of "social justice." Social justice, it is well to remind these "forward-looking" professors, means in practice class justice, class justice means class war and class war, if we are to go by all the experience of the past and present, means hell.

The inadequacy of social justice with its tendency to undermine the moral responsibility of the individual and at the same time to obscure the need of standards and leadership may be made clearer if we consider for a moment the problem of government with the utmost degree of realism. Thus consid-ered, government is power. Whether the power is to be ethical or unethical, whether in other words it is subordinated to true justice, must depend finally on the quality of will displayed by the men who administer it. For what counts practically is not justice in the abstract, but the just man. The just man is he whose various capacities (including the intellect) are acting in right relation to one another under the hegemony of the higher will. We are brought back here to the problem of the remnant. Those who strive for the inner proportion that is reflected in the outer world as justice have always been few. The remark of Aristotle that "most men would rather live in a disorderly than in a sober manner" remains true, at least in the subtler psychic sense. Though one agree with Aristotle as to the ethical unsoundness of the majority, it does not follow that the ethical State is impossible. Human nature, and this is its most encouraging trait, is sensitive to a right example. It is hard, indeed, to set bounds to the persuasiveness of a right example, provided only it be right enough. The ethical State is possible in which an important minority is ethically energetic and is thus becoming at once just and exemplary. Such a minority will also tend to solve the problem of union. The soul of the unjust man is, according to Aristotle, torn by every manner of faction. The just man, on the contrary, is he who, as the result of his moral choices based on due deliberation, choices in which he is moved primarily by a regard for his own happiness, has quelled the unruly impulses of his lower nature and so attained to some degree of unity with himself. At the same time he will find that he is moving towards a common centre with others who have been carrying through a similar task of self-conquest. A State that is controlled by men who have become just as the result of minding their own business in the Platonic sense will be a just State that will also mind its own business; it will be of service to other States, not by meddling in their affairs on either commercial or "idealistic" grounds, but by setting them a good example. A State of this kind may hope to find a basis of understanding with any other State that is also ethically controlled. The hope of coöperation with a State that has an unethical leadership is chimerical. The value of political thinking is therefore in direct ratio to its adequacy in dealing with the problem of leadership. The unit to which all things must finally be referred is not the State or humanity or any other abstraction, but the man of character. Compared with this ultimate human reality, every other reality is only a shadow in the mist.

It follows from what I have said that ethical union, whether in the single man or among different men or on the national or international scale, is attainable so far as it is attainable at all, not by expansive emotion nor by any form of machinery or organization (in the current sense of the word), but only by the pathway of the inner life. Some persons will remain spiritually anarchical in spite of educational opportunity, others will acquire at least the rudiments of ethical discipline, whereas still others, a small minority, if we are to judge by past experience, will show themselves capable of the more difficult stages of self-conquest that will fit them for leadership. Our traditional education with all its defects did something to produce leaders of this ethical type, whereas the utilitarian-sentimental education which has been tending to supplant it is, as I have been trying to show, lacking in the essentials of the inner life and so is not likely to produce either religious or humanistic leaders. Most Americans of the present day will, indeed, feel that they have refuted sufficiently all that I have said, if they simply utter the word "service." One may suspect, however, that the popularity of the gospel of service is due to the fact that it is flattering to unregenerate human nature. It is pleasant to think that one may dispense with awe and reverence and the inner obeisance of the spirit to standards, provided one be eager to do something for humanity. "The highest worship of God," as Benjamin Franklin assures us blandly, "is service to man." If it can be shown experimentally—and a certain amount of evidence on this point has accumulated since the time of Franklin—that service in this sense is not enough to chain up the naked lusts of the human heart, one must conclude that the supreme exemplar of American shrewdness and practicality did not, in the utterance I have just cited, show himself sufficiently shrewd and practical. The gospel of service is at all events going to receive a thorough trial, if nowhere else, then in America. We are rapidly becoming a nation of humanitarian crusaders. The present reign of legalism is the most palpable outcome of this crusading. It is growing only too evident, however, that the drift towards license is being accelerated rather than arrested by the multiplication of laws. If we do not develop a sounder type of vision than that of our "uplifters" and "forward-lookers," the history of free institutions in this country is likely to be short, and, on the whole, discreditable. Surely the first step is to perceive that the alternative to a constitutional liberty is not a legalistic millenium, but a triumph of anarchy followed by a triumph of force. The time may come, with the growth of a false liberalism, when a predominant element in our population, having grown more and more impatient of the ballot box and representative government, of constitutional limitations and judicial control, will display a growing eagerness for "direct action." This is the propitious moment for the imperialistic leader. Though the triumph of any type of imperialistic leader is a disaster, especially in a country like our own that has known the blessings of liberty under the law, nevertheless there is a choice even here. Circumstances may arise when we may esteem ourselves fortunate if we get the American equivalent of a Mussolini; he may be needed to save us from the American equivalent of a Lenin. Such an emergency is not to be anticipated, however, unless we drift even further than we have thus far from the principles that underlie our unionist tradition. The maintenance of this tradition is indissolubly bound up with the maintenance of standards. The democratic contention that everybody should have a chance is excellent provided it mean that everybody is to have a chance to measure up to high standards. If the democratic extension of opportunity is, on the other hand, made a pretext for lowering standards, democracy is, in so far, incompatible with civilization. One might be more confident of the outcome of the struggle between a true and a false liberalism that has been under way since the founding of the Republic, if the problem of standards was being dealt with more adequately in our education, above all in our higher education. The tendency here, however, is, as I have noted, to discard standards in favor of "ideals"; and ideals, as currently understood, recognize very imperfectly, if at all, that man needs to be disciplined to a law of his own, distinct from the law of physical nature. One might view this idealistic development with more equanimity if one were convinced with Professor John Dewey that the growing child exudes spontaneously a will to service. If we look, however, on this form of spontaneity as a romantic myth, we shall be forced to conclude that we have been permitting Professor Dewey and his kind to have an influence on our education that amounts in the aggregate to a national calamity; that with the progress of ideals of this kind our higher education in particular is, from the point of view of a genuinely liberal training, in danger of becoming a vast whir of machinery in the void; finally, that, in the interest of our experiment in free institutions, we need educational leaders who will have less to say of service and more to say of culture and civilization, and who will so use these words as to show that they have some inkling of their true meaning.

* * * * The American situation can be understood only with reference to the larger background—the slow yielding in the whole of the Occident of traditional standards, humanistic and religious, to naturalism. I have defined in its main aspects

the movement that has supervened upon this emancipation from the past as Baconian, Rousseauistic, and Machiavellian; in other words, as utilitarian, sentimental, and imperialistic. The individualist should, however, make a better use of his liberty; the less traditional he becomes, the more he should strive to get at standards positively and critically. The result of such a striving would, I have tried to show, be a movement that might be best defined as Socratic, Aristotelian, and Christian, that would, in short, put prime emphasis in its different stages on definition, habit, and humility. What has actually been witnessed in the Occident, as a result of the failure to work out critical equivalents of traditional standards, has been a series of violent oscillations between a humanitarian idealism and a Machiavellian realism. Humanitarian idealism is still firmly entrenched in this country, especially in academic circles, where it seems to be held more confidently, one is almost tempted to say more smugly, with each succeeding year. Europeans, on the other hand, have suffered certain essential disillusions. It is becoming increasingly difficult for them to believe that the idealists have discovered any effective counterpoise to the push for power. "We are much beholden," says Bacon, "to Machiavel and others that wrote what men do, and not what they ought to do." The gap between what men do and what they ought to do is turning out to be even wider under the humanitarian dispensation than under that of mediaeval Christianity.

Yet the Machiavellian solution is in itself impossible. If the Occident does not get beyond this type of realism, it will simply reënact all the pagan stupidities and hasten once more to the pagan doom. Moreover, the latter stages of the naturalistic dissolution of civilization with which we are menaced are, thanks to scientific "progress," likely to be marked by incidents of almost inconceivable horror. The danger of power without wisdom, of a constantly increasing material organization combined with an ever-growing spiritual anarchy, is already so manifest that unless there is a serious search for a remedy we may conclude that the instinct for self-preservation that is supposed to inhere in mankind is a myth. Surely the first step will be to put in his proper subordinate place the man of science with his poison gases and high explosives, and that without a particle of obscurantism. The tendency of physical science to bring the whole of human nature under a single law can be shown to be at the bottom of some of the most dangerous fallacies of the present time—for example, the socialistic dream of "scientific" politics. "Thus the whole of society," says Mr. J. Ramsay MacDonald, "its organization, its institutions, its activities, is brought within the sway of natural law, not merely on its descriptive and historical side, but on its experimental side, and administration and legislation become arts pursued in the same way as the chemist works in his laboratory." The man of science is flattered in the conceit of his own importance by this inordinate exaltation of the "law for thing." Yet he should, in the interest of science itself, reject the whole point of view as pseudo-scientific; for science needs the support of civilization and the chief force that is now making against civilization is, next perhaps to emotional unrestraint, pseudo-science.

Mr. MacDonald and his kind almost invariably look upon themselves as "idealists." This should serve to remind us that the terms idealism and realism as now employed, however much they may clash superficially, have at least this much in common: they are both rooted in a naturalistic philosophy. Anyone who transcends this philosophy ceases in about the same measure to be either a humanitarian idealist or a Machiavellian realist. He becomes aware of a quality of will that distinguishes man from physical nature and is yet natural in the sense that it is a matter of immediate perception and not of outer authority. I have said that the neglect of this quality of will by both utilitarians and sentimentalists has encouraged a sophistical definition of liberty; that this type of liberty has owed its appeal to its flattery of spiritual indolence, perhaps the most fundamental human trait that is open to direct observation. Anyone who has once perceived this trait in himself and others, and followed it out in even a few of its almost innumerable ramifications, will be in no danger of overlooking the old Adam after the fashion of the "idealists." The insistence on the putting aside of spiritual indolence and the exercise of the higher will is found in every genuinely spiritual doctrine, above all in genuine Christianity. Traditionally the Christian has associated his liberty and his faith in a higher will with grace. "Where the Spirit of the Lord is, there is liberty." I myself have been trying to come at this necessary truth, not in terms of grace, but in terms of work, and that on the humanistic rather than on the religious level. I am not so arrogant as to deny the validity of other ways of affirming the higher will, or to dismiss as obsolete the traditional forms through which this will has been interpreted to the imagination. I am attempting a contribution, I cannot remind the reader too often, to a specific problem—to the distinction, namely, between a sound and an unsound individualism. My argument should appeal primarily, so far as it appeals to any one, to those who, as a result of having broken with the traditional forms on grounds insufficiently critical, are in danger of losing the truths of the higher will entirely; who are mere modernists at a time when there is a supreme need of thoroughgoing and complete moderns.

In Germaine de Staël (1766–1817) Babbitt finds a representative of her time, as well as a modern who substitutes the virtues of expansion for the virtues of concentration. He discovers in her life and writings the kind of cosmopolitanism that rounds out national originality with international comprehension and sympathy. But such a cosmopolitanism, Babbitt declares, amounts to moral disintegration, especially when discipline and standards of selectivity are surrendered to enthusiasm, sympathy, and shallow comprehensiveness. True cosmopolitanism, he insists, must be the mediation between extremes and must be allegiant to a common standard that prevails against the powers of individual and national self-assertion. Madame de Staël, temperamentally and intellectually a Rousseauist, in rejecting the restrictive principles revealed an expansive view of taste and of genius. She believed that creative genius should be effusive and the critical pursuit merely acquiescent. Babbitt centers on her book De l'Allemagne, *which not only romanticizes that "nation of noble enthusiasts" but also gives excessive attention to German romantic writers. Her preoccupation with differences rather than identities concomitantly instances, Babbitt concludes, the limitations of her taste and historic sense. Madame de Staël is, then, an example of Rousseau's disciples, who, as "corrupters of the conscience," introduce confusion into morality. (From* The Masters of Modern French Criticism *[Boston and New York: Houghton Mifflin Co., 1912], pp. 1–33.)*

MADAME DE STAËL

The first year of the nineteenth century was appropriately marked by the publication of Madame de Staël's *Literature Considered in its Relations to Social Institutions.* This relationship between literature and society upon which the new century was to insist more than any previous century had been forced upon its notice by the very suddenness of its separation from the past. As Stendhal was to say later: "How could you expect a man who had been on the retreat from Moscow to care for literature written for the men who had taken off their hats at Fontenoy to the English column and said, 'Fire first, gentlemen'?" "Nothing in life should be stationary," wrote Madame de Staël in the *Germany,* "and art is petrified when it no longer changes. Twenty years of revolution have given the imagination other needs than those it felt when the novels of Crébillon portrayed the love and society of the time." Chateaubriand, at variance with Madame de Staël on so many other points, agreed with her that men's characters had been profoundly transformed by the Revolution and that literature should reflect this transformation.

We should err, however, in supposing that the public in general at the beginning of the nineteenth century felt the need of changes in art and literature to express a changed society. The Empire as a whole was a period of artificiality and formalism. This would seem less strange if those who had learned nothing and forgotten nothing politically had alone shown zeal in maintaining the Old Régime in literature. On the contrary, the men who had innovated most rashly in other ways were often conspicuous for their literary conservatism. Men who had toppled over altars and beheaded a king were ready to kneel down superstitiously in the little Temple of Taste; like Byron who, according to Goethe, showed no respect for any law human or divine except the law of the three unities. An occasional writer who felt a new spirit stirring vaguely within him, and set out to be original, only succeeded in becoming odd. Thus Népomucène Lemercier (Népomucène le Bizarre), after precipitating a bloody riot by the liberties he took with the unities and verbal decorum in his play *Christophe Colomb,* afterwards declared in his *Cours de littérature,* that a tragedy must fulfil precisely twenty-six rules or conditions under penalty of ceasing to be.

The society of the Empire, made up as it was largely of parvenus and of persons whose education had been broken off abruptly by the Revolution, was almost naïvely willing to be schoolmastered. It wished to get on the easiest terms that tincture of humane literature that was deemed necessary not only to good taste but to good breeding. Hence no doubt the popularity during the first twenty or thirty years of the century of the *Lycée* of La Harpe, the last eminent critical authority of the Old Régime; for no one was better fitted than he to give a first general initiation into literary tradition. Sainte-Beuve calls the critics of the Empire the small change of Boileau—Boileau, conceived, of course, after the late neo-classical fashion, as the policeman of Parnassus, the vigilant guardian of literary orthodoxy. Sainte-Beuve points out that they had not only the limitations but the merits of the older type of critics: they were preëminently judicial. They felt themselves supported, moreover, in their judgments by a public opinion that had grown weary of the chaos and anarchy of the Revolution, and are even less important in themselves than as the mouthpieces of this opinion.

Geoffroy, the representative critic of the period, was fitted by his past to play the pedagogue. He had been professor of "eloquence" at Paris before the Revolution and taught school in the village where he concealed himself during the Terror. Geoffroy, however, cannot be dismissed as a mere political and literary reactionary, though in a sense he was both. He makes frequent use of the historic method and is guided in his actual judgments even more by vigorous good-sense than by a regard for formal requirements. At the age of fifty-eight, he created a new *genre*, the dramatic feuilleton, and for twelve years ruled the playwrights and actors of his time with a rod of iron. Like Jeffrey, with whom he has been compared, he belongs only partly to the old critical order by his method, but entirely to it by his temper, which was hard, imperious, and vituperative. According to an epigram, he died as a result of having sucked inadvertently the tip of his own pen. His violence, like that of his opponents, is due to the same poisonous intrusion of politics into literature that one finds at about the same time in England. No wonder that a man who has to repel almost daily charges of venality and gluttony should in the long run become pugilistic. Quite apart from politics, however, Geoffroy believed in the virtues of *la critique amère;* and something may as a matter of fact be said in behalf of a tonic bitterness in criticism. Unfortunately, he not only flourished the ferule too openly, but had against him the deeper currents of his time. He stood at most for a minor movement of concentration in an age which was in its underlying tendency expansive, and which, caring little for discipline, aspired towards a vast widening out of knowledge and sympathy. Of this underlying expansive tendency the true representative is Madame de Staël.

I

It has been said that the rôle of Madame de Staël was to understand and make others understand, that of Chateaubriand to feel and teach others to feel; which is only another way of saying that Chateaubriand is more intimately related to romanticism than Madame de Staël. That "unnatural amount of understanding" in Madame de Staël of which Schiller complained sets her off sharply from the romanticists and connects her with the eighteenth century. Her style is of that age; it lacks, however, the epigrammatic neatness of the eighteenth century before Rousseau, and though not always free from the sentimentality and declamation that the late eighteenth century had caught from Rousseau at his worst, it lacks the imaginative freshness and warmth of coloring of Rousseau at his best. It has its own merits as a medium for conveying ideas, but it is deficient in both the old art and the new poetry.

Madame de Staël belongs no less decisively to the Old Régime in preferring society to nature and solitude. Napoleon, in his ten years' duel with her, discovered that he could inflict sufficient torment simply by keeping her at a distance from Paris. She was especially impatient with those who suggested that she had a compensation for her enforced absence from the capital in the panorama of the Alps that unfolded itself before her at Coppet. She spent years in the presence of this panorama, as has been pointed out, without receiving from it the suggestion of a single image. However, her often quoted remark that she would travel five hundred leagues to meet a man of parts, but would not open her window to look at the Bay of Naples, gives a somewhat exaggerated idea of her indifference to nature.

In spite of her excess of understanding, her love of the drawing-room and her comparative coolness towards nature, Madame de Staël is nevertheless a disciple of Rousseau. We merely need to define carefully this discipleship. She might have said, though in a somewhat different sense from Rousseau, that "her heart and her head did not seem to belong to the same individual." Like Renan she was fond of attributing the conflict of which she was conscious in herself to a mixed

heredity. "To be born a French woman," she says, "with a foreign character, with French taste and habits and the ideas and
feelings of the North, is a contrast that wrecks one's life." In
the *Germany* Madame de Staël says that Rousseau introduced
an alien element into French literature, an element that is
Northern and Germanic. Now the element that Madame de
Staël conceived to be common to Rousseau and herself and at
the same time to distinguish the Germans, manifests itself
especially in the power of "enthusiasm." She is, then, not only
temperamentally an enthusiast, but also an enthusiast by the
direct influence of Rousseau as well as by the Rousseauism
that she received from Germany.

The more we study the literary revolution at the beginning
of the nineteenth century, the more it becomes plain that
everything hinges on the word enthusiasm. The romantic
movement in its modern phase is even more a renascence of
enthusiasm than a renascence of wonder, or rather wonder
itself is only one aspect of the new enthusiasm. The process by
which the word enthusiasm itself changed in the course of the
eighteenth century from a bad to a good meaning, by which the
enthusiast and original genius supplanted the wit and man of
the world, is one of the most important in literary history and
can scarcely be traced too carefully.

Illuminating passages on the nature of the new enthusiasm and at the same time on Madame de Staël's relationship
to Rousseau will be found in her very youthful *Letters on the
Writings and Character of Jean-Jacques Rousseau.* "Is it not
in our youth," she exclaims in the preface to that work, "that
we owe the most gratitude to Rousseau, to the man who succeeded in making a passion of virtue, who wished to convince
by enthusiasm and made use of the good qualities and even the
faults of youth to render himself its master." Elsewhere she
says that "he invented nothing but set everything afire"—
even to the point it would appear of setting virtue afire. Virtue
thus becomes an involuntary impulse, a "noble enthusiasm," a
"movement which passes into the blood and sweeps you along
irresistibly like the most imperious passions." In other words,
for Madame de Staël as for Rousseau, virtue is a mere process
of emotional expansion, related to the region of impulse below

the reason rather than to the region of insight above it. Rousseau and his followers introduce universal confusion into morality, as Joubert says, by thus conceiving of virtue not as a bridle but as a spur. Of Madame de Staël in particular, he said that she had a native ethical gift which was corrupted by her notion of enthusiasm. "She took the fevers of the soul for its endowments, intoxication for a power, and our aberrations for a progress. The passions became in her eyes a species of dignity and glory."

It would not, however, be entirely fair to Madame de Staël to see in her conception of morality a mere Rousseauistic intoxication. The two ruling passions of her life were hatred of Napoleon and love for her father, and as she grew older she showed herself more and more not merely the daughter but the disciple of Necker. Both her rationalism and her emotionalism were tempered by the traditional views of morality and religion of the Swiss protestant. In her political thinking again, both on her own account and as a follower of her father, she departed from Rousseau in putting her chief emphasis on liberty. In the very passage where she says that Rousseau invented nothing but set everything afire, she goes on to say that "the sentiment of equality which produces many more storms than the love of liberty, and which causes questions to arise of a quite different order,—the sentiment of equality in its greatness as well as in its pettiness stands out in every line of Rousseau's writings." Rousseau was nearer to the French in this respect than Madame de Staël. In making the love of liberty the mainspring of the Revolution, she was under more illusions about the French character than Napoleon, who knew that the deeper craving of the French was for equality, even equality under a despot.

Rousseauistic enthusiasm remains after all the essential aspect of Madame de Staël's genius. She differs however from many of the posterity of Jean-Jacques in being intellectually as well as emotionally expansive. In so far as she desired only expansiveness and refused either an inner or an outer check, she was unbalanced and did not escape the Nemesis that pursues every form of lack of balance, especially, perhaps, lack of emotional balance. Yet it may be said in her behalf that the

half-truths on which she insisted were the half-truths that the
age needed to hear, and that the excess by which she erred
was—in spite of the charges of masculinity brought against
her by her contemporaries—the excess of the feminine virtues.
She really had the largeness and generosity of outlook that her
theory required, and hers was above all a magnificently hospitable nature. The welcome that she extended at Coppet to
visitors from the ends of Europe symbolizes fitly the breadth
of her intellectual hospitality. She was cosmopolitan not only
in the influences she received but in those she radiated. As
Napoleon complained, she taught people to think to whom it
would never otherwise have occurred to do so.

II

Any one who conceives of life as expansively as did Madame de
Staël, comes inevitably to be interested less in form than in
expression. The partisan of form is fastidious and exclusive,
whether his sense of form rests on a living intuition or on the
acceptance of certain traditional standards. Now Madame de
Staël almost entirely lacked the living intuition of form and
had repudiated the traditional standards. She was led by her
interest in expression to exalt the variable element in literature, to see it not absolutely but relatively; above all, as we
have seen, to look on it as the expression of society and therefore as changing with it. Saint-Evremond had opposed a keen
sense of historical relativity to the overweening faith of the age
of Louis XIV in the fixity and finality of its own standards.
But Madame de Staël did not get her historical sense from
Saint-Evremond, so far as she may be said to have had one at
all at the time of writing her book on *Literature;* it is rather a
development of what is already in germ in Rousseau. For Rousseau, unhistorical as he was in many respects, treated one of
the literary forms, the drama, from the relative and expression-
istic point of view. In the *Letter to D'Alembert* he maintains
that the only possible kind of play is the problem play; furthermore that the dramatist is not free to choose his problem,
but has it imposed upon him by the taste of his country and
time. Thus the *Oedipus Rex* did not succeed because of its

absolute human appeal, but because it expressed the taste of
an Athenian audience of the fifth century B.C. If it were put on
the stage to-day it would infallibly fall flat. Curiously enough
Saint-Evremond made precisely the same use of the same illustration, and both Saint-Evremond and Rousseau would seem
to have been convicted of error by recent successful revivals of
the Oedipus as an acting play.

The use of the historical method in the book on *Literature*
is much obscured by the utterly unhistorical conception of perfectibility, that faith in a mechanical and rectilinear advance of
the human race which so many people still hold naïvely, imagining themselves to be evolutionists. Madame de Staël assumes the superiority of Roman over Greek philosophy simply
because it comes later. She was at least led in this way to
suspect something of value in those mediaeval centuries which
La Harpe had dismissed as mere "chaos and night."

We find in the *Literature,* along with many other passages
that anticipate at least faintly the *Germany,* the first form of
the celebrated distinction between the two literatures, that of
the North and that of the South (she does not however as yet
apply to the former the epithet romantic). She shows the
limitations both of her taste and of her historic sense when,
after deriving the southern or Graeco-Roman tradition ultimately from Homer, she seeks for the headwaters of the northern literatures in Ossian! This love of Ossian was one of the
few things she had in common with Napoleon. She relates that
when Talleyrand presented Bonaparte to the Directorate on
his return from Italy, he assured them that General Bonaparte
"detested luxury and display, wretched ambitions of ordinary
spirits, and that he loved the poetry of Ossian, especially because it detaches one from the earth." She adds that the earth
would not have asked anything better than to have him detach
himself from it.

But let us come to the more mature expression of Madame
de Staël's views. Her *Germany* bears the marks not only of her
travels in Italy, Austria, and Germany during the ten years
that had elapsed since the publication of the *Literature* but
also of important personal influences. We are told that the
proper rule to follow in accounting for the ideas of a woman is,

Cherchez l'homme; and we cannot entirely neglect this rule even in the case of Madame de Staël, the most intellectual of modern women. Heine complained that throughout the *Germany* he could hear with disagreeable distinctness the falsetto voice of August Wilhelm Schlegel. It is not surprising that with such a guide she not only gave undue attention to certain German romantic writers, but inclined to romanticize Germany in general. She was especially indignant at a phrase of the letter in which Savary, Duke of Rovigo, announced to her the confiscation of the *Germany* and her banishment: "Your last work is not French." Yet in a sense Savary was right. The Germany that she paints becomes (somewhat like the Germania of Tacitus) a sort of Arcadia, against which the French corruption "sticks more fiery off." The book brought up before Heine the image of a "passionate woman eddying about like a whirlwind through our tranquil Germany, exclaiming everywhere delightedly, 'O how sweet is the peace that I breathe here!' She had got overheated in France and came among us to cool off. The chaste breath of our poets was so comforting to her boiling and fiery heart. She looked upon our philosophers as so many different kinds of ices; she sipped Kant like a vanilla sherbet and Fichte like a pistachio cream. 'O what a charming coolness reigns in your woods!' she kept constantly exclaiming; 'what a ravishing odor of violets! How peacefully the canary-birds twitter in their little German nests! You are good and virtuous; you haven't as yet any idea of the moral depravity that prevails among us in France in the rue du Bac!' "

This legend of an idyllic Germany, a land of sentimental dreamers and philosophers who refused to interest themselves in anything less than the universe, survived in France to some extent until the rude awakening of 1870. To this nation of noble enthusiasts Madame de Staël opposes the drily analytical French. It is at bottom the same contrast that Coleridge and Carlyle elaborated in England. The German is not, like the Frenchman, imprisoned in the uninspired understanding (*Verstand*), but dwells in the region of the imaginative and synthetic reason (*Vernunft*). The psychological elements of the opposition thus worked up into a fine metaphysical distinction, are already manifest in the quarrel between Rousseau the enthusiast, and Voltaire the mocking analyst. We are simply witnessing the international triumph of Rousseau over Voltaire. The closing pages of the *Germany* in which she exalts enthusiasm as the distinctive German virtue and at the same time warns the French against the spirit of cold reasoning and calculation are, as she herself says, the summing up of her whole work. They are also, we are told, the pages that give the best idea of her actual conversation.

Madame de Staël is really arguing against a social order the ultimate refinements of which were necessary, as we have seen, for her own happiness. In her whole attack on French society, its artificiality and conventionalism and its abuse of ridicule, in her charge that the spirit of imitation had killed spontaneity and enthusiasm, she simply repeats, often less tellingly, the arguments of Rousseau. "It is unbelievable," says Rousseau of the French, "to what a degree everything is stiff, precise and calculated in what they call the rules of etiquette. . . . Even if this people of imitators were full of originals it would be impossible to discover the fact, for no man dares to be himself. *You must do as other people do;* that is the first maxim in the wisdom of the country. . . . You might suppose they were so many marionettes nailed to the same board or pulled by the same wire." "An aristocratic power," Madame de Staël complained in turn, "good form and elegance, had triumphed over energy, depth, feeling, wit itself." It had pronounced "an ostracism against everything strong and individual. These proprieties, slight in appearance and despotic at bottom, dispose of the whole of life; they have by degrees undermined love, enthusiasm, religion, everything save egotism, that irony cannot touch because it exposes itself to censure and not to ridicule." A certain conception of decorum, a "certain factitious grandeur not made for the human heart," as Rousseau had put it, always stood in the way of naturalness. "In the pictures and bas-reliefs in which Louis XIV is painted," says Madame de Staël, "at one time as Jupiter, at another as Hercules, he is represented as naked or clothed simply in a lion skin, but always with his big wig on his head."

This idea of decorum, as Rousseau had already pointed out, had been especially fatal to naturalness in the drama (*la scène moderne ne quitte plus son ennuyeuse dignité* [the modern stage never parts with its tiresome dignity]). "We rarely escape," says Madame de Staël in turn, "from a certain conventional nature which gives the same coloring to ancient as to modern manners, to crime as to virtue, to murder as to gallantry." The pathway of escape from this pale conventionality is a more thorough study of history. "The natural tendency of the age is towards historical tragedy." If she had said towards historical melodrama, she would very nearly have proved herself a prophetess.

The weapon with which society punishes those who depart from its notions of decorum and good taste is ridicule. "In France," says Madame de Staël, "the memory of social proprieties pursues talent even into its most intimate emotions, and the fear of ridicule is the sword of Damocles that no festival of the imagination can make it forget." The whole error arises from confounding taste in the literary with taste in the society sense. Madame de Staël therefore makes her main attack on "good taste," and its tendency to be merely negative and restrictive. Taste in the literary sense should get beyond petty fault-finding, based on rules and formal requirements, and become generous and comprehensive and appreciative. Taste in poetry derives from nature and like it should be creative. The principles of this taste are therefore entirely different from those that depend on social relations. She relates how she attended at Vienna the public course of A. W. Schlegel and was "dumbfounded at hearing a critic eloquent as an orator, who far from attacking faults—the eternal food of jealous mediocrity—merely sought to revive creative genius." "Next to genius what is most like it is the power to know it and admire it."

This is the message that the chief romantic critics of France, England and Germany managed to get uttered in some form or other at the beginning of the nineteenth century. "The rules," says Madame de Staël, "are only barriers to keep children from falling." These barriers are to be set aside and no new restrictive principle is to be imposed on either critic or creator, whose rôles indeed are very much confounded. Genius is to be purely effusive and the critic, instead of serving as a check on genius, is only to enter sympathetically and comprehensively into its effusions.

One might suppose that such an expansive view both of taste and of genius would not stop short of pure impressionism. Since there is no norm that can set bounds to the creative writer in the unfolding of his originality or to the comprehension and sympathy with which the critic enters into this originality, taste would seem bound to become entirely fluid. Germany is as a matter of fact praised as the land where there is no taste in the French sense, and where every man is free to follow his own impressions. Criticism, if it does not judge, may at least reveal the individual, and in this respect Madame de Staël anticipates Sainte-Beuve. "Each character," she says, "is almost a new world for any one who knows how to observe with finesse, and I am not acquainted in the science of the human heart with any general idea completely applicable to particular cases." Sainte-Beuve for his part had such a predilection for Madame de Staël that she has been called the heroine of the *Lundis.*

III

Though Madame de Staël is interested in differences rather than identities, the differences that interest her most after all are not so much those between individuals as those between nationalities. To the claims of the French and the classicist to possess a monopoly of good taste, what she really opposes are the claims of national taste. "It is national taste alone," she says, "that can decide about the drama. We must recognize that if foreigners conceive of the art of the theatre differently from us, it is not through ignorance or barbarism but in accordance with deep reflections that are worthy of consideration." Few persons have been more preoccupied than she with questions of national psychology. In *Corinne,* for example, we have not merely the conflict and interplay of different characters, but of different civilizations; and as usual the French do not show to advantage in contrast with other nationalities. Napoleon himself is said to have written the article in the *Moniteur* in which Madame de Staël is attacked for having made of the amiable but hopelessly superficial Comte d'Erfeuil the typical Frenchman.

Her conception of the relation of nationalities to one another simply reproduces on a larger scale the Rousseauistic
conception of the proper relation of individuals. Each nationality is to be spontaneous and original and self-assertive, and
at the same time infinitely open and hospitable to other national originalities. Nationalism in short is to be tempered by
cosmopolitanism, and both are to be but diverse aspects of
Rousseauistic enthusiasm. The first law for nationalities as for
individuals is not to imitate but to be themselves. Thus Madame
de Staël is indifferent to the work of Wieland because it seems
to her less a native German product than a reflection of French
taste (*l'originalité nationale vaut mieux* [national originality is
better]). Having, however, made sure of its own originality
each nation is then to complete itself by foreign borrowings.
For example, "in order that the superior men of France and
Germany may attain to the highest degree of perfection, the
Frenchman must be religious and the German somewhat
worldly. Piety is opposed to the dissipation of spirit which is
the fault and grace of the French nation; the knowledge of men
and society would give the Germans in literature the taste and
dexterity they lack." "The nations should serve as guides to
one another. . . . There is something very strange in the difference between one people and another: the climate, the
aspect of nature, language, government, finally and above all
the events of history,—a power even more extraordinary than
all others,—contribute to these diversities, and no man, however superior he may be, can guess what is developed naturally
in the mind of the man who lives on another soil and breathes
another air. It is well then in every country to welcome foreign
thoughts, for this kind of hospitality brings fortune to him
who exercises it."

Madame de Staël thus appears as the ideal cosmopolitan,
as the person who has perhaps done more than anyone else to
help forward the comparative study of literature as we now
understand it. But is there not something utopian in the whole
conception, is there any adequate counterpoise to the inordinate emphasis that is placed on the centrifugal elements of
originality and self-expression? When individual or national
differences are pushed beyond a certain point what comes into

play is not sympathy but antipathy. Madame de Staël admits that her cosmopolitanism is only for the few. The ordinary Frenchman and German, for instance, remind her in their relationship to one another of the fable of La Fontaine in which the stork cannot eat off the plate or the fox out of the long-necked bottle. It is not sure that even the few will have sufficient comprehension and sympathy to overleap the invisible barriers that are set up by individual and national idiosyncrasy. We hear of the tact needed by Madame de Staël to keep in check the antipathies that were quivering just beneath the surface in the international élite she had gathered together at Coppet. Between Schlegel and Sismondi, for example, there existed what Sainte-Beuve calls *une haine de race* [a racial hatred].

A still better test of the theory is the meeting of Madame de Staël with Goethe and Schiller at Weimar, perhaps the best instance on record of ideal cosmopolitan contact. Crabb Robinson, who was at Weimar at this time, insinuated to Madame de Staël that she did not understand Goethe's poetry; whereupon her black eyes flashed and she replied, "I understand everything that deserves to be understood." As for Goethe and Schiller, the letters they exchanged with one another during her visit do not make altogether agreeable reading. Schiller denied her any sense for what Germans call poetry, declared it a sin against the Holy Ghost to speak even one word according to her dialect, was overwhelmed by her volubility, and felt when she finally left as though he were just recovering from a severe illness. Goethe complains that she had no idea of duty and wished to settle in a five minutes' conversation the kind of questions that should only be debated in the depths of a man's conscience between himself and God. Both are agreed that she took her departure none too soon. Later, enlightened by the publication of the *Germany,* Goethe dilates on the importance of a meeting that seemed at the time, he admits, a mere surface play of personal and national antipathies: "That work on Germany which owed its origin to such social conversations must be looked on as a mighty implement, whereby in the Chinese wall of antiquated prejudices that separated us from France, a broad gap was broken; so that across the Rhine and in consequence of this across the Channel, our neighbors at last took

closer knowledge of us; and now the whole remote West is open
to our influences."

IV

Possibly the most important chapter in the *Germany* is that in
which Madame de Staël takes up again her distinction between
the literature of the South and that of the North and definitely
describes the two traditions as classic and romantic, thus
giving international currency to the application that the Schle-
gels had made of these epithets to two distinct literary schools.
Classic had always passed as the norm of perfection. But
Madame de Staël refuses to discuss the relative superiority of
classic and romantic taste. "It is enough to show," she says,
turning determinist for the moment, "that this diversity of
tastes derives not only from accidental causes, but also from
the primitive sources of imagination and thought." She here
appears as a disciple of Herder and the other German primitivists who had themselves merely elaborated the primitivism
of Rousseau on a national scale. In true Rousseauistic fashion
we are to advance by looking backward, we are to progress by
reverting to origins; only in this way can we escape from the
artificial and the imitative and recover the spontaneous and
the original. Our choice is not between classic poetry and
romantic poetry, "but between the imitation of the one and the
inspiration of the other." "The literature of the ancients is
among the moderns a transplanted literature, romantic or
chivalrous literature is indigenous among us and has been produced by our religion and our institutions." Writers who imitate the ancients have to conform to strict rules because they
cannot consult their own nature and memories, all the religious
and political circumstances that gave rise to the ancient
masterpieces having changed. "Poems imitative of the antique
are rarely popular because they are not related at present to
anything national." Since popularity is to be the test of poetry,
we are to look in estimating its worth, not merely backward
but downward. "French poetry being the most classic of all
modern poetries is the only one which is not diffused among

the people, whereas the stanzas of Tasso are sung by the gondoliers of Venice, and the Spanish and Portuguese of all classes know by heart the verses of Calderon and Camoens," etc.

The truth in passages of this kind is of course mixed up with the usual sophistries of the primitivist. The chief Rousseauist venom of the whole point of view is found in the elimination of the aristocratic and selective element from the standard of taste, and in the assumption that the proper judges of poetry are the illiterate. Emerson says that we descend to meet. This is no doubt true of certain kinds of meeting, of the kind that takes place at an afternoon tea, let us say; and Emerson probably did not mean much more than this. But the phrase may evidently have another and, from the humanistic point of view, far more sinister meaning. Instead of disciplining himself to some form of perfection set above his ordinary self, a man sinks down from the intellectual to the instinctive level, on the ground that he is thus widening his human sympathies. Thus Tolstoy, whose book on art is indeed the *reductio ad absurdum* of Rousseauism, rejects Sophocles and Shakespeare because of their failure to make an immediate emotional appeal to the Russian peasant.

Moreover Madame de Staël, to judge from her choice of examples, seems to be in some confusion as to the nature of popular poetry. It is not clear that Tasso is more "popular" than Boileau, whom Madame de Staël attacks as the extreme type of classic artificiality. Boileau himself says that many of his lines became proverbs at their birth. They still remain proverbs, whereas the verses of Tasso are no longer sung by the gondoliers of Venice. In general to look for poetry at all among gondoliers and the like is, under existing conditions, at least, to chase an Arcadian dream. For at the very time that one side of our civilization is sentimentalizing about the primitive, another side of this same civilization is just as surely killing it. At the present rate the poetry of the people, poetry that is spontaneous in the Rousseauistic sense, will soon have given way all over the world to the yellow journal or the equivalent.

The special type of mediaevalism worked out by the

German romanticists and diffused by Madame de Staël, that is
the mediaevalism that would have the European nations break
with the classical tradition and return each to its own infancy,
had its own value as a revolt against formalism. But it tended
to get rid of form along with formalism. Recent research has
shown more and more clearly that, wherever in the East or
West, we find what the French call *le grand art*, art that rises
above the merely decorative and renders the more essential
aspects of human nature itself, we are dealing with some survival of the great Greek tradition of form. The man who turns
away from the masterpieces of this tradition to study the *Nib-
elungenlied*, or the *Chanson de Roland*, or the Irish Sagas is
running the risk, even when he is not blinded by national
enthusiasm, of impairing his sense of form.

Moreover mediaevalism is not only likely to involve a loss
of form, but a loss of ideas. No amount of talk about the men of
the Middle Ages being of our own blood and religion will alter
the essential fact that the main movement of the modern mind
has been away from the mediaeval point of view. If we are
seeking, not for some tower of ivory into which we may retire
from the present, but for men who had problems similar to our
own, we shall find these men in certain periods of classical antiquity. The Frenchman of to-day is nearer to Horace in his
outlook on life than to the author of the *Chanson de Roland*.
An instructor in government recently said to me that the most
modern book on his subject was Aristotle's *Politics*. This may
prove that we are becoming pagans again, but we are not going
to alter the fact by romantic dreaming.

To be sure, the mediaeval primitivists, though they have
rarely shone as men of ideas, have been in many cases not
merely romantic dreamers, but also precise investigators, and
in this way they have related themselves to one side of the
modern spirit. I once asked a young American mediaevalist
what his chosen period actually meant for him. A rapt expression came into his eyes and he replied that for him the Middle
Ages were all a beautiful dream. To judge, however, by what
he actually published one would suppose rather that they were
an unusually dry philological fact. And this is unfair to the
Middle Ages. For if the romantic mediaevalist by his delvings

into the popular and the primitive has cut himself off in large measure from modern thought, he has also cut himself off, in at least an equal degree, from the thought of the Middle Ages. The works (mainly in Latin) in which this thought is to be found are not in the least popular or primitive or national, in Madame de Staël's sense, but derive along manifold lines from Greece and Rome and Judaea.

This literature that expressed the mind of the Middle Ages was in the highest degree cosmopolitan, but cosmopolitan in the older and what may turn out to be the only genuine sense,—that is, it rested primarily on a common discipline and not on a common sympathy. Renan, who in his conception of the ideal relations between France and Germany, is perhaps the most distinguished of Madame de Staël's French followers, dreams of an international fraternity of savants, "an empyrean of pure ideas, a heaven in which there is neither Greek nor barbarian, neither German nor Latin." Saint Paul in the passage that Renan is here paraphrasing says that these and like distinctions disappear for those who have become "one in Christ." Now Christ, for Saint Paul, is evidently the living intuition of a law that is set above the ordinary self; by taking on the yoke of this law men are drawn together as to a common centre. Renan's notion that simply by collaborating in the expansion of scientific knowledge men can achieve the union that, according to Saint Paul, is only to be achieved by spiritual concentration, may turn out to be utopian; and it is the fate of the utopist to suffer sudden and severe disillusions. Renan had his disillusion in 1870. He expected the new Christ to come from Germany, as some one has put it, and instead he got Bismarck. He was pained to see how fiercely German national sentiment blazed up in scholars whom he had regarded as being before all scientific internationalists, and how mercilessly they gloated over the downfall of France. On the other hand, many a Frenchman, who had been indulging like Sully Prudhomme in humanitarian effusions, suddenly awoke in 1870 as from a dream and found that his love of mankind was as naught compared with his love of his own land. "Let us suppress these unhealthy outbursts of national self-love," cries Renan. But in the name of what principle? In a crisis, the altruistic impulse either towards other individuals or towards other nations is likely to seem to most men pale and unsubstantial compared with the putting forth of personal or national power.

The modern cosmopolitan is to be blamed not for developing on a magnificent scale the virtues of expansion but for setting up these virtues as a substitute for the virtues of concentration. He would have us believe that every man can fly off on his own tangent, and then in some mysterious manner, known only to romantic psychology, become every other man's brother; and that the same process can be repeated on the national scale. There may after all be something in the traditional idea that in order to come together men need to take on the yoke of a common discipline. But the procedure of the Rousseauist is always to get rid of law or discipline on the ground that it is artificial or conventional, and to set up in its stead some enthusiasm or sympathy. Madame de Staël and the romanticists were strong in their attacks on formalism, but in discarding the idea of law itself along with the conventionalities in which it had got embedded they were almost incredibly weak. They are at least equally weak in the various sentimental sophistries and pseudo-mystical devices to which they resorted to prove to themselves and others that it is possible to have one's cake and eat it too, in other words, to have the virtues of centrality while in the very process of flying off from the centre.

As I have already said, there is something of this romantic sophistry in Madame de Staël's idea that a true cosmopolitanism may rest solely on the rounding out of national originality with international comprehension and sympathy. To stop at this stage is simply to dodge the more difficult half of the problem. It is excellent to be internationally comprehensive and sympathetic, but only as a preparation for being internationally selective. Few moments are more perilous for a country than the moment when it escapes from its narrow traditional discipline and becomes cosmopolitan. Unless some new discipline intervenes to temper the expansion, cosmopolitanism may be only another name for moral disintegration. Nations no less than individuals, as history tells us only too plainly, may descend to meet. Their contact with one another may result not in that ideal exchange of virtues of which Madame de Staël dreamed, but in an exchange of vices. A French traveler relates that on penetrating to a remote hill town in India he found on the mantel-piece of the only room for the use of Europeans in the local club "a collection of French books for exportation, all that frightful literature by which foreigners judge us." On somewhat the same principle the programme of the Moulin Rouge was recently posted about the streets of Paris in five languages. One touch of lubricity, as some one has put it, makes the whole world kin. A man may become cosmopolitan like young Grandet in Balzac, who travelled so much and saw so many standards of morality in different countries that he finally lost all standards himself and became a profligate. Madame de Staël was herself well aware of the danger of an indefinite widening out of one's horizons. "To see everything and understand everything," she says, "is a great cause of uncertainty." *L'étendue même des conceptions nuit à la décision du caractère* [The extensiveness of conceptions is itself harmful to resolution of character].

But what is the value of a breadth that has been gained at the expense of judgment and lacks sufficient counterpoise in character? True cosmopolitanism, it would appear, like almost everything else that is worth having, is a mediation between extremes. We may have universal contact as at present, and an international confederacy of scientists, and plenty of persons who, in Rousseau's phrase, are ready "to embrace the whole of mankind in their benevolence," and yet we may fall short of being true cosmopolitans because there is still lacking the centripetal force, the allegiance to a common standard, that can alone prevail against the powers of individual and national self-assertion. "The pathway of modern culture," says Grillparzer, "leads from humanity, through nationality, to bestiality." Long before this final stage is reached there may be a sharp reaction from the half-truths of the Rousseauist.

V

The unit of Madame de Staël's thinking, it should be observed, is the nation and not the race. The nation as she conceives it,

though she is not specially clear or consistent on this point, is
not so much a mere product of environment as a sort of spiritual entity, a body of men united by common memories and
achievements and aspiring to common ends. The idea of race is
evidently much more naturalistic, and, as treated by many
writers, has become almost zoölogical. No one would of course
deny the importance of the racial factor, but the attempts that
have been made to formulate it accurately have been curiously
unsatisfactory. The endless theorizing that has gone on about
race during the past century may indeed be seen in the retro-
spect to have been the happy hunting-ground of the pseudo-
scientist. And this pseudo-science is often used to produce a
sort of emotional intoxication that may take the form either of
exultation at one's own superiority or else of contempt for the
(supposedly) inferior breeds. It gives a man a fine expansive
feeling to think that he is endowed with certain virtues simply
because he has taken the trouble to be born a Celt or a Teuton
or an Anglo-Saxon. What an exhilaration, for example,
Fichte's audience must have felt when he told them that there
was no special word for "character" in German because to be a
German and to have character were synonymous. The Germans were an *Urvolk*, the elect not of God but of nature; and so
character instead of having to be painfully acquired gushed up
from the primordial depths of their being.

Fichte speaks as a primitivist, and there is a clear connection between primitivism and modern determinism. Though
Madame de Staël was also a primitivist, and although she felt
the force of the deterministic argument as based especially,
perhaps, on the influence of climate and of the historical
"moment," she nevertheless shrank from accepting it. She
admits that "no one can change the primitive data of his birth,
his country, his age," etc. Yet she is loath to admit that "circumstances create us what we are." "If outer objects are the
cause of everything that takes place in our soul, what independent thought would emancipate us from their influence? The
fatality which descended from heaven filled the soul with a
sacred terror, whereas that which binds us to the earth only degrades us." This distinction between the psychological effects
of the two types of fatality, that of Calvin, let us say, and that

of Taine, would seem to be confirmed by the naturalistic novel and other developments in France and elsewhere during the second half of the nineteenth century.

The influence of Madame de Staël at home and abroad would require a separate study. Wherever this influence made itself felt, as in Italy for example, it stimulated national sentiment, on the one hand, and on the other, undermined pseudo-classic formalism, especially in the drama. The French romanticists had rather a slender stock of ideas, but for such ideas as they had they drew largely on Madame de Staël. Hugo does not mention her in the *Préface de Cromwell*, but the relationship between the *Germany* and this manifesto of romanticism can be easily established.

Madame de Staël's influence in both France and Italy is associated with that of another critic who was in some respects her disciple and who acted upon her in turn—Claude Fauriel, the friend and admirer of Manzoni. Perhaps no one did more than Fauriel for the establishment of the new scholarship in France at the beginning of the nineteenth century. Sainte-Beuve calls him the "secret initiator of most of the distinguished spirits of this time in literary method and criticism." (I speak elsewhere of Fauriel's influence on Sainte-Beuve himself.) Fauriel covered a territory that would nowadays be divided among at least a score of specialists—Sanskrit, Provençal, early Italian, Basque, Celtic dialects, etc. He had a truly Rousseauistic passion for the primitive (we are told that among plants he preferred the mosses). The unconscious felicities of instinct appealed to him more than any form of deliberate art. In this sense we may say with Sainte-Beuve that he was the "most anti-academic mind by vocation that had ever appeared in France." He was in fact a sort of French Herder, less enthusiastic and less enamored of general ideas, but with more scholarly precision. Yet though he was, as Sainte-Beuve estimates, twenty years ahead of his times, though he began most of the distinctively modern forms of investigation, he did not at any moment break abruptly with the past. He marks the gradual transition from the point of view of the eighteenth to that of the nineteenth century.

Appearing in the Atlantic Monthly *in 1898, and based on Babbitt's walking tour of Spain as a Harvard undergraduate taking his junior year abroad, this piece shows him at his best as an essayist. Here the critical austerity of his judgment and the polemicism of his style, so characteristic of most of his writings, are subdued. Grace and charm inform what Babbitt, writing as a detached observer, reports about his journey from the Pyrenees to Gibraltar. He not only captures spirit of place but also peers into the Spanish soul. An appreciation of the landscape and the people impells Babbitt's responses. He glimpses the deep shadows and the sunny places of Spain's "smiling landscapes and such dreary desolation." His awareness of tensive paradox and antithesis and of perplexities and emotions is both subtle and tangible. Babbitt shows also a concern with the essentials of Spanish life, with the moral destiny of "the land of the unexpected." Pointing to the traditions of an old absolutism as these merge, disquietingly, with a new frivolity, he perceives the difficulty that Spain will encounter in passing from the medieval to the modern state of mind without falling into anarchy. At this early stage of his career, Babbitt is already speaking as humanist teacher and critic, "in obedience to the unrelenting exactions of conscience," to use a phrase of his friend Paul Elmer More. (From* Spanish Character and Other Essays, *ed. Frederick Manchester, Rachel Giese, and William F. Giese [Boston and New York: Houghton Mifflin Co., 1940], pp. 1-20; originally printed in the* Atlantic Monthly *82 [1898]: 190-97.)*

LIGHTS AND SHADES OF SPANISH CHARACTER

There is something enigmatical and peculiar in the make-up of the Spaniard—*du je ne sais quoi*, as a Frenchman might express it. In trying to fathom Iberian ways of thought and feeling, we are frequently forced to fall back on the supposition of a recent writer, that "there is something Spanish in the Spaniard which causes him to behave in a Spanish manner." I remember that when I visited Spain, a few years ago, I was somewhat disappointed in the appearance of the country itself, though it has all the beauty of line and color of a land for the most part devoid of turf and trees. I found, however, an ample compensation in the interest afforded by this intense idiosyncrasy of the national temperament. Abandoning the beaten paths of travel, I spent several months journeying over the Peninsula on foot, from the Pyrenees to Gibraltar. In this way, I was enabled to get beyond the French civilization of Madrid, and penetrate to the old Spanish civilization which still lingers in the villages and provincial towns. But even with these opportunities for observation I was often at a loss to formulate my impressions of the Spaniards. This arose partly from the strong Moorish and Oriental element which combines in them so strangely with European traits, partly from Spain itself being pre-eminently the land of puzzling anomalies. Both in the country and in the national character a shining virtue usually goes hand in hand with an egregious fault. In no like area in Europe, perhaps not in the world, do there exist such extremes of dryness and moisture, heat and cold, fertility and barrenness, such smiling landscapes and such dreary desolation. And contrasts such as we find between the arid steppes of Aragon and the *huerta* of Valencia, between the bleak uplands of Castile and the palm groves of Elche, between the wind-blown wastes of La Mancha and the *vega* of Granada, are not without counterpart in the character of the inhabitants. What, for instance, can be affirmed of a Catalan which will also hold true of a native of Seville? I remember that a theater audience at Madrid thought it the height of comic incongruity when a stage valet declared that he was a mixture of Galician and Andalusian. ("*Yo soy una mezcla de Gallego y Andaluz.*") It is hard, indeed, to avoid a seeming abuse of paradox and antithesis in speaking of Spain—"that singular country, which," in the words of Ford, "hovers between Europe and Africa, between civilization and barbarism; that land of the green valley and barren mountain, of the boundless plain and broken sierra; those Elysian gardens of the vine, the olive, the orange, and the aloe; those trackless, vast, silent, uncultivated wastes, the heritage of the wild bee; . . . that original unchanged country, where indulgence and luxury contend with privation and poverty, where a want of all that is generous or merciful is blended with the most devoted heroic virtues, where ignorance and erudition stand in violent and striking contrast."

We almost refuse to credit Madame d'Aulnoy's account of the mingled squalor and magnificence, barbarism and refinement, that existed at Madrid toward the end of the seventeenth century, when Spain, isolated from the rest of Europe, was still free to express her antithetical nature. Throughout nearly everything Spanish there runs this chiaroscuro, this intense play of light and shade. In the history of what other nation do we find such alternations of energy and inertia, such sudden vicissitudes of greatness and decay? On the one hand, Spanish religion in the sixteenth century culminated in the Inquisition; and on the other, it attained to the purest spirituality and Christian charity in Santa Teresa, Fray Luis de Leon, and San Juan de la Cruz, the last of the great mystics, the splendid sunset glow of medieval Catholicism. The brilliant literature of the Golden Age died away abruptly into platitude and insignificance. Among the masterpieces of this literature itself we pass with little interval from heights of mysticism and strains of lyric eloquence to the works of the picaresque writers, recounting the exploits of rogues and vagabonds. Spanish society, which until recently had no middle class, suggested to Cervantes the perfect antithesis of Don Quixote and Sancho Panza; and in Sancho Panza himself, the Spanish peasant of Cervantes' time and of today, there is the contrast between his shrewd mother wit and his ignorance and credulity. Spain has left almost entirely uncultivated that intermediary region of lucidity, good sense, and critical discrimination which France has made her special domain.

Perhaps the first requisite to getting a clear notion of the Spaniard is to realize in what respects he is *not* like the Frenchman. We should not allow ourselves to be misled by any supposed solidarity of the Latin races. In certain essential traits the Spanish differ from the French almost as much as the Hindus from the Chinese, and in somewhat the same manner. The chief thing that strikes one in French literature is the absence of what the Germans call *Innigkeit,* of inwardness, it is the subordination of everything in man to his social qualities; among the Spaniards, on the other hand, there is vastly greater capacity for solitude and isolation. In France, reason, insufficiently quickened by the imagination, easily degenerates into dry rationalism; whereas in the land of Don Quixote the imagination tends to break away from the control of the senses and understanding, and is unwilling to accept the limitations of the real, and then follows the inevitable disenchantment when the world turns out to be different in fact from what it had been painted in fancy. *Engaño* and *desengaño,* illusion and disillusion, eternal themes of Spanish poetry!

Intimately related to this intemperate imagination of the Spaniard is his pride, his power of self-idealization, his exalted notion of his personal dignity. He is capable of almost any sacrifice when appealed to in the name of his honor—the peculiar form his self-respect assumes—and of almost any violence and cruelty when he believes his honor to be offended. The Spanish classic theater revolves almost entirely around this sentiment of honor, which is medieval and Gothic, and the sentiment of jealousy, which is Oriental. It was by working upon his pride and sense of honor far more than upon his religious instinct that Rome induced the Spaniard to become her champion in her warfare against the modern spirit. He looked upon himself as the *caballero andante* [knight-errant] who sallied forth to do heroic battle for Mother Church.

This self-absorption of the Spaniard has interfered with his acceptance of the new humanitarian ideal. Don Juan, in Molière's play, tells his valet to give alms to the beggar, not for the love of God, but for the love of humanity. In fact, since the time of Molière man has been substituting for the worship of God and for the old notion of individual salvation this cult of Humanity, this apotheosis of himself in his collective capacity. He has idealized his own future, and thus evolved the idea of progress. He has dwelt with minute interest on his own past, and has thus given rise to the historical spirit. He has ministered with ever increasing solicitude to his own convenience and comfort, and has sought to find in this world some equivalent for his vanished dream of paradise. The individual has so subordinated himself to this vast common work that he has almost lost the sense of his independent value. "The individual," said M. Berthelot only the other day, "will count for less and less in the society of the future."

The Spaniard, however, refuses thus to identify the interests of his individual self with the interests of humanity. He is filled with that subtle egotism, engendered by medieval religion, which neglected man's relation to nature and his fellows, and fixed his attention solely on the problem of his *personal* salvation. In the olden time, it was not uncommon for a pious Spaniard, on dying, to defraud his earthly creditors in order that he might pay Masses for the welfare of his soul; and it was said of such a man that he had "made his soul his heir." The Spaniard remains thus self-centered. He has little capacity for trusting his fellow men, for co-operating with them and working disinterestedly to a common end; he is impatient of organization and discipline. And so, as someone has remarked, he is warlike without being military. We may add that he is overflowing with national pride without being really patriotic. He still has in his blood something of the wild desert instinct of the Arab, and the love of personal independence of the Goth. "You would rather suspect," says an old English author, speaking of the Spaniards, "that they did but live together for fear of wolves." As a public servant the Spaniard is likely to take for his motto, *"Après moi le déluge,"* or, as the proverb puts it, *"El último mono se ahoga"* (The last monkey gets drowned).

In the Spaniard's indifference to bodily comfort and material refinements we find traces of the Oriental and medieval contempt for the body.

> *Le corps, cette guenille, est-il d'une importance,*
> *D'un prix à mériter seulement qu'on y pense?*
>
> [The body, that trifle, is it of any consequence,
> Of a value that is even worth thinking about?]

However, those happy days of Spanish abstemiousness which Juan Valera describes have passed, never to return; that golden era before the advent of French cookery, when all classes, from grandee to muleteer, partook with equal relish of the national mixture of garlic and red peppers; when window-glass was still a rarity in the Peninsula; when, if a tenth part of the inhabitants of Madrid had taken it into their heads to bathe, there would have been no water left to drink, or to cook those *garbanzos* (chick-peas) so essential in the Spanish dietary. But in spite of the spread of modern luxury, which Señor Valera looks upon with ascetic distrust, the Spaniards still remain in the mass the most temperate people in Europe.

The cruelty of the Spaniard—or rather, his callousness, his recklessness of his own life and of the lives of others—is another medieval and Oriental survival; and then, too, there underlies the Spanish temperament I know not what vein of primitive Iberian savagery. Madame d'Aulnoy relates that on a certain day of the year it was customary for court gallants to run along one of the main streets of Madrid, lashing furiously their bare shoulders; and when one of these penitents passed the lady of his choice among the spectators, he bespattered her with his blood, as a special mark of his favor. Insensibility to the suffering of animals, though general in Spain, is not any greater, so far as my own observation goes, than in the other Latin countries. Possibly, medieval religion, in so exalting man above other creatures, in refusing to recognize his relations to the rest of nature, tended to increase this lack of sympathy with brute creation. The Spanish peasant belabors his ass for the same reason that Malebranche kicked his dog—because he has not learned to see in it a being organized to feel pain in the same way as himself.

Closely akin, also, to the Spaniard's medieval and aristocratic attitude toward life is his curious lack of practical sense and mechanical skill. "The good qualities of the Spaniards," writes Mr. Butler Clarke, "alike with their defects, have an old-world flavor that renders their possessors unfit to excel in an inartistic, commercial, democratic, and skeptical age." Juan Valera admits this practical awkwardness and inefficiency of the Spaniard, but exclaims, "Sublime incapacity!" and discovers in it a mark of his "mystic, ecstatic, and transcendental nature." The Spaniard, then, finds it hard to light a kerosene lamp without breaking the chimney, much as Emerson made his friends uneasy when he began to handle a gun. Unfortunately, Nature knows how to revenge herself cruelly on those who affect to treat her with seraphic disdain, and on those who, like the Spaniards, see in a lack of prudence and economy a proof of aristocratic detachment. "*Qui veut faire l'ange fait*

la bête [He who wishes to become an angel becomes a beast]."
After centuries of mortal tension, man has finally given over
trying to look upon himself as a pure spirit. (Indeed, in the case
of M. Zola and his school, he has tried to look upon himself as a
pure animal.) He has been gradually learning to honor his
senses and to live on friendly terms with Nature. The Spaniard, however, has refused to adjust himself to the laws of time
and space. He is unwilling to recognize that the most sublime
enterprises usually go amiss from the neglect of the homeliest
details. He has failed to develop those faculties of observation
and analysis by which man, since the Renaissance, has been
laying hold upon the world of matter with an ever firmer grasp.
The splendid sonorities of the Spanish language serve in its
poetry as a substitute for the exact rendering of nature, and
take the place of a precise mastery of facts in the speech of the
orator in Cortes. The Spaniard is reluctant to mar the poetry of
existence by an excessive accuracy. Steamboats are advertised
in Spanish newspapers to start at such and such an hour *more
or less* (*mas ó menos*). Procrastination is the national vice. As
I walked along the alameda at Saragossa, shortly after
arriving in Spain, the words I caught constantly rising above
the hum of voices were, "*mañana, mañana por la mañana,
mañana*" (tomorrow, tomorrow morning, tomorrow). "In
Spain," says Ford, "everything is put off until tomorrow—
except bankruptcy." "A thing in Spain is begun late, and
never finished," runs a native proverb (*En España se empieza
tarde, y se acaba nunca*); and again, "Spanish succor arrives
late or never" (*Socorro de España ó tarde ó nunca*).

Along with this Oriental disregard for the value of time
there is a dash of Oriental fatalism. I remember once talking
the matter over with an old peasant, as we walked together
over the pass of Despeñaperros into Andalusia. "In this accursed world," he ended by saying, "a man who is born a
cuarto" (a copper coin) "is not going to turn out a *peseta*" (a
coin of silver). A curious comparison might be made between
this true Eastern fatalism of the Spaniard, the fatalism of pre-
destination, and that fatalism of evolution which seems to be
gaining ground with us.

Another Oriental and medieval trait in the Spaniard is his

lack of curiosity. *"Quien sabe?"* (Who knows?) is the formula of his intellectual indifference, just as *"No se puede"* (It is impossible) is the formula of his fatalism. The modern world is coming more and more to seek its salvation in the development of the reason and intelligence; and from this point of view Renan is consistent in exalting "curiosity" above all other virtues. Christianity, on the other hand, may justly be suspected of having insufficiently recognized from the start the rôle of the intellect, and at times has inclined to show a special tenderness toward ignorance. Pascal was but true to the tradition of the Christian mystics when he branded the whole process of modern scientific inquiry as a form of concupiscence—*libido sciendi,* the lust of knowing. When he felt the rise within him of the new power of reason which threatened the integrity of his medieval faith, he exclaimed in self-admonishment, "You must use holy water and hear Masses, and that will lead you to believe naturally and will *make you stupid."* Spain, for several centuries back, has applied with great success this panacea of Pascal for any undue activity of the reason. The abject ignorance into which she has fallen is the result, then, partly of Christian obscurantism, and in part of Oriental incuriousness.

Which is worse, after all, some of us may be prompted to ask in passing, this incuriousness of the Spaniard, or that eager inquisitiveness of his antipode the American, which leads him to saturate his soul in all the infinite futility of his daily newspaper? Spain may at least owe to her ignorance some of that wisdom of little children so highly prized by Christianity. "There is more simplicity, kindliness, and naïveté in Spain than in the rest of Europe," writes Wilhelm von Humboldt to Goethe. Other Western countries are showing signs at present of intellectual overtraining. The impression we get from a typical Parisian Frenchman of today is that the whole energy of the man's personality has gone to feed the critical intellect, at the expense both of what is below and of what is above the intellect—of the body and the soul. The critical intellect of the Spaniard has been so stunted and atrophied by centuries of disuse that he has lost the very sense of his deficiency. Education is as truly the last object of his concern as it is the first of the American's.

Juan Valera, who has analyzed with great acuteness the causes of Spanish decadence, says that Spain's head was turned in the sixteenth century by her sudden accession to world-wide dominion, coinciding as it did with her triumph, after seven centuries of conflict, over the Moors. She became filled with a fanatical faith in herself, with a "delirium of pride," and since then has hugged with desperate tenacity, as embodying absolute and immutable truth, those medieval forms to which she ascribed her greatness. In the meanwhile, the rest of the world has been quietly changing from a medieval to a Greek view of culture. It has been discovering that growth is not in one, but in a multitude of directions, and that the nation no less than the individual is greatest which can take up and harmonize in itself the largest number of opposing qualities. France, indeed, has been almost fatally crippled by her attempt to carry into modern times the principle of medieval exclusiveness. Sainte-Beuve traces to the persecution of the Jansenists and the expulsion of the Huguenots a loss of balance in the French national character. It was perhaps no idle fancy that led the Parisian Nefftzer to exclaim, as he heard the boom of the German guns about the city in the siege of 1870, "We are paying for Saint Bartholomew's Day!" The history of Spain bears still more tragic witness to the truth of Emerson's saying that exclusiveness excludes itself. Nearly all her skill in finance, manufacture, and agriculture departed from her with the banishment of the Jews and Moriscos; and the Inquisition shut that intellectual element from her life which was needed as a corrective of her over-ardent imagination and narrow intensity.

However, modern ideas have fairly got a footing in Spain during the past forty years, and new and old have been arrayed against each other with a truly Iberian vividness of contrast. This battle between medieval and modern is the favorite topic of recent Spanish literature. It has been treated, often with great power, by novelists like Galdós, Alarcón, and Valera, and has inspired the work of poets like Nuñez de Arce and Campoamor. It is curious, this spectacle of a nation hesitating between contradictory ideals. Spain looks doubtfully on our scientific and industrial civilization, and in the very act of

accepting it feels that she is perhaps entering the path of per-
dition. She does not share our exuberant optimism, and has
misgivings about our idea of progress. She cannot, like other
Western nations, throw herself with fierce energy upon the
task of winning dominion over matter, and forget,

> In action's dizzying eddy whirl'd,
> The something that infects the world.

She is haunted at times by the Eastern sense of the unreality
of life. It is no mere chance that the title of the most famous
play of Spain's greatest dramatist is *La Vida es Sueño* (Life is
a Dream). This note, which is heard only occasionally in English, and notably in Shakespeare, recurs constantly in Spanish
from the Couplets of Manrique to Espronceda. Wisdom, often
for the Spaniard as always for the Oriental, reveals herself by
some strange process of solitary illumination, comparable to
the awakening from a dream. "The mysterious virgin," she
calls herself in Espronceda's poem, "on whom man bestows his
last affections, and in whom all science becomes mute."

> *Soy la vírgen misteriosa*
> *De los últimos amores*, etc.

Whereas Bacon, speaking for the West, says that the way of
knowledge is one that no man can travel alone.

We might augur more hopefully of Spain's attempt to
enter upon the path of modern progress if she had been more
happily inspired in the choice of a model. Wilhelm von Humboldt, one of the few philosophical observers of Spain, remarks
that her greatest misfortune is her geographical position. All
her ideas come to her through France, and France is above all
dangerous to her. In that ideal cosmopolitanism of which
Goethe dreamed, each country was to broaden itself by a wise
assimilation of the excellencies of other nationalities. The
actual cosmopolitanism which has arisen during the present
century has perhaps resulted in an interchange of vices rather
than of virtues. I have sometimes been tempted to see a symbol of this cosmopolitanism in a certain square at Florence
whose fine old native architecture has given way to a cheap
imitation of the Parisian boulevard; and over the front of one

of these modern structures appear in flaming letters the words "Gambrinus Halle"!

In theory, Spain should have sent hundreds of her young men to German universities and to English and American technical schools, in order that they might thus acquire the scientific method of the Teuton and the practical and executive instinct of the Anglo-Saxon. She should have fostered among her sons an interest in commerce, in manufacture, and above all in agriculture; they should have been encouraged to go forth and reclaim the waste tracts of their native land, plant forests, and heal that long-standing feud between man and Nature which in Spain is written on the very face of the landscape.

Instead of this, she has turned for her exemplar to France, to the ideal, infinitely seductive and infinitely false, embodied in Paris. She has been guided in this choice by her incurably aristocratic instinct. It is estimated that in the days of Spanish greatness only three million out of a population of nine million consented to work; and Spain still remains a nation of aristocrats. Every true Castilian still aspires to be a *caballero,* or horseman; the Spaniard is unwilling to come down from his horse and put his shoulder to the work of modern civilization. I find in an old English author the following judgment on Spain, which has lost little of its truth: "The ground is uncultivated partly through the paucity and partly through the pride of the people, who breed themselves up to bigger thoughts than they are born to, and scorn to be that which we call plowmen and peasants. . . . And if you take men of that nation, before they have spoiled themselves, either by getting some great office at home or else by much walking abroad, to seek some employment or fortune there, you shall find them for the most part to be of noble and courteous and quiet minds, in the very natural constitution thereof. Whereas, if you show them a new and sweeter way of life, either at home or abroad, it intoxicates them so with the vanities and vices of the world that they are many of them quickly wont to suck the venom in, and become the very worst of men. So that naturally I hold them good; and that by accident and infection they grow easily to be stark naught."

The Spaniards, then, have sucked in the venom of the Parisian boulevard, and have raised up in their capital a showy façade of borrowed elegance to which nothing in the country corresponds. I know of no more startling contrast, even in Spain, than to pass suddenly from some gray, poverty-stricken village of Old Castile into the factitious glare and glitter of the Fuente Castellana at Madrid. The highest ambition of thousands of young Spanish provincials is to swagger about in close-fitting frock coats, and seek for political preferment, any meaner occupation being unworthy of such noble hidalgos. Government places are few compared with the number of applicants; they are ill paid and of uncertain tenure, and the officeholder has little choice except to steal or starve. The vicious traditions of the old absolutism have thus united with the new frivolity to produce in the modern Spanish official that harmonious blending of corruption and incompetency with which we are familiar.

However, we must remember how little these *afrancesados,* these café-haunting Frenchified Spaniards of Madrid, really represent the nation. In Spain, even more than in France and Italy, the germs of promise for the future are to be sought anywhere rather than in the upper classes. Even among the upper classes, if we are to judge from recent literature, there are those who do not accept the French ideal of *l'homme moyen sensuel,* who would have the Spanish character come under certain modern influences, without therefore sacrificing its own native gravity and religious seriousness. It is encouraging to note in many of the Spanish books published of late years something of that robustness and virility wherein lies the natural superiority of the Spaniard over the other Latins. Spain has as yet no decadent writers, no Zola and no Gabriele d'Annunzio.

To speak, then, of the lower classes, there is a singular agreement among those who have really mingled with them as to their natural possibilities for good. "I have found in Spain," says Borrow, "amongst much that is lamentable and reprehensible, much that is noble and to be admired, much stern, heroic virtue, much savage and horrible crime; of low, vulgar vice very little, at least amongst the great body of the Spanish nation. . . . There is still valor in Asturia, generosity in Aragon, probity in Old Castile." But how far will these old-world virtues of the Spanish peasantry be able to withstand the contact with nineteenth-century civilization? Will not the profound poetry of their simple instinctive life fade away at its touch, and the racy originality of their native ways be smothered under its smug uniformity? Will they be able, in short, to make the difficult passage from the medieval to the modern habit of mind without falling into anarchy and confusion? More than any other land, Spain came under the control of that Jesuitical Catholicism issued from the Council of Trent which has poisoned the very life-blood of the Latin races; which, rather than lose its hold upon the minds of men, has consented through its casuists to sanction self-indulgence; which has retarded by every means in its power the development of those virtues of self-reliance and self-control that more than any others measure a man's advancement in the modern spirit; and now that the Spaniards are escaping from the artificial restraint of their religion they are left, passionate and impulsive children, to meet the responsibilities of nineteenth-century life. From my observation of the common people, I should say that already the power of the priesthood is broken, that respect for the institution of monarchy is undermined, and that there is a rapid drift toward republicanism joined to a profound distrust of the present rulers. The *desengaño,* or rude disillusion, they are likely to experience before the end of the present struggle may result in some fierce outburst, boding disaster to the political jobbers at Madrid. Yet no prudent man would risk a prophecy about Peninsular politics; for Spain is *le pays de l'imprévu,* the land of the unexpected, where the logical and obvious thing is least likely to happen; and that is perhaps one of the reasons why she still retains her hold on the man of imagination.

Whatever comes to pass, we may be sure that Spain will not modify immediately the mental habits of centuries of spiritual and political absolutism. In attempting to escape from the past, she will no doubt shift from the fanatical belief in a religious creed to the fanatical belief in revolutionary formulae, and perhaps pass through all the other lamentable phases of Latin-country radicalism. Yet if space allowed I could give reasons for the belief that there are more elements of real republicanism in Spain than in France or Italy. This remark, as well as nearly everything else I have said, I mean to apply especially to the Castiles, Aragon, and the northwestern provinces, the real backbone of the Peninsula.

In any case, those who have a first-hand knowledge of Spain will be loath to place her on that list of "dying nations" to which Lord Salisbury recently referred. She is still rich in virtues which the world at present can ill afford to lose. It remains to be seen whether she can rid herself of the impediments which are rendering these virtues ineffectual. Will she be able to expel the Jesuit poison from her blood? Will she learn to found her self-respect on conscience, instead of on the medieval sentiment of honor, and come to rely on action, the religion of the modern man, rather than on María Santísima? Chief question of all, will she succeed in taming her Gotho-Bedouin instincts, and become capable of the degree of orderly co-operation necessary for good government? Alas! the Spaniards themselves relate that the Virgin once granted various boons to Spain, at the prayer of Santiago, but refused the boon of good government, lest then the angels forsake heaven, and prefer Spain to paradise.

Babbitt studied Sanskrit and Pāli at Harvard and at the Sorbonne. We have much to learn, he believes, from the Eastern teachers and expositors of Karma. He also believes that Christianity and Aristotelianism, on the one side, and Buddhism and Confucianism, on the other, are mutually illuminating. Babbitt's lifelong interest in oriental philosophy and religion and in the relations between East and West is underlined in a number of essays and crystallized in "Buddha and the Occident," which serves as the introduction to his translation of the ancient Pāli classic of Buddhist wisdom, The Dhammapada. *In Buddha he finds a religious teacher who combined humility with self-reliance and a cultivation of the positive critical spirit, even as in early Buddhism Babbitt finds answers that support the humanism that he lived and taught. Buddha embodied the humanistic and religious qualities, or "path," that lead to "an increase in peace, poise, centrality": a discriminating temper, a rigorous tracing of cause and effect, a right use of meditation, and, above all, an emphasis on spiritual vigilance and strenuousness, or as Buddha himself declares, "Those who are in earnestness do not die, those who are thoughtless are as if dead already." Babbitt, it is sometimes claimed, was much closer to Buddhism than his writing indicates. In Buddhism he certainly found a confirmation of the transcendent view of life. "Buddha and the Occident" is undoubtedly his spiritual testament, his final witness. (From* The Dhammapada, *trans. from the Pāli by Irving Babbitt [New York: Oxford University Press, 1936], pp. 65–121; first written in 1927; selections appear as "Romanticism and the Orient" in the* Bookman *74 [1931]: 349–57, and in* On Being Creative and Other Essays *[Boston and New York: Houghton Mifflin Co., 1932], pp. 235–61.)*

BUDDHA AND THE OCCIDENT

The special danger of the present time would seem to be an increasing material contact between national and racial groups that remain spiritually alien. The chief obstacle to a better understanding between East and West in particular is a certain type of Occidental who is wont to assume almost unconciously that the East has everything to learn from the West and little or nothing to give in return. One may distinguish three main forms of this assumption of superiority on the part of the Occidental: first, the assumption of racial superiority, an almost mystical faith in the preëminent virtues of the white peoples (especially Nordic blonds) as compared with the brown or yellow races; secondly, the assumption of superiority based on the achievements of physical science and the type of "progress" it has promoted, a tendency to regard as a general inferiority the inferiority of the Oriental in material efficiency; thirdly, the assumption of religious superiority, less marked now than formerly, the tendency to dismiss non-Christian Asiatics *en masse* as "heathen," or else to recognize value in their religious beliefs, notably in Buddhism, only in so far as they conform to the pattern set by Christianity. Asiatics for their part are ready enough to turn to account the discoveries of Western science, but they are even less disposed than they were before the Great War to admit the moral superiority of the West. A certain revulsion of feeling seems to be taking place even in Japan which has gone farther than any other Oriental land in its borrowings from the Occident.

On any comprehensive survey, indeed, Asiatics, so far from having a mean estimate of themselves, have had their own conceit of superiority, not only with reference to Occidentals but with reference to one another. Many Hindus have held in the past, some no doubt still hold, that true spirituality has never appeared in the world save on the sacred soil of India. No country, again, not even ancient Greece, has been more firmly convinced than China that it alone was civilized. A statesman of the Tang period addressed to the throne a memorial against Buddhism which begins as follows: "This Buddha was a barbarian." One of the traditional names of China "All-under-Heaven" (*Poo-Tien-shia*) is itself sufficiently eloquent.

In general Asia offers cultural groups so widely divergent that one may ask if there is not something artificial in any attempt to contrast an Asiatic with a European or Western point of view. A symposium on this topic was recently held in Paris to which about one hundred and fifty French and foreign writers and scholars contributed. According to one of these contributors, M. Sylvain Lévi of the *Collège de France*, it is absurd to bring together under one label "a Syrian of Beyrut, an Iranian of Persia, a Brahman of Benares, a pariah of the Deccan, a merchant of Canton, a mandarin of Peking, a lama of Thibet, a yacut of Siberia, a daimio of Japan, a cannibal of Sumatra, etc." When stated in such general terms the question of East versus West has, as a matter of fact, little or no meaning. It may, however, turn out to have a very weighty meaning if properly defined and limited. Other contributors to the Paris symposium, though they express a singular variety of opinions about Asia, occasionally show some inkling of what this meaning is. They are helped to their sense of the contrast between Europe and Asia by another continental contrast—that between Europe and America; and here they are in substantial agreement. America stands for the purely industrial and utilitarian view of life, the cult of power and machinery and material comfort. It is in order to escape from this baleful excess of Americanism that Europe is inclined to turn towards the East. "Europe," we read in the symposium, "is, as a result of her almost mortal sufferings of recent years, ready to bow her head and humble herself. It will then be possible for Oriental influences to make themselves felt. An immense continent will remain the refuge and the fortress of the Occidental spirit: the whole of America will harden herself and proudly close her mind, whereas Europe will heed the lesson of the Orient." One may perhaps sum up the sense of passages of this kind by saying that in its pursuit of the truths of the natural order Europe had come to neglect the truths of humility—the truths of the inner life. In the literal sense of the word, it has lost its orientation, for it originally received these truths from the Orient. One remembers Arnold's account of this former contact between East and West: first, the impact of a Europe drunk with power upon Asia.

> The East bowed low before the blast
> In patient deep disdain;
> She let the legions thunder past,
> And plunged in thought again.

And finally the heeding of the voice of the East, in other words the acceptance of the truths of the inner life in their Christian

form, by a Europe that had grown weary of her own materialism:

> She heard it, the victorious West,
> In sword and crown arrayed,
> She felt the void that mined her breast,
> She shivered and obeyed.

The problems that arise today in connexion with the relations of East and West are far more complex than they were in
Graeco-Roman times. The East now means not merely the
Near East, but even more the Far East. Moreover, the East,
both Near and Far, is showing itself less inclined than formerly
to bow before the imperialistic aggression of the Occident "in
patient deep disdain." On the contrary, a type of nationalistic
self-assertion is beginning to appear in various Oriental lands
that is only too familiar to us in the West. Japan in particular
has been disposing of her Buddhas as curios and turning her
attention to battleships. The lust of domination which is
almost the ultimate fact of human nature, has been so armed in
the Occident with the machinery of scientific efficiency that
the Orient seems to have no alternative save to become efficient in the same way or be reduced to economic and political
vassalage. This alternative has been pressing with special
acuteness on China, the pivotal country of the Far East. Under
the impact of the West an ethos that has endured for thousands of years has been crumbling amid a growing spiritual be-
wilderment. In short the Orient itself is losing its orientation.
The essence of this orientation may be taken to be the affirmation in some form or other of the truths of the inner life. Unfortunately, affirmations of this kind have come to seem in the
Occident a mere matter of dogma and tradition in contrast
with a point of view that is positive and experimental. It is
here that the study of great eastern teachers, notably Confucius and Buddha, may prove helpful. The comparative absence of dogma in the humanism of Confucius and the religion
of Buddha can scarcely be regarded as an inferiority. On the
contrary one can at least see the point of view of a young
Chinese scholar, Mr. H. H. Chang, who complains that the
man of the Occident has introduced unnecessary theological
and metaphysical complications into religion: he has been too

prone to indulge in "weird dogmas" and "uncanny curiosity."
He has been guilty to a degree unknown in the Far East of
intolerance, obscurantism, and casuistry. Pascal, one of the
most profound of religious thinkers, attacked casuistry in its
Jesuitical form but himself supplies an example in what Mr.
Chang means by weird dogmas. Man, says Pascal in substance, is unintelligible to himself without the belief in infant
damnation.

The Far Eastern doctrine that is probably freest from the
undesirable elements that Mr. Chang enumerates is the
authentic teaching of Buddha. Scholarly investigation has already proceeded to a point where it is possible to speak with
some confidence not only of this teaching but of Buddha
himself. One may affirm indeed that few doctrines and per-
sonalities of the remote past stand out more clearly. There is
practical agreement among scholars that the material found in
the Pāli Canon, the basis of the form of the religion known as
the Hīnayāna or Small Vehicle, which prevails in Ceylon,
Burma, and other countries, is on the whole more trustworthy
than the records of the Mahāyāna or Great Vehicle, which, variously modified, prevails in Thibet, China, Korea, and Japan.
The psychological evidence on this point, which is overwhelming, is supplemented by historical evidence—for example, the
Asokan inscriptions. By psychological evidence I mean evidence of the same kind as is supplied by numerous passages of
the New Testament, passages that give one the immediate
sense of being in the presence of a great religious teacher.
Anyone who can read the Sermon on the Mount and then proceed to speculate on the "historicity" of Jesus must simply be
dismissed as incompetent in matters religious.

On the basis then of evidence both psychological and historical one must conclude that if the Far East has been comparatively free from casuistry, obscurantism, and intolerance,
the credit is due in no small measure to Buddha. It is so difficult to have a deep conviction and at the same time to be tolerant that many have deemed the feat impossible. Yet not only
Buddha himself but many of his followers achieved it. For
example, the tolerant spirit displayed by the Emperor Asoka
who probably did more than any other person to make Bud-

dhism a world religion, simply reflects the spirit of the
Founder. An apologue of Buddha's which has been widely
popular in both East and West, is relevant to this topic of tolerance. Once upon a time, Buddha relates, a certain king of
Benares, being bored and desiring to divert himself, gathered
together a number of beggars blind from birth, and offered a
prize to the beggar who should give him the best account of an
elephant. The first beggar who examined the elephant chanced
to lay hold upon the leg, and reported that an elephant was like
a tree-trunk; a second, laying hold of the tail, declared that an
elephant was like a rope; a third, who seized an ear, insisted
that an elephant was like a palm leaf; and so on. Whereupon
the beggars proceeded to dispute with one another and finally
fell to fisticuffs and the king was highly diverted. Even so,
says Buddha, ordinary teachers, who have grasped this or that
small member of the truth, quarrel with one another. Only a
Buddha can apprehend the whole. The thought that in matters
spiritual we are at best blind beggars fighting with one another in our native murk is not conducive to a narrow and
fanatical intensity. The rounded vision is so difficult, so alien,
one is tempted to say, to human nature, that one is not surprised to learn that Buddhas are rare, only five at the most in a
kalpa or cosmic cycle, a period, according to Hindu computation, of something over four billion years.

The apologue I have just cited suggests that Buddha was
more prone to humour than most religious teachers. The contrast in this respect between certain portions of the Pāli Canon
(notably the Jātaka tales) and the Christian Bible is striking.
Another trait possessed by Buddha that is in itself humanistic
rather than religious is urbanity. The doctrine of the mean that
Buddha proclaimed even in the religious life is not unrelated to
the absence in Buddhism of the casuistical and obscurantist
element. There is a sense, one should remember, in which
casuistry is legitimate and indeed inevitable. The general principle needs to be adjusted to the infinitely varying circumstances of actual life. There is casuistry in this sense in the
first main division of the Pāli Canon (*Vinaya*)—the division
which deals with the details of discipline in the Order (*Sangha*)
founded by Buddha. The danger here is that a minute outer

regulation should encroach unduly on the moral autonomy of the individual. Buddha, as we shall presently see more fully, was at special pains to assert this autonomy. A second peril of casuistry is that it should not only substitute outer authority for individual conscience, but that it should be made a cover for the kind of relaxation that Pascal attacks in the *Provincial Letters.* Buddha would have the members of his Order avoid this relaxation without falling into the opposite extreme of asceticism and mortification of the flesh. This is in substance his doctrine of the middle path.

The obscurantism that denies unduly the senses has usually been associated in the Occident with the obscurantism that denies unduly the intellect. Buddha's avoidance of this latter form of obscurantism is a matter of even more interest than his avoidance of the ascetic extreme. The conflict between the head and the heart, the tendency to repudiate the intellect either in the name of what is above or what is below it, which has played such an enormous rôle in the Occident from some of the early Christians to Bergson, is alien to genuine Buddhism. The supreme illumination of Buddha was associated with the precise tracing of cause and effect, with the following out of the so-called causal nexus. His discriminating temper appears in the care with which he uses general terms, always a crucial point in any doctrine. He gives one the impression of a person who has worked out his ideas to the ultimate degree of clarity, a clarity that is found not merely in separate propositions but in the way in which they are woven into an orderly whole. During his youth, we are told, he passed through a period of groping and hesitation, but after his illumination he never seems to grope or hesitate. This firm intellectual grasp, joined to a dominant and unwavering purpose, no doubt contributed to the effect of authority that he produced upon his contemporaries and continues to produce upon us. In his personality he strikes the reader of the old records as massive, some might say even a bit ponderous, and at the same time supremely self-reliant and aggressively masculine. One has the sense of getting very close to Buddha himself in the verses of the *Sutta Nipāta* descriptive of the true sage. A few lines of this passage, which I render literally, are as follows:

The wise man who fares strenuously apart,
Who is unshaken in the midst of praise or blame,
Even as a lion that trembles not at noises,
Or as the wind that is not caught in a net,
Or as the lotus that is unstained by the water—
A leader of others and not by others led,
Him verily the discerning proclaim to be a sage.

In human nature, as it is actually constituted, every virtue has its cognate fault. The unflinching analysis practised by the early Buddhists runs very easily, especially when divorced from intuition, in some sense or other of that much abused word, into scholastic dryness. There are portions of the Buddhist writings that remind one in this respect of the less attractive side of the Aristotelian tradition in the West. The Buddhist again inclines at times, like the Aristotelian, to be unduly categorical and so to achieve a sort of false finality. The Buddhist commentators, for example, give what they conceive to be a definitive enumeration of the different noises that characterize a normal town! Furthermore, large portions of the Buddhist books seem to the Western reader to have damnable iteration, to push beyond permissible grounds the sound maxim that repetition is the mother of memory. It is well to remember that most of this repetition is only a mnemonic device that would never have been employed if the canonical material had from the outset been committed to writing. And then, too, in the midst of tracts of wearisome repetition and arid categorizing one encounters not infrequently passages that are vividly metaphorical and concrete and lead one to infer in Buddha a rare gift for aphoristic utterance; though even these passages, if one may be allowed to speak of such matters from a profane literary point of view, can scarcely match in sheer epigrammatic effectiveness certain sayings of Christ.

If the doctrine and personality of Buddha stand out so distinctly from the ancient records, how, it may be asked, has there been so much misapprehension regarding both? Certain reasons for this misapprehension are obvious; it may be well to clear these away before coming to other reasons which lie less near the surface. In the first place, much confusion has been caused in the Occident by the failure to distinguish between Mahāyāna and Hīnayāna. Various eminent thinkers and writers of the nineteenth century got their chief impression of Buddhism from the extravagant theosophy of the *Lotus of the Good Law* as translated by Eugène Burnouf. Even those who, without knowing Pāli, have gone to the more authentic documents have been frequently misled by the translations. The special pitfall here is the general terms. Though these terms, as I have said, are used by Buddha himself with considerable precision, they have no exact Occidental equivalents. Translators seem at times to have given up in despair the task of rendering all the discriminations of a subtle and unfamiliar psychology. Thus it is estimated that Fausböll, to whom we are deeply indebted for the first edition of the *Dhammapada* in the West, has in his version of the *Sutta-Nipāta* translated fifteen different Pāli words by the one English word "desire."

Moreover, to come to less obvious sources of misapprehension, serious study of the Far East got under way during a period that was in its predominant temper either romantic, or again, scientific and rationalistic. Neither the romanticist nor the pure rationalist is qualified to grasp what is specifically Oriental in the Orient. The romanticist seeks in the East what he seeks everywhere, the element of strangeness and wonder. His interest is in differences rather than in identities; as a consequence, this form of Orientalism has amounted chiefly in practice to the pursuit of picturesqueness and local colour. Closely allied to this pursuit is the quest of some place of refuge from an unpalatable here and now. A familiar example is "The Road to Mandalay," which tells of the satisfaction that the British private finds in Buddhist Burma of his craving for a "neater sweeter maiden in a cleaner greener land." I may be accused of taking too seriously Kipling's trifle, but after all this romantic imperialist has enjoyed a certain prestige as an interpreter, not only of the Anglo-Indian East, but of the real East. The central passage of "The Road to Mandalay" may therefore serve as well as any other to illustrate the Oriental aspect of the immense literature of escape that has grown up in connexion with the romantic movement.

Ship me somewheres East of Suez, where the best is like the worst,

Where there ain't no Ten Commandments, an' a man may raise a
    thirst;
For the temple bells are callin' an' it's there that I would be,—
By the old Moulmain Pagoda lookin' lazy at the sea.

If the temple bells are calling the British private to "raise
a thirst," to what, one may inquire, are they calling the native
Burman? Certainly not to be "lazy" and irresponsible. Kipling
himself would no doubt warn us against pursuing any such unprofitable inquiry, in virtue of the principle that "East is East
and West is West, and never the twain shall meet." The fact is
that they are meeting more and more, with the attendant
danger that this meeting will be only on the material level.
Kipling's line is rightfully resented by Orientals: it is true
about in the sense that John is John and James is James and
never the twain shall meet, or, if there is any difference between the two statements, it is one of degree and not of kind.

If we refuse then to admit that the point of view of Buddhist Burma is necessarily unintelligible to us and turn for
information to an authentic document like the *Dhammapada,*
what we find is that a central admonition of Buddha may be
summed up in the phrase: Do not raise a thirst! Nothing
perhaps throws more light on what actually goes on in Burma
today than the type of education given to the children of the
country by the members of the Buddhist Order. This education
consists largely in the memorizing of certain sacred texts. One
of the passages especially favoured for this purpose, we learn
from a recent book on Burma, is Buddha's discussion of the
nature of true blessedness, which runs in part as follows:

> To wait on mother and father, to cherish child and wife and
> follow a quiet calling, this is true blessedness.
> To give alms, to live religiously, to protect relatives, to
> perform blameless deeds, this is true blessedness.
> To cease from sin, to refrain from intoxicating drinks, to per-
> severe in right conduct, this is true blessedness.
> Reverence and humility, contentment and gratitude, the
> hearing of the Law of righteousness at fitting moments, this is
> true blessedness.
> Patience and pleasant speech, intercourse with holy men, re-
> ligious conversation at due seasons, this is true blessedness.

Penance and chastity, discernment of the noble truths and
the realization of peace, this is true blessedness.

The author of the book on Burma proffers the further
information that, as a result of memorizing such verses, the
children acquire "boundless charity and rigid self-control"—a
statement one is inclined to receive with some scepticism. Like
Kipling, though in an entirely different way, he is probably
substituting an idyllic for the real Burma. But if only a frac-
tion of what he says is true, we should seek to divert the attention of our own children from radio sets and motion-pictures
and set them to memorizing Buddhist verses!

Though particular utterances of Buddha, like the discourse on True Blessedness I have just quoted, may offer little
difficulty, it must be admitted that his teaching is not easy for
the Westerner to grasp in its total spirit. Even the person
who affirms an underlying unity in human nature and is more
interested in this unity than in its picturesque modifications in
time and space, should at least be able to see the point of view
of the scholar who affirmed that he had turned to the study of
Buddhism in order that he might enjoy "the strangeness of the
intellectual landscape." A chief reason for this strangeness is
that the doctrine of Buddha cuts across certain oppositions
that have been established in Western thought since the
Greeks, and have come to seem almost inevitable. There has,
for example, from the time of Heraclitus and Parmenides been
an opposition between the partisans of the One and the partisans of the Many, between those who see in life only change
and relativity and those who in some form or other affirm an
abiding unity. The Platonic affirmation in particular of a world
of ideas that transcends the flux so combined with Christianity that it has come to be almost inseparable from our notion of
religion. Religion, as we understand it, seems to require faith
in a spiritual essence or soul that is sharply set apart from the
transitory, and in a God who is conceived as the supreme
"idea" or entity. Buddha denies the soul in the Platonic sense
and does not grant any place in his discipline to the idea of
God. Superficially he seems to be on the side of all the "flow-
ing" philosophers from Heraclitus to Bergson. The schoolmen
of the Middle Ages would have accounted him an uncom-

promising nominalist. We are told that, at the voice of a Buddha proclaiming the law of mutability in both Heaven and earth, the bright gods who had deemed themselves immortal feel a shiver of apprehension like that occasioned by the roar of the lion in the other beasts of the field. Buddha is so disconcerting to us because doctrinally he recalls the most extreme of our Occidental philosophers of the flux, and at the same time, by the type of life at which he aims, reminds us rather of the Platonist and the Christian.

Buddha also differs from the religious teachers with whom we are familiar by his positive temper. The idea of experiment and the idea of the supernatural have come to seem to us mutually exclusive. Yet Buddha may perhaps be best defined as a critical and experimental supernaturalist. If he deserves to be thus defined it is not because of the so-called magic powers (*iddhi*)—the power of supernormal memory, of levitation and the like. If we accepted only a small part of what we read in the ancient records about the thaumaturgical accomplishments not merely of Buddha but of a number of his followers, we should have to conclude that man has certain psychic capacities that have been atrophied through long disuse. In general, however, the ancient Buddhist maintained an extreme reserve in regard to the magic powers. He granted them at most a very subordinate rôle in religion. He is far removed in this respect from a Pascal who avowed, like St. Augustine before him, that he would not have accepted Christianity had it not been for its miracles.

One is justified in asserting on other than thaumaturgical grounds that the genuine teaching of Buddha is steeped in the supernatural. According to the tradition, when Buddha begged his way through the streets of his native town, his father, King Suddhodana, demurred; whereupon Buddha said that he was merely following the practice of all his race. When the King protested that no one of his race had ever been a mendicant, Buddha replied that he referred, not to his earthly lineage, but to the race of the Buddhas. As a matter of fact, what is specifically supernatural, not merely in the Buddhas but in other religious teachers, for example, in St. Francis, is their achievement of certain virtues. Of these the virtue that marks most immediately the obeisance of the spirit to what transcends nature and has therefore always been held, by those who believe in such virtues at all, to command the others, is humility. In the present naturalistic era the very word humility has tended to fall into disuse or, if used at all, to be used incorrectly. One needs to be reminded, for example, that humility and modesty are not at all synonymous. Matthew Arnold says that Emerson was one of the most modest of men, Mr. Brownell that he was one of the least humble. Both statements are conceivably correct. Of Buddha, one is tempted to say that he was humble without being modest. It is not easy to ascribe modesty to a teacher who made claims for himself even more sweeping than those put forth by the Founder of Christianity. Regarding these claims one is reminded of an anecdote that may also serve to illustrate the peculiar vein of humour in the Buddhist writings. A certain Buddhist recluse, we are told, being puzzled by a knotty point of doctrine and finding no mortal who could solve his difficulty, at last by appropriate meditations mounted from heaven to heaven but was still unable to discover anyone who could enlighten him. Finally he came to the paradise of Brahmā, and propounded the question to the divinity himself. Brahmā said, "I am Brahmā, the Supreme Being, the Omniscient, the Unsurpassed," etc. "I did not ask you," replied the recluse, "whether you were Brahmā, the Supreme Being, the Omniscient and Unsurpassed, but whether you could answer my question." Whereupon Brahmā took him to one side and explained that the angels of his retinue thought him omniscient, but that in fact no one could give the desired enlightenment save Buddha.

That Buddha should put himself above all other animate beings, whether men or gods, and at the same time be humble is, from the Christian point of view, highly paradoxical. The essence of humility in Christianity is the submission not merely of man's will but of the will of Christ himself to the will of a divine personality. If one is to understand how Buddha avoids asserting any such personality and at the same time retains humility one needs to reflect on what it means to be a critical and experimental supernaturalist. It means first of all that one must deny oneself the luxury of certain affirmations about ultimate things and start from the immediate data of consciousness. It is hard to see, for example, how one can affirm, on strictly experimental grounds, a personal God and personal immortality. If a man feels that these tremendous affirmations are necessary for his spiritual comfort, he should turn to dogmatic and revealed religion which alone can give them, adding with Dr. Johnson that "the good and evil of Eternity are too ponderous for the wings of wit." The person who assumes a genuinely critical attitude is finally forced to accept in some form or other the maxim that man is the measure of all things. If one is told in the words of Plato that not man but God is the measure of all things, the obvious reply is that man nowhere perhaps gives his own measure so clearly as in his conceptions of God; and that is why, as Goethe would add, God is so often made a jest. What one is able to affirm without going beyond immediate experience and falling into dogma is, in Arnold's phrase, a great power not ourselves that makes for righteousness, a phrase that reminds one of Buddha's conception of the *dhamma*, or human law, as one may render it, in contradiction to the law of physical nature. Not being able to find any personality human or divine superior to his own, Buddha got his humility, as he himself tells us, by looking up to the Law.

Let us consider more carefully what this obeisance to the *dhamma* means when disengaged, as Buddha seeks to disengage it, from dogma and metaphysical assumption and envisaged as one of the immediate data of consciousness. Numerous Western philosophers from Descartes down have professed to start from these data. On comparing the results they have reached with the results reached by Buddha one is conscious of some central clash. At the risk of being unduly schematic, one may say that the tendency of Western philosophers has been to regard as primary in consciousness either thought (*cogito ergo sum*) or feeling (*sentio ergo sum*). Buddha, for his part, is neither a rationalist nor, again, an emotionalist. No small confusion has resulted from trying to fit him into one or the other of these alien categories. He gives the primary place to will, but to a quality of will that has been almost inextricably bound up in the Occident with the doctrine of divine grace and has been obscured in direct proportion to the decline of this doctrine. The question of the priority of will in this sense, as compared either with intellect or emotion, and the question of humility that is bound up with it, is one * * * that involves an opposition not merely between Buddha and this or that Occidental philosopher, but between the Asiatic outlook on life in general and that which has tended to prevail in Europe. The granting of the primacy to intellect or mind, in any sense those terms have had since Anaxagoras, would seem to be incompatible with humility. It is a task of absorbing interest to trace the struggle between Christian voluntarism with its subordination of man in his natural self—including the intellect—to God's will, and a resurgent rationalism. In tracing a subject of this kind one becomes aware of a main problem in the spiritual life of the Occident to which I have already referred; reason has repeatedly aspired to rise out of its due place and then the resulting reactions against its presumption have encouraged various forms of obscurantism.

Among the doctrines in which reason has thus aspired unduly, with a corresponding tendency of pride to prevail over humility, Stoicism stands preëminent: first, because many important modern philosophies—for example, those of Descartes, Spinoza, and Kant—have in their practical bearing on life and conduct much in common with Stoicism; secondly, because misleading comparisons have been made between the Buddhist and the Stoic. The Buddhist reminds one of the Stoic by the severity of the self-control he inculcates, also by his self-reliant spirit. He relies, however, in this discipline, not, like the Stoic, upon a "reason" supposed to coincide with the cosmic order, but upon a will that transcends it. Reliance upon this will gives the psychic equivalent of the Christian submission to the divine will, in other words, of humility. The Stoic is a monist; the Buddhist is like the Christian, an uncompromising dualist. So far from "accepting the universe" in the Stoic sense, he rejects so much of it that the alarmed Occidental is inclined to ask whether anything remains.

Practically the difference between monist and dualist converges upon the problem of evil. The Stoic is a theoretic optimist; Buddha, though very untheoretic here as elsewhere, is extraordinarily insistent upon the fact of evil. "This alone I have taught," he says, "sorrow and the release from sorrow." Buddha's emphasis on sorrow may seem to some incompatible with the urbanity I have attributed to him; for nothing is more contrary to the urbane temper than absorption in a single idea. He really aims at wholeness, a type of wholeness that it is hard for us to grasp because breadth is for us something to be achieved expansively and even by an encyclopaedic aggregation of parts; whereas the wholeness at which Buddha aims is related in fact, as it is etymologically, to holiness and is the result of a concentration of the will. To define the quality of will that Buddha would have us put forth psychologically— that is, by his own method—is to go very far indeed in an understanding of his doctrine.

The modern man is normally, as the Germans phrase it, a "yes-sayer" and a "becomer" and glories in the fact. Buddha on the other hand is probably the chief of all the "no-sayers"; specifically he says no to everything that is implicated in the element of change even to the point of defining the highest good as "escape from the flux." "What is not eternal," he says, "does not deserve to be looked on with satisfaction." In his rejection of the transitory for the eternal he is, as I have just remarked, neither metaphysical nor theological, but psychological. One needs only to take a glance at the four noble truths of Buddha to perceive that his doctrine is in its genuine spirit a psychology of desire. The four noble truths themselves need to be interpreted in the light of the three "characteristics," which, we are told, only a Buddha can properly proclaim: namely, (1) the impermanence of all finite things; in this sense (2) their lack of "soul" or their "unreality"; and therefore (3) their final unsatisfactoriness. As one becomes aware of the fact of impermanence and of its implications, one tends to substitute for the ignoble craving for what is subject to corruption the noble craving for the "incomparable security of a Nirvāna free from corruption."

Buddha's attitude towards the "soul," it should be observed, differs decisively from that of the Vedantists in India and from the somewhat similar doctrine of Plato in the West.

His objection to those who assert a soul and other similar entities is not metaphysical but practical: they are thereby led to think they have transcended the transitory when they have not done so and are thus lulled into a false security. Buddha can scarcely be regarded as an idealist in any sense the term has ever had in the Occident. He is not an idealist in the Platonic sense, in spite of numerous and important points of contact between his teaching and that of Plato, because of the central clash I have just indicated. Still less is he an idealist in the other two main senses of the word: he does not hope, like Rousseau and the sentimentalists, to unify life in terms of feeling; nor again, after the fashion of philosophers like Hegel, to unify it in terms of intellect. The unification that Buddha seeks is to be achieved by the exercise of a certain quality of will that says no to the outgoing desires with a view to the substitution of the more permanent for the less permanent among these desires and finally to the escape from impermanence altogether. His assertion of this quality of will is positive and empirical to the last degree.

I have already tried to make clear that Buddha is not merely a great religious personality but a thinker so trenchant as to invite comparison with the chief figures in Occidental thought. An interesting comparison suggests itself at this point with the thinker who has had a preponderant influence on recent Occidental philosophy—Immanuel Kant. Anyone who glances through the three critiques of Kant will be struck by the phrase *a priori* which recurs innumerable times and gives the key to the whole body of doctrine. To Kant it seemed that a resort to some kind of *apriorism* was necessary if one was to bind together and unify the elements of experience that the empirical method of Hume seemed to dissolve into a flux of unrelated impressions. Buddha would have opposed Hume not on *apriorist* but empirical grounds. He would have asserted a quality of will peculiar to man not as a theory but as a fact, as one of the immediate data of consciousness. Buddha may be defined indeed, in contradistinction to a naturalistic empiricist like Hume, as a religious empiricist. One may perhaps best illustrate what it means to assert positively and critically a religious will in man by a study of Buddha's way of dealing with the three questions that must, according to Kant, confront every philosopher: What can I know? What must I do? What may I hope?

In virtue of its intellectualist temper Western philosophy has always shown a strong predilection for the first of these questions, the so-called problem of knowledge. The drift of the modern philosophy of the West towards epistemological inquiry has been marked since Descartes. From the time of Locke one is tempted to define this philosophy as a long debauch of epistemology. The various subsidiary questions that have been discussed—the question of substance, of innate ideas, of causation, of time and space, both in themselves and in their relation to one another—all finally converge upon the question as to the relation of appearance to reality. This endless epistemological debate would be justified if it could be shown to have prepared the way for a more adequate reply to Kant's second question: What must I do? The Christian supernaturalist would not, however, grant that it has. The false dualism set up by Descartes has been eliminated, he would admit, but he would add that the true dualism has been eliminated along with it—the opposition, namely, between God's will and man's. The Buddhist sets up a similar opposition between a higher and a lower will, not, however, on dogmatic but on psychological grounds. Western thinkers from St. Augustine to William James who have sought to deal with the will psychologically are in agreement with one another and with Buddha in at least one particular: will is revealed above all in the act of attention or concentration. The office of a Buddha is to proclaim the truths to which man must attend if he would escape from sorrow. The "causal nexus" or "chain of dependent origination" that leads to the rise of sorrow is extraordinarily difficult to grasp. To the Occidental indeed it is likely to seem a hopeless puzzle. The essential link in the chain is at all events "ignorance." Strictly speaking, one does not in the Buddhist sense overcome ignorance merely by acquiescing in the four noble truths. Anyone who does not get beyond this stage is compared to a cowherd counting another's kine. A man may possess the noble truths and so escape from sorrow only by acting upon them. Knowledge follows upon will. The term faith has had various meanings in Buddhism as in Christianity. The original meaning is faith to act. In so far, the Buddhist is in agreement with the Christian voluntarist when he proclaims that we do not know in order that we may believe, but we believe in order that we may know.

In its primary emphasis on will, the doctrine of Buddha is not a system in the Occidental sense but a "path." A Buddha is simply one who has trodden this path and can report to others what he has found. In this sense he is the Tathāgata. He who would tread the same path must not be diverted from concentration on the goal by anything to the right or to the left. Everything is to be set aside which does not, in Buddha's own phrase, make for "quiescence, knowledge, supreme wisdom, and Nirvāna." Anyone who entered the Buddhist order in the hope of finding a solution for his merely speculative difficulties was doomed to disappointment. We are told that one of the brethren once came to Buddha with a list of such difficulties—for example, whether the world is finite or infinite, eternal or not eternal, whether soul and body are one or separate, whether the saint exists or does not exist after death, etc.—and complained to him that he had received no enlightenment on these points. Buddha replied to him in substance that human nature is sick of a disease. His own rôle he conceived to be that of the physician. Anyone who refused to act on his teaching until he had an answer to such questions Buddha compared to a man who had been wounded by a poisoned arrow and was unwilling to receive medical aid until he had learned whether the man who had wounded him was of light or dark complexion, belonged to the Brahman or warrior caste, etc. No one was ever more unfriendly than Buddha to persons who had "views." One must indeed agree with a German student of Buddhism that the dislike of mere speculation is the distinguishing mark of the authentic doctrine. One may, however, refuse to agree with him that this practical and unmetaphysical temper is a weakness. Some questions Buddha would dismiss because they are intrinsically unthinkable; others because they are not worthy of thought—do not, in his own phrase, make for edification. Among the questions that he thus dismisses are several that have been persistently debated in Occidental religion and philosophy.

In defining the topics with which the man who has re-nounced the world may properly concern himself Buddha makes a distinction similar to that of Christ between the things of God and the things of Caesar. So far from encour-aging the members of his order to take a part in political life, he would not even have them discuss politics.

Though a Buddha may proclaim to those seeking to enter the path the truths on which they may profitably concentrate and at the same time set them a persuasive example, he is not to be regarded in the full Christian sense as a Saviour. In the last analysis a man must, according to Buddha, save himself. Though both Christian and Buddhist associate salvation with the putting forth of a similar quality of will, no small difference between the two results from the fact that the Christian asso-ciates this quality of will in a greater or lesser degree with divine grace. He would even tend to regard as blasphemous Buddha's dictum: "Self is the lord of self. Who else can be the lord?" To be sure, Christians themselves have varied widely in their views of grace. Some would receive the grace imme-diately, others mediately through the Church. The Jansenist, for example, with his emphasis on the inner light seems spirit-ually autonomous, at least so far as outer authority is con-cerned, compared with the Jesuit. But even the inner light of the Jansenist, implying as it does complete dependence on the divine will, is something far removed from the spiritual auton-omy of the Buddhist, an autonomy so complete that in de-scribing it one is constrained to employ at the risk of grave misunderstanding the terms self-reliance and individualism; for in the West the doctrine of self-reliance, from the ancient Cynics and Stoics down to Emerson, has been associated with pride rather than humility. The Buddhist type of individ-ualism again is at the opposite pole from the type with which we are familiar nowadays—the type which combines a gospel of self-expression with the evasion of moral responsibility. Buddha seems to the Occidental to allow insufficiently for self-expression, at the same time that he gives the widest possible extension to the doctrine that a man is simply reaping, in the good or evil that befalls him, the fruits of his own sowing. These fruits seem even more inevitable than in Christianity, inasmuch as man is accountable to Law and not to a more or less arbitrary and capricious divine will. He cannot ascribe his failure to make the salutary effort to any denial of grace nor can he look to a Saviour to do for him what he is unable to do for himself. He cannot, again, substitute for self-reliance a reliance upon rites and ceremonies, a reliance reckoned by Buddha among the "ten fetters." At the very end of his life Buddha exhorted his followers to be "refuges unto themselves." A still more individualistic flavour is given to such utterances by the positive and critical element in Buddhistic teaching to which I have already called attention. Buddha would not have his followers receive spiritual truth merely on his own authority, nor again on that of tradition. As a result of the primary emphasis on Law the temper of the Buddhist is more impersonal than that of the Christian. An effusion like Pascal's *Mystère de Jésus,* profoundly religious in its own way, would have seemed to him to involve a morbid exacerbation of personality.

A statement of this kind applies above all to the original doctrine. The spirit of passionate devotion (*bhakti*) that developed in so striking a fashion in Hinduism has its equivalent in later Buddhism. In general much that I have been saying would need to be modified or even exactly reversed, if I were attempting an account of the various forms of Mahāyāna. Thus some of these forms developed a confidence in rites and ceremonies as aids to salvation that probably goes beyond anything of the kind that has been witnessed in Christianity. The example of the prayer-mill will occur to everybody. Mahāyāna has again in many of its forms encouraged the very type of theosophic and metaphysical speculation that Buddha himself repudiated. A debate regarding the relation of appearance to reality was carried on for centuries in connexion with this movement which is probably at least equal in subtlety to corresponding epistemological inquiries in the Occident. To be sure Buddha was himself prodigiously subtle. This subtlety, unlike that of the Mahāyānist, was, however, psychological rather than metaphysical. Finally the spiritual autonomy or self-reliance encouraged by the original doctrine receives far less emphasis in Mahāyāna, and is at times abandoned entirely. In direct proportion to the completeness of this abandonment, Buddha ceases to be a man and becomes a god or saviour. The teaching of a higher will is retained, but is so modified as to approximate at times to the Christian doctrine of grace. The abandonment of spiritual self-reliance was often conscious and deliberate. According to the reasoning of certain Mahāyānists in Japan, men may formerly have been capable of achieving salvation by their own efforts, but, in view of their present degeneracy, their only hope is in the grace and mercy of Amitabha. At the same time debates arose between the partisans of grace and of good works (in the ritualistic sense) not unlike those which have gone on in certain periods of Christianity. Analogies of this kind are indeed so numerous that some have suspected a direct or indirect influence upon Mahāyāna of a distinctly gnostic type of Christianity. There is a sense, one should add, in which Buddhist believers of all types have been comparatively individualistic. They have not on the whole been submitted to a rigid outer authority. Above all the Buddhist world has never known any organization for enforcing outer authority comparable in elaborateness and effectiveness to the Roman Catholic Church, itself modeled in important respects on Roman imperial organization. One may sum up the whole subject by saying that though Mahāyāna and Hinayāna have much in common in their strictly ethical teaching, Mahāyāna has tended to give to this teaching a radically different doctrinal setting.

Keeping this general contrast in mind we may return to Buddha's positive and psychological method of dealing with the problem of the will. In the contrast he establishes between the expansive desires and a will that is felt, with reference to these desires, as a will to refrain, he is, as I have said, an uncompromising dualist. By exercising this quality of will a man may gradually put aside what is impermanent in favour of what is more permanent and finally escape from impermanence altogether. The chief virtue for Buddha is therefore the putting forth of this quality of effort, spiritual strenuousness, as one may say. His last exhortation to his disciples was to practise this virtue (*appamāda*) unceasingly. Anyone who has grasped all that it implies has gone far in his understanding of the genuine doctrine.

We are told that the exposition by a Buddhist missionary of aphorisms on the importance of spiritual effort, similar no doubt in substance and possibly even in form to the second chapter of the present *Dhammapada*, led to the conversion of Asoka, an event of incalculable importance for the culture of the Far East. Asoka showed that he had caught the very spirit of the Sakya sage when he proclaimed to his subjects: "Let all joy be in effort." "Let small and great exert themselves." Asoka was active in every sense of the word; so was Buddha himself for that matter, as should be sufficiently clear to anyone who considers the attention he must have given to details in the founding of his religious order. But, though Buddha and Asoka were men of action in every sense of the word, it goes without saying that they were less interested in outer than in inner action. Buddha brings all forms of work into relation with one another, asserting the final superiority of the form by which one wins to self-mastery. He develops the paradox of religion that the man who is outwardly idle may be at once more strenuously and more profitably employed than the man who is outwardly active. On one occasion a rich Brahman farmer to whom Buddha had presented himself for alms reproached him with being an idler. Buddha replied that he was engaged in an even more important form of tillage than that of the soil. "Faith is the seed, penance the rain, understanding my yoke and plough, modesty the pole of the plough, mind the tie, thoughtfulness my ploughshare and goad . . . exertion my beast of burden." As a result of this spiritual husbandry one achieves the "fruit of immortality." Everything indeed hinges upon the quality of one's working, whether one sets out to be a carpenter, a king, or a saint.

The term *Karma* (work), though sometimes used in much the same sense as *appamāda*, a term reserved for the salutary exercise of the higher will, is applied more commonly to the doctrine of the deed in general, to the affirmation in the widest possible sense that "what we have been makes us what we are." The belief in Karma in this extended sense with its correlative belief in reincarnation, was not, it is scarcely necessary to add, peculiar to Buddha. It has been all but universal in India from early times and has also appealed to important

Western thinkers like Plato. However, according to the view of
the orthodox Buddhist, the Master did not base his acceptance
of Karma on traditional grounds but on immediate perception.
To be sure the nature of the insight of a Buddha as well as the
way in which Karma fulfills itself are both numbered among
the "unthinkables." This much, at most, is certain, that the
state of Buddhahood is conceived as a state of pure vision and
that among the truths comprised in this vision is the truth
that as a man sows even so he shall reap. A Buddha is supposed to be immediately aware not merely of his own Karma,
but, at will, of the Karma of others. An ordinary Buddhist and
even a non-Buddhist may acquire in some degree the supernormal memory that this type of vision implies, though their
illumination in this particular is, we are told, compared with
that of an Arhat Buddha, as the light of a candle compared
with the blaze of the noonday sun. One may note in passing
that as a result of the insistence on the accountability of the
individual not merely for his conduct in his present life but for
that of his remoter past, two ideas coalesce in Buddhism that
have tended to fly apart in the West—the idea of sudden conversion and the idea of habit. Sudden conversion is admitted
by the Buddhist, but is usually represented as the result of a
long habituation. The impressions and acts that have been
associated with these impressions, not merely in one's present
brief span of life but in one's secular past, lie hidden in what
the modern psychologist would term the unconscious, and
tend to give a bias to one's character and conduct both now
and in one's secular future. Karma thus envisaged is a sort of
fate, but a fate of which a man is himself the author and which
is not at any particular moment entirely subversive of moral
freedom.

　　It is in their respective attitudes towards the unconscious
that the difference between a genuine supernaturalist like
Buddha and the primitivist is especially manifest. The primitivist is ready to surrender to the swarming images of the unconscious at the expense both of his intellect and of his higher
will, in the hope that he may thus enjoy a sense of creative
spontaneity. Buddha, on the contrary would put the intellect,
felt as a power of discrimination, in the service of the higher

will. He holds that it is possible by this coöperation to explore the unconscious, uncovering and finally eradicating the secret germs that, if allowed to develop freely, will result in future misery. Insight, as Buddha understands it, is marked by an increasing awareness. It is at the opposite pole from the diffuse reverie that has been so encouraged by our modern return to nature. A man's wisdom is measured by the extent to which he has awakened from the dream of sense. Goethe is very Buddhistic when he says that error bears the same relation to truth that sleeping does to waking. The very word Buddha means the Awakened. "Right awareness" is indeed the seventh stage of the Buddhist "path," immediately preceding the final stage of "right meditation."

We come here to what is for Buddha fundamental in religion. To many things that have been regarded as indispensable in other faiths—for example, prayer and belief in a personal deity—he grants a secondary place or even no place at all; but without the act of recollection or spiritual concentration he holds that the religious life cannot subsist at all.

Certain scholars have tended to emphasize the relationship between the Samkhya and Yoga Philosophies and Buddhism. Too little is known, however, about the historical development of the Hindu philosophical systems to justify one in asserting any specific borrowings from them on the part of Buddha. Moreover, as I have already pointed out, Buddhism is in its true spirit not a philosophical system at all but a "path." If one takes, however, Yoga, not in its systematic but in its psychological sense, one is justified in affirming a deep kinship between it and Buddhist teaching. In this psychological sense India, from a period even far anterior to Buddha, has been dominated,—one is at times tempted to say, obsessed,—by the idea of Yoga. One will be helped in understanding this word by keeping in mind its etymology which relates it to the Latin *jugum* and our word yoke. Metaphorically a man practises Yoga when he yokes or reins in the impulses of the natural man, though the term is usually reserved for the putting forth of this special quality of will in meditation. The yoking of self in meditation is at times compared to the actual yoking of horses or oxen. Buddha himself is described with some justification in one of the later Buddhist writings as the great *yogi*. A religious teacher cannot be explained merely in terms of environment. He does, however, presuppose an immense previous development, the turning of the attention of a multitude of men in a given direction, in this case to the quality of will, by which man may transcend his natural self. In much the same way the appearance of a Darwin or a Pasteur is not explained by the primary concentration on the natural order that has been under way in the Occident for several centuries past; it does, however, presuppose some such development. Buddha is supposed to have received from previous masters of Yoga an initiation into all the stages of meditation with the exception of the last or Nirvānic stage. This last stage is declared by Buddha, who is not in general friendly to absolutes and ultimates, to work that final emancipation from the transitory at which the whole doctrine aims. From this point of view Nirvāna has been the subject of much, and, as it seems to the Buddhist, unintelligent discussion in the Occident. As a rule, the Western student is repelled by Nirvāna, to which he gives a nihilistic interpretation, and at the same time is attracted by Buddha's compassionateness. Buddha taught a boundless love, it would appear, that had as its goal mere nothingness. One must, however, if one is to avoid grave misunderstanding, interpret both "love" and Nirvāna with reference to the special quality of will put forth in meditation. As I have already said, this will is in all its aspects a will to refrain and in its more radical aspects a will to renounce. What the Buddhist renounces are the expansive desires. Nirvāna is, in its literal meaning, the going out or extinction of these desires—especially of the three fires of lust, ill-will, and delusion. The notion that what ensues upon this extinction is mere emptiness is not genuinely Buddhistic. The craving for extinction in the sense of annihilation or non-existence (*vibharatanhā*) is indeed expressly reprobated in the Buddhist writings. The Buddhist quest is at bottom not for mere cessation but for the eternal. Negatively Nirvāna is defined as "escape from the flux," positively as the "immortal element." Strictly speaking, what is above the flux cannot be defined in terms of the flux, and "mind" is for Buddha an organ of the flux. Anyone therefore who demands at the outset a firm intellectual formulation of Nirvāna has, from the Buddhist point of view, missed the point. The notion of Nirvāna that one may get in this way has about as much value, to use an image that Buddha employs in a slightly different connexion, as the theories that a chick that has not broken its way through its shell might form of the outside world. The important fact is that the chick is able to peck its way through the shell; even so, says Buddha, man has the power of will, if he would but exercise it, to tread the path and achieve its fruition. If one inquire as to the nature of this fruition one is simply told that the saint can no longer be confined in the categories of ordinary consciousness; he has become "deep, immeasurable, unfathomable like the mighty ocean."

Though the nature of this fruition cannot be defined abstractly it can to some extent be described psychologically and concretely; all the more so in that Nirvāna is normally attained in the present life. According to Pascal, those alone deserve commendation who have succeeded in combining properly a sense of man's grandeur with a sense of his misery. Buddha seems to deserve this commendation, though his way of conceiving of man's grandeur in particular is not altogether in consonance with Christianity. This grandeur consists in the fact that the Buddhas appear as men and that the human state is in general more favourable than any other to the attainment of sanctity. Not merely Buddha himself, but many of his followers are supposed to have achieved Nirvāna and to have been in a position to compare this experience with what may be experienced in ordinary consciousness. We have already seen that Buddha subordinated the first of Kant's three questions, "What can I know?," to the second, "What must I do?" A similar subordination appears in his answer to the third question, "What may I hope?" In a verse of doubtful syntax, Pope has told us that man never is but always to be blessed. Buddha, on the contrary, aims at a present blessedness and does not encourage one to entertain any hope that is likely to divert one from this blessedness and the kind of effort by which it is attained. It goes without saying that he did not cherish the humanitarian hope: he did not, like the youthful Wordsworth, make "society his glittering bride," or like Tennyson look for-

ward to a "far-off divine event." He was free from the nos-
talgic longing, the vague out-reaching of the imagination with
which this type of hope has been so often associated. Compared with that perfect emancipation of the spirit at which he
aims, even the older form of hope, that of bliss in a world to
come, is deemed unworthy of the true disciple.

> The strong gods pine for my abode,
> And pine for me the sacred seven:
> But thou, meek lover of the good,
> Find me and turn thy back on heaven.

One should add that the "Nirvāna here and now" (*Sam-
ditthakam Nibbanam*) of the Buddhist has much in common
with the "release in this life," (*jivan-mukti*) of the Hindu
philosopher. One may, however, affirm confidently that no religious teacher was ever more opposed than Buddha in his
scheme of salvation to every form of postponement and procrastination. He would have his followers take the cash and let
the credit go—though the cash in this case is not the immediate pleasure but the immediate peace.

The peace in which the doctrine culminates is not, the
Buddhist would insist, inert but active, a rest that comes
through striving. In general the state that supervenes upon
the turning away from the desires of the natural man is not, if
one is to believe the Buddhist, a state of cool disillusion. One
may apply to it, indeed, the term enthusiasm, though the
enthusiasm is not of the emotional type with which we are so
familiar, but rather of the type which has been defined as
"exalted peace." Buddha himself seems to speak from an immeasurable depth of calm, a calm that is without the slightest
trace of languor. The innumerable images of the founder of the
faith scattered throughout the Far East strive to render this
effect of meditative tranquillity, at times, as in the great
Buddha of Kamakura in Japan, with notable success. Anyone
who like Buddha does not indulge "the desire of the moth for
the star," and the psychic restlessness that it encourages, is
likely to seem to an Occident permeated with romanticism to
lack not merely poetry but religion. Mr. Chesterton, for
example, seeks to prove, from this point of view, the superiority of the Christian over the Buddhist saint. "The Buddhist

saint," he says, "always has his eyes shut, while the Christian saint always has them very wide open. The Buddhist saint has a sleek and harmonious body, but his eyes are heavy and sealed with sleep. The mediaeval saint's body is wasted to its crazy bones, but his eyes are frightfully alive. The Buddhist is looking with peculiar intentness inwards. The Christian is staring with frantic intentness outwards," etc. There are no doubt saints and saints. The London papers published a few years ago the following dispatch from India: "A new saint has appeared in the Swāt Valley. The police are after him." But a saint, whether Buddhist or Christian, who knows his business as a saint is rightly meditative and in proportion to the rightness of his meditation is the depth of his peace. We have it on an authority which Mr. Chesterton is bound to respect that the kingdom of heaven is within us. It would be interesting to hear Mr. Chesterton explain how a saint can find that which is within by "staring frantically outwards." Failing like many others to discriminate between romanticism and religion, Mr. Chesterton has managed to misrepresent both Buddhism and Christianity. The truth is, that though Christianity from the start was more emotional in its temper than Buddhism, and though an element of nostalgia entered into it from an early period, it is at one in its final emphasis with the older religion. In both faiths this emphasis is on the peace that passeth understanding.

Matthew Arnold is therefore infelicitous from both a Christian and a Buddhist point of view in defining religion merely as morality touched by emotion. The numerous persons who have seen in the original teaching of Buddha in particular only the ethical element have been guilty of grave misapprehension. The path to religion leads through morality—on this point Buddha is most explicit; but as one approaches the goal one enters into an entirely different element: the saint who has attained the Nirvānic calm is, we are told repeatedly, "beyond good and evil."

The confusion regarding the relation of religion in general and Buddhism in particular to emotion is still more serious. The Western student, I have said, is likely to be repelled by Nirvāna but is almost invariably attracted by the prominence

Buddha gives to love or compassion. It is not as a matter of fact easy to over-emphasize this side of his teaching. "The boundless good-will" that he urges us to cultivate, "even as a mother at the risk of her life watches over her own child, her only child," embraces not only man but the whole animate world. Buddhist love can, however, like Nirvāna, be understood only in connexion with the special form of activity that is put forth in meditation. It does not well forth spontaneously from the natural man but is, like Christian charity, the supernatural virtue *par excellence*. The current confusion on this point is perhaps the most striking outcome of the sentimentalism of the eighteenth century and of the emotional romanticism of the nineteenth century that prolonged it. This confusion may be defined psychologically as a tendency to substitute for a superrational concentration of will a subrational expansion of feeling. How many persons, for example, exalt the "love" of St. Francis who, in their total outlook on life, are almost inconceivably remote from the humility, chastity, and poverty from which, in the eyes of St. Francis himself, the love was inseparable! The emotionalists have been busy with even more august figures than St. Francis, for example with Christ himself. They have also inclined, although this tendency is less familiar, to interpret Buddha subrationally. The latter tendency is probably best exemplified in Schopenhauer who founds ethics upon a distinctly subrational sympathy (or pity) and then proceeds to associate this type of sympathy with Buddha and with the wisdom of the East in general. Schopenhauer knew little about the authentic teaching of Buddha, but his error is so fundamental that it is doubtful whether he would have corrected it even if he had been more adequately informed.

The real Buddha, I have tried to make clear, though an enthusiast, was not an emotionalist. For the Buddhist, emotion, like morality, lies on the way to religion; but as one approaches the goal one enters, as I have said, into a different element—an element of unalloyed calm. It would never have occurred to Buddha and his early followers to measure a man's humanity, much less his religion by his "droppings of warm tears." The tears shed by Ananda, the favourite disciple, on learning from the Master of his approaching end, tears that seem to us so touching, were regarded by the Arhats or true saints as a mark of his spiritual immaturity. They had been so schooled in the truths of impermanence that they were not to be shaken even by the passing of a Buddha. A religious peace so perfect as this seems to us to exclude tenderness to a degree that is slightly inhuman. For the Buddhist, however, the peace and a love that has grown "great" and "immeasurable," have a common source—namely, a right use of meditation.

Moreover one should not forget that though Buddha was very pitiful, he was also very stern. His love is not of the kind that is subversive of justice. In the case of Buddha, as in that of Christ, love and justice seem to be so perfectly harmonized as to constitute but a single virtue. Later in both Buddhism and Christianity, the principle of compassion tends to get divorced, in some degree at least, from justice. The cult of the goddess of mercy in Mahāyāna lands has certain analogies with the cult of the Virgin in the West. The sympathy of the modern humanitarian, though it also tends to override justice, and though it has also, as I have already said, been frequently associated with Christ or Buddha, needs to be judged rather differently—as something more unmistakably subrational.

By its predominant emphasis on the will to refrain, Buddhism is likely to seem to the Occidental unduly negative. The peace and all-embracing charity that the saint is supposed to attain can, however, scarcely be regarded as merely negative. Moreover, though the fruit of the doctrine is often presented negatively as "release from sorrow," it is also presented positively as happiness. The Buddhist temper, like that of the Christian and unlike that of the Stoic, is cheerful. Rhys Davids, who spent a life-time in contact with the original documents, insists on the "exuberant optimism" of the early Buddhists. The phrase would seem to call for some qualification. The true Buddhist, like the true Christian, takes a gloomy view of the unconverted man; but, though holding that life quantitatively is bad, he is, regarding a certain quality of life, unmistakably buoyant. Joy rightly receives due emphasis in St. Paul's admirable list of the fruits of the spirit. The same virtue appears in the equivalent lists proclaimed by Asoka to his subjects: the joy in both cases arises from an exercise of the will to refrain. The early members of the Buddhist Order at all events were not unfamiliar with what Pascal terms total and blissful renunciation (*renonciation totale et douce*). "Let us live happily, then, though we call nothing our own!" Buddhism, indeed, at least in its original form, is more frankly eudaemonistic than Christianity. Traditionally the motive suggested to the Christian for renouncing the world has been the love of God. Buddha would have one make a similar renunciation with an eye primarily to one's own advantage. The phrase "enlightened self-interest" has come to have unfortunate connotations. The meaning given to "enlightened" and "self-interest" by Buddha is at all events at a wide remove from the meaning given to the same terms by the utilitarian. Aristotle is nearer to Buddha when he counsels a man to be a true lover of himself. Doctrines that urge one not to think of one's self at all but to act purely for the love or greater glory of God, or in more recent times, purely for the love of humanity, have a certain abstract nobility; but it may be doubted whether they are as deeply grounded as the doctrine of true self-love in the facts of human nature. To be sure, the doctrine of true self-love, like any other doctrine that may be set up, is easily abused. We hear of the prevalence in Buddhist lands of a literal and unimaginative computation of merits and demerits according to the law of Karma, a sort of spiritual book-keeping that may lead one to be self-regarding in the wrong sense. The complaint is also made that, as a result of Buddha's insistence that a man's first duty is to himself, Buddhists are, as compared with Christians, lacking in the spirit of mutual helpfulness.

It is hard to see why the teaching of self-love should result thus undesirably, if it is made sufficiently plain that the self that one loves is not only a higher self, but a self that one possesses in common with other men. As for the ordinary, or natural self, Buddha often uses language that reminds one of Christianity. His paradox of true self-love, interpreted in the light of renunciation, does not turn out so very differently from the Christian paradox of dying that one may live. According to Buddha, anything that is impermanent is not only unreal but finally illusory. In virtue of his psychological method, however, he does not as a rule dwell, after the fashion of the Hindu philosopher, on illusion in general (*māyā*) but on conceit or the illusion of the ego (*manas*). The eliminations imposed by the putting aside of the false or illusory self are, even from the point of view of the austere Christian, extremely drastic. Failure to make these eliminations is due to a failure to exercise the higher will, the will to refrain. One may say indeed that, according to Buddha, the root diseases of human nature are conceit and indolence, and that the conceit itself turns out at last to be only an aspect of the indolence; so that, even as spiritual strenuousness is the supreme Buddhist virtue, so spiritual slackness or supineness is the unpardonable offence. One must constantly keep in mind, however, that both the strenuousness and its opposite have reference primarily, not to the outer world, but to meditation. "Meditate therefore," says Buddha, "and be not indolent lest later ye have reason to repent."

Meditation is, indeed, so paramount in Buddhist belief and is carried so far that one is forced to consider in connexion with it one of the most difficult of all questions—that of mysticism. The first step in dealing with this baffling term would seem to be to limit it. The tendency on the part of certain authorities so to widen the term as to make it identical with religion itself is inadmissible. Bossuet, for example, although genuinely religious, was, so far from being mystical, positively unfriendly to mysticism. One is aided in dealing with the word mystic, as in dealing with *yoga*, by a reference to its etymology. Etymologically the mystical state implies an actual closing of the eyes. In the true mystic there is always a considerable blunting and even complete suppression of ordinary consciousness in favour of what is conceived to be a wholeness of some kind or a more genuine unity. Buddhist meditation is undoubtedly mystical in this sense. For example, we learn regarding Buddha himself the realistic detail that on a certain occasion he was not disturbed in his contemplation by a thunderbolt that struck near him, killing two peasants and four oxen. One is reminded of the *henôsis* or mystic absorption in the One of a Plotinus. Yet right at this point one needs to make sharp discriminations. The teaching of Plotinus and the neo-Platonists in general, however much it may agree with that of Buddha in this or that particular, is in its total tendency, radically divergent. This divergence is nowhere more apparent than in the quality of the mysticism the two teachings have fostered. On the immensity of the neo-Platonic influence, especially of Plotinus, not merely on European culture but on the culture of the Near East, it is scarcely necessary to dilate. Through the treatise of the pseudo-Dionysius and other channels this influence penetrated into Christianity itself. It received a fresh impetus in the early Renaissance from such works as Ficino's commentary on the *Symposium.* The confusion between the neo-Platonic interpretation of Plato and a genuine Platonism has not been dissipated even to the present day. It is possible to detect the persistent neo-Platonic strain in mystics so far apart in time as Eckhardt, Boehme, and Blake.

The first obvious contrast between Buddha and the mystics who have been in greater or lesser degree neo-Platonic, appears in their respective attitudes towards the problem of evil. For Plotinus evil has no intrinsic reality, it is only an absence of the good. One may recognize in Plotinus himself an element of genuine spirituality—he is very far from being like Buddha a clear-cut figure—and one may at the same time insist on the danger of this notion that evil is mere deprivation. It tends to discredit everything that is felt negatively and restrictively, to associate the pursuit of the good with expansive longing rather than with renunciation. The nostalgia that has assumed so many forms in Western religion and literature is not unrelated to the neo-Platonic influence. The reaching out towards the "infinite" in this sense is at all events alien to a teacher who held that the higher will in man is primarily an inhibition, and who is in this sense, as I have said, an uncompromising dualist.

The true humility of the Christian with its subordination of man in his natural self to a divine will is also sharply dualistic. The mystic of the neo-Platonic type tends, on the contrary, to blunt the edge of this dualism or even to suppress it entirely. He is less concerned than the Christian with man's sinfulness or than the Buddhist with his spiritual indolence felt as a positive evil. With the resulting decline in humility, he is inclined to substitute for the sense of one's dependence on the divine an assertion of identity with it. The Roman Catholic Church has given recognition to mystics who exhibit traits that to the ordinary person seem pathological. It may be doubted, however, whether with its secular experience it has ever countenanced any mystic capable of announcing, as Sister Katrei announced to Eckhardt, that she had "become God."

Eckhardt's own mysticism has, along with marked neo-Platonic elements, points of contact with the mediaeval school that exalted intellect above will. In general it is important to determine the attitude of a mystic towards intellect both in itself and in its relation to will. The neo-Platonic mystic reminds one of the Buddhist in that his ultimate is an indefinable. The Buddhist holds, however, that in order to achieve his ultimate he needs to exercise the sharpest discrimination. One is tempted to say, although the phraseology is not Buddhistic, that in treading his "path," he would use his intellect as an instrument of the higher will. The neo-Platonist, on the contrary, tends to fall away from the form of concentration that seems so salutary to the Buddhist, in favour of expansiveness. He then wins a more or less mystical unity at the expense of discrimination. The maxim *omnis determinatio est negatio* is sound in itself. When, however, negation is conceived neo-Platonically as mere absence of the good, an interpretation of the maxim follows that is not conducive to self-limitation or to limitation of any kind. It is at all events highly important to know whether the union with a larger whole—the goal of every mystic—is won by the multiplication or the obliteration of distinctions. The intellect when left to its own devices is prone, as one may already see in Plotinus, to forget its secondary and instrumental rôle and to set up absolutes or, what amounts to the same thing, to devise some metaphysical denial of that dualism which is the scandal of reason and is nevertheless one of the immediate data of consciousness. This monistic trend, even when it does not take on a mystical colouring, results in its extreme form, and that from the Taoists of ancient China down to Hegel and Croce, in the assertion of a *coincidentia oppositorum* or identity of contradictories, and finally to a denial of the distinction that it would seem most important to preserve—that between good and evil. The intellectual running together of opposites has, as every student of our modern "return to nature" is aware, its emotional equivalent, which also frequently takes on a mystical colouring. Mysticism of this latter type would seem to be at the opposite pole from that of Buddha. The early Buddhists practised certain "unpleasant meditations" on the decay and corruption of the body which will be found to justify their title. One may cite by way of contrast the utterance of the "mystic" Novalis: "One touches heaven when one touches a human body"; or the somewhat grotesque equivalent of this utterance in Walt Whitman, who has also been termed a mystic: "I dote on myself, there is that lot of me and all so luscious." When Whitman speaks of the "mystical deliria" of the senses he uses the word mystical in a sense, one scarcely need point out, that would have seemed to Buddha sheer madness. The primitivistic revery that is at the basis of the mysticism of a Novalis or a Whitman cannot, like genuine meditation, be regarded as a form of action. It results rather from a dissipation of attention, a relaxation of one's grip on the world of spiritual values and even on the facts of the natural order; so much so at times as to suggest that it has its source in actual physical debility.

The foregoing analysis, if correct, would seem to justify the conclusion that the record of so-called mysticism in the Occident has been in general highly dubious; that the modern return to nature in particular, though it has revealed new sources of poetry, offers in its mystical aspects, and that from either a Christian or a Buddhist point of view, a mere subrational parody of genuine meditation. It is well to remember that the Far East has also had a primitivistic movement of immense extent in Taoism and that, either as a result of Taoist intrusion or other influences, the Mahāyānist seems to have developed at times a quality of meditation more or less pantheistic and in so far unlike that found in the original doctrine. Anyone who seeks to meditate in Buddha's sense must be, as regards the intellect, keenly discriminating, and, as regards the higher will, strenuous; whereas according to Wordsworth, in what one is tempted to call his Taoist phase, the man who wishes to commune with nature must combine passivity with a distrust of the "meddling intellect."

In this matter of meditation as in other respects one scarcely needs to insist on the immensity of the psychic gap that separates the Buddhist Orient from the Occident of today. It is because of this gap, at least as much as because of insufficient information, that so many Western treatises on Buddhism are almost unconsciously partisan, at times violently partisan. Renan maintained that one could not be polite in a Parisian omnibus without violating the rules of the company. Even so anyone who sets out to be a Buddhist today would find himself in conflict with some of the underlying assumptions of our civilization. An Occidental is as likely to be as much disconcerted on a first reading of the Buddhist *Nikāyas* as one may suppose an ancient Buddhist would be if set down in a modern powerhouse. The phenomenal world that alone seems to us real and to which we therefore cling desperately he would have us look upon as a flying mist of illusion. On the other hand the Nirvāna towards which Buddha urges us to strive affects us as mere nothingness. It is to be feared that he would have held our opinions on this point in scant esteem. The truth of his discipline, he would have insisted, can be apprehended only by putting it into practice. Knowledge in matters religious waits upon will. It is the result of doing certain things. So far from doing these things, we are doing almost the exact opposite. He would therefore have dismissed us as mere theorists. In general, it may be a help in elucidating this subject to reverse the usual question as to what we are to think of Buddha and ask rather what Buddha would think of us. This latter question is one that can be answered with certainty, assuming that Buddha remained Buddha and was not swept off his feet by our wonderfulness; for we are very wonderful. The Oriental even at the present day is astounded by our material achievements.

In its essence Buddhism is, as I have said, a psychology of desire, so that all that is needed for a reply to the question what Buddha would think of us is to compare positively and critically our attitude towards the expansive desires with that of Buddha. The movement that became predominant in the Occident with the emergence of the middle class in the eighteenth century and which still continues, may be defined in its two main aspects as utilitarian and sentimental. The outstanding characteristic of the movement in both of these aspects has been its enormous expansiveness. The utilitarian is wont to pursue an ever expanding production as an end in itself. The point of view of an eminent American economist has been summed up in the formula: "Pigs for more pigs for more pigs." A world of frenzied producers requires as its complement a world of frenzied consumers. The expert in advertising has been gravely praised of late for making two desires grow where only one grew before. The extirpation of desire in the Buddhist sense, or even the limitation of desire in the humanistic sense, would plainly be injurious to trade. If need is felt of a counterpoise to the acquisitive life, recourse is had, not to a genuinely restrictive principle but to the sympathy and spirit of service recommended by the sentimentalists, which is at bottom only another form of expansion. To both types of expansionist I have been defining, Buddha's psychology of desire seems intolerably astringent. To Buddha, on the other hand, a view of life that combines the extreme of outer activity with the extreme of spiritual indolence would have seemed one-sided to the point of madness. The current notion that it is possible to establish a collective peace and brotherhood among men who are individually filled with every manner of restlessness, would have seemed to him positively delirious. We are wont to deal with the question of war and peace at its extreme periphery,—for example war or peace between nations. Like the Christian, the Buddhist would begin at the centre— with the issue of war or peace in the heart of the individual. Any conquest that the individual may win over his own inordinate desires will be reflected at once in his contact with other men. If the individual happens to be one in high station, such a conquest may have almost immediate consequences in the field of political action. One may illustrate interestingly from the history of Buddhism. About 273 B.C., Asoka, grandson of that Chandragupta who defeated in the Punjab and drove back the Macedonian garrisons left by Alexander the Great, succeeded to a realm more extensive than modern British India. He had it in his power to drench the world in blood. He actually made a beginning—and then came his conversion to Buddhism. The result may be told in his own words as they appear in the edicts which he caused to be engraved on rocks or pillars throughout his vast empire. In one of his rock edicts he tells of his "profound sorrow" at the hundreds of thousands who had been slain in his war on the Kalingas, as well as at the misery that had been brought upon a multitude of non-combatants. "If a hundredth or a thousandth part of these were now to suffer the same fate it would be a matter of regret to his Majesty." A mighty emperor who not only repented of his lust of dominion but had his repentance cut into the rock for the instruction of future ages—this under existing circumstances is something to ponder on. The type of statesman with whom we are familiar in these latter days is wont to indulge his own will to power as well as that of the national group to which he belongs, and then, when the untoward consequences appear, to evade responsibility. Nearly everyone, for example, who was concerned with the outbreak of the Great War has been proclaiming his own blamelessness and at the same time pointing an accusing finger at someone else. We shall discover perhaps even more unedifying aspects of human nature than this search for scapegoats if we probe this whole question of war and peace by a Buddhistic method; if, in other words, we envisage it from the point of view of the inner life and then deal with the inner life itself positively and critically, in the opposition it offers between the principle of control and the expansive desires. According to an ancient Sanskrit epigram the uncultivated man and the thoroughly cultivated man are alike in having few and simple desires; the man who has reached the stage of half-way knowledge, on the other hand, is insatiable. Precisely this type of insatiableness has appeared in the modern man who has become too critical to accept the traditional controls but not critical enough to achieve new ones. In tracing the process by which in our modern period the principle of control in human nature has been weakened in favour of a sheer expansiveness one needs to attend carefully to the fortunes of the doctrine with which this principle had been traditionally associated— the doctrine of divine grace. An important aspect of the senti-

mental movement has been primitivism. The primitivist inclines to look for goodness not to the grace of God but to the
grace of nature. Instead of the inner workings of the spirit on
which both Christian and Buddhist put so much emphasis, he
proclaims a "wise passiveness." The utilitarian, representing
the other chief aspect of the modern movement, has obscured
the truths of the higher will in the Christian or any other form,
by his tendency to transfer action from the inner life to the
outer world, to put a material in place of a spiritual efficiency.
One can trace this development with special clearness among
Protestants, notably perhaps among Calvinists. Calvin
granted to God so much and to man so little in his scheme of
salvation that his followers inclined to turn their efforts from
the inner life where they seemed to be of no avail to the outer
world, and then, in the type of prosperity achieved by this kind
of working, to see a sign that they were in the divine favour.
This development has rightly received attention from those
who have studied the rise of modern capitalism with its exaltation of the acquisitive life.

At all events, an outstanding feature of the humanitarian
movement on both its utilitarian and its sentimental side has
been its expansiveness, its reaching out for more and ever for
more. The representatives of this movement are not willing to
admit that they are foregoing the benefits that not merely
Buddha but the religious and humanistic teachers of the Occident as well have associated, not with expansion, but with
concentration. On the contrary they have proclaimed a
progress that is supposed to lead in the direction of peace and
fraternal union among men. In short, though resolved to renounce nothing, they hope to enjoy all the fruits of renunciation. They would seem to illustrate, on a large, perhaps an
unprecedented scale, a trait that is universally human but is
specially visible in the half-educated man—the proneness
namely to harbour desires that are not only numerous but
often incompatible. The explanation of this tendency to reach
out after certain ends and at the same time seek to evade the
means is only too obvious: though the ends are desirable the
means are difficult and disciplinary. The readiness of men to
succumb to schemes for acquiring sudden wealth is familiar. It
probably offers only a faint image of their proneness to yield to

the lure of teaching that seems to hold out the hope of spiritual riches without any corresponding effort. In America—and America is the paradise of the half-educated—substantial material rewards await anyone who can devise some new and painless plan for getting "in tune with the infinite."

The revolution in the very basis of ethics implied in the setting up of utilitarian or sentimental substitutes for religion has not perhaps attracted an amount of attention commensurate with its importance. The gravity of this revolution would probably have been more manifest had it not been accompanied by a sort of revolution in the dictionary. The words that had been used traditionally to sum up certain ethical and religious ideas were retained but with a modification of the traditional meanings. The modern movement indeed, especially since the eighteenth century, illustrates another trait of the imperfectly cultivated man: he not only has numerous and frequently incompatible desires, but he dissimulates this incompatibility both from himself and others by a vague and confused use of general terms, or it may be, by a transfer of general terms from one scheme of values to another. For example, the sentimentalist has associated words like virtue and conscience not, as traditionally, with a will to refrain, but with expansive emotion. The utilitarian again has also inclined to eliminate the will to refrain and the inner effort it involves in favour of a mere outer working. This shifting of emphasis is reflected above all in the changed meaning of the word comfort. Material comfort has come more and more to seem to the modern man a satisfying substitute for spiritual comfort. To be sure, one does not know what secret qualms may torture the modern man or at least an occasional modern man as he is whirled he knows not whither in an ever-increasing mass of interlocking machinery. To all outer appearances, however, most men no longer crave the security and serenity which are of the essence of religious comfort and have allowed these terms, like the term comfort itself, to be appropriated by the utilitarians. An American life insurance company recently advertised as follows: "Buddha, who was born a prince, gave up his name, succession and his heritage to attain security. But . . . we do not have to give up the world; we have only to see a life insurance agent who can sell us security for the future, the most direct step to serenity of mind."

The issues raised by this advertisement evidently involve much more than one's attitude towards Buddha. For example, the differences of outlook between Christ and Buddha are inconsequential compared with the difference between them both and the man who believes that serenity and security are something one may purchase from the agent of a life insurance company. In general, a collateral benefit of any comprehension one may achieve of Buddha is that it will help one to a better understanding of Christ. One will be less likely to confound him with the humanitarian phantom that has for several generations past tended to usurp his place. This usurpation has been made plausible, as I have said, by a tampering with general terms; it has also illustrated on a large scale another human proclivity—the proclivity namely to read one's self into the great figures of the past. Thus both primitivists and utilitarians have sought to refashion Christ in their own image. For instance the author of a recent *Life of Christ*, Giovanni Papini, complains that the "exhausting mercantile superstition of our day" has led to an utterly one-sided activity. The desirable opposite of this utilitarian one-sidedness is, he would have us believe, not another form of action but the sheer inaction (*Wu wei*) of the ancient Chinese Taoist, which he proceeds to identify not merely with the primitivism of Rousseau but also with the wisdom of Christ. On the other hand, another recent interpreter of the gospel narrative, Mr. Bruce Barton, wishing to commend Christ to an age that plumes itself above all on its efficiency, presents him as a master of the art of advertising and an ancestor of the modern man of business.

If the man of the West has been falling away from religion in the fashion I have indicated, it is not to be supposed that the man of the East has maintained himself on the level of religious insight that one finds in Buddha and his early followers. On the contrary, it would probably be even more difficult to find an *arhat* in the full Buddhist sense in contemporary Asia than it would be to discover any complete exemplar of Christian sanctity in the Occident. Furthermore, if we are to trust certain passages in the Pāli Canon, Buddha's own contemporaries, who were as definitely concentrating on religious problems as the present age is on material efficiency, did not find his teaching easy to grasp. "Profound, O Vaccha, is this doctrine," Buddha is represented as replying to a puzzled inquirer, "recondite and difficult of comprehension, good, excellent and not to be reached by mere reasoning, subtle and intelligible only to the wise; and it is a hard doctrine for you to learn who belong to another sect . . . and sit at the feet of another teacher." There is also the tradition of the "private Buddhas" who did not see fit to give their wisdom to the world. Nay, it is related of Gotama himself that, after having attained supreme illumination, he hesitated about attempting to bestow it upon mankind "held spellbound by its lusts." Finally Brahmā Sahampati himself appeared before him and entreated him not to disappear from the world without proclaiming the Doctrine. "There are those," he added, "who will understand." Buddha finally assented, exclaiming: "The door is open to the deathless."

If it was not easy for Buddha's contemporaries to enter the door thus opened, to attune their ears to "sweet airs breathed from far past Indra's sky," the task is doubly difficult for the unmeditative Occidental; for it is plain that one cannot have even an inkling of the nature of the insight Buddha professed without some grasp on the idea of meditation. From this point of view the Occidental is likely to find the Buddha of certain schools of Mahāyāna more accessible, Buddha conceived less as a master of meditation than as a Lord of compassion; such a conception, however, finds comparatively little support in the older records. To be sure, the Mahāyānist, even though he grant the greater historical authenticity of the Pāli Canon, is prone, like certain Christians, to take refuge in a theory of development and to allege in particular the paramount place given to compassion as proof of the superiority of the developed over the original doctrine. Theories of development are, however, when applied to religion, dubious, whether the religion be Buddhism or Christianity. Peripheral development there may well be—for example, in Buddhist or Christian art; but development at the centre is another matter. A great religion is above all a great example; the example tends to grow faint in time or even to suffer alteration into something very different. Buddhism seems to have the most vitality today in Hīnayāna rather than in Mahāyāna lands. The reason may be that in the former lands there has been less sophistication of the figure of the Founder.

The whole question is related to a topic that is now being actively discussed: namely, what is the specifically Oriental element in the Orient and what should be the attitude of the Occident towards this element? According to a recent French writer, Europe, appalled at the one-sided American cult of mass production and mechanical efficiency, feels that it may finally have to choose between Henry Ford and Gandhi. There is much in the teaching of Gandhi, however, that is more sug- gestive of Tolstoy than of the genuine Oriental seer. Buddha, on the other hand, not only stands for an idea that is typically, though not exclusively, Asiatic—the idea of meditation—but he deals with meditation and the form of effort it requires in a more positive and critical fashion perhaps than any other re- ligious teacher. The significance of his teaching for the Occi- dent, so far as it has any, would seem to be here. The scientific naturalists profess at present to have a monopoly of positive and critical method. The attempt, however, to bring the whole of human experience under the natural law, so far from being genuinely positive and critical, involves a lapse at some point into mere dogma and metaphysical assumption. It would seem desirable, then, that those who object on either humanistic or religious grounds to the over-reaching attitude of the scientific naturalists should not burden themselves with any unneces- sary metaphysical or theological baggage, and that their appeal should be to experience rather than to some counter- dogma. As is well known, the more thorough-going naturalists have been tending more and more to discard speculative philosophy in favour of psychology; and herein they are at one with Buddha. One is conscious, however, of some underlying discrepancy between Buddha and the naturalistic psycholo- gists, and that precisely at the point where, in spite of serious divergences, these psychologists are in accord with one another. One may illustrate from the behaviourists and the psycho-analysts, who may be taken to represent the extreme opposing wings of contemporary psychology. The psycho-analyst is introspective, at least to the extent that he is concerned with certain desires and impulses of the natural man as reflected in states of consciousness. The behaviourist, on the other hand, is so eager to be "objective," to avoid even the suspicion of introspection, that he is ready to deny instinct as understood by the psycho-analyst and even consciousness itself. There is a sense in which Buddha agrees with both behaviourist and psycho-analyst. Like the psycho-analyst he reduces the human problem to a psychology of desire, and then deals with desire itself in terms of conflict and adjustment. Like the behaviourist, again, he would deal with man neither metaphysically nor theologically but positively, and from this point of view is ready to assert that "man is what he does." If in his total position he seems so widely removed from both psycho-analyst and behaviourist, the explanation is that he affirms as a matter of immediate perception a principle of control in man that all schools of naturalistic psychology deny in favour of some form of monism. If the quality of will proclaimed by Buddha and other religious teachers is a fact, it is plainly a fact of overwhelming importance; so much so that any view of life that fails to reckon with it will finally turn out to be nugatory. If one affirms that man is what he does and then, like the behaviourist, conceives of doing merely in terms of reactions to outer stimuli, the result is a monstrous mutilation of human nature. A similar failure to take account of the higher will vitiates the psycho-analytical idea of adjustment. Religion also looks upon life as a process of adjustment. This process as envisaged by the Christian is summed up once for all in Dante's phrase: "His will is our peace." A reading of works like the *Dhammapada* suggests that the psychological equivalent of this form of adjustment was not unknown to the Buddhist.

It is true that in a naturalistic era like the present the refusal to recognize a super-rational factor in human nature has a certain plausibility. At such a time a psychology that does not discriminate qualitatively between the behaviour of a man and that of a frog, may seem to have some support in the facts. One might, again, take psycho-analysis more seriously if it applied to the genuinely religious Buddha as perfectly as it does to the pseudo-religious Rousseau and his innumerable spiritual progeny. It is well, therefore, if one does not wish to fall victim to the fallacies of the naturalist, to turn from an age like our own which tends to see in life only a free expansion of wonder and curiosity to certain periods of the past that were more preoccupied with the problem of religious or humanistic control. The situation with which Buddha had to cope in his affirmation of the principle of control was not so different from our own as one might infer from his remoteness in time and place. He lived in an age of extreme philosophical sophistication. Naturalistic doctrines were being proclaimed very similar in their practical implications to scientific determinism. One of these doctrines, especially subversive of moral responsibility, Buddha declared to be the worst of all, just, he added, as a hair garment is the worst of garments, hot in summer, cold in winter, uncomfortable at all seasons.

In general, there is an irreconcilable opposition between Buddhism and any philosophy or psychology ancient or modern, that tends, on any grounds whatsoever, to obscure the truths of the higher will. Buddha's emphasis on this will is so fundamental that, according to a German authority, his teaching may be summed up in the lines of Goethe:

> Von der Gewalt die alle Menschen bindet
> Befreit der Mensch sich der sich überwindet—
>
> [The man who subdues himself frees himself
> From the power that binds all men—]

lines that recall a sentence of Milton's: "He who reigns within himself and rules passions, desires and fears, is more than a king." One should not forget, however, that, though Buddhism is hostile to all doctrines that deny a principle of control in human nature, it is not necessarily in accord with every doctrine that affirms such a principle. The sayings of Goethe and Milton I have just quoted would have met the approval of a Stoic. Milton's use of the word king is indeed very much in the Stoical tradition. Yet the wisdom of Buddha, whatever it may be, is not, as I have already remarked, Stoical. One needs to keep in mind here the ordinary contrast between Stoic pride and Christian humility, for the same contrast exists between the Stoic and the Buddhist. The source of Stoical pride would seem to be an usurpation on the part of reason of a primacy that does not belong to it, with a resulting attempt to bring all the facts of experience under a single law, the law of "nature." The Stoic thus comes to deny dualism in his metaphysical theory at the same time that he asserts it in his ethical practice. In other words, he seeks to base the principle of control on a philosophy of immanence; whereas both Christianity and Buddhism are, though on different postulates, transcendent. Everything will be found to hinge finally on the idea of meditation. This idea has suffered a steady decline in the Occident, along with the transcendent view of life in general, in the passage from the mediaeval to the modern period. Yet it is not certain that religion itself can survive unless men retain some sense of the wisdom that may, according to Dante, be won by sitting in quiet recollection. The meditation of the Buddhist involves like that of the Christian the exercise of transcendent will; this will is not, however, associated, as it normally is in the meditation of the Christian, with that of a personal deity. Persons of positive and critical temper who yet perceive the importance of meditation may incline here as elsewhere to put less emphasis on the doctrinal divergence of Christianity and Buddhism than on their psychological agreement.

REFERENCE NOTES

Introduction

PAGE

ix   where labor is cheap?: Malcolm Cowley, "Humanizing Society," in *The Critique of Humanism: A Symposium*, ed. C. Hartley Grattan, pp. 68, 84.

x   of moral Fascism": Allen Tate, "Humanism and Naturalism," *Reactionary Essays on Poetry and Ideas*, p. 114. This essay first appeared under the title "The Fallacy of Humanism," *Criterion* 8 (1929), 661–81, and then in *The Critique of Humanism: A Symposium*, ed. C. Hartley Grattan, pp. 131–66.

x   of modern life": Walter Jackson Bate, *Criticism: The Major Texts* (New York: Harcourt, Brace and Co., 1952), p. 547.

x   mind and experience": F. O. Matthiessen, *American Renaissance: Art and Expression in the Age of Emerson and Whitman* (London and New York: Oxford University Press, 1941), p. 231.

xi   time and fashion": Paul Elmer More, "Criticism," *Shelburne Essays*, 7th ser. (New York: G. P. Putnam's Sons, 1910), pp. 219, 220.

xiii   our contemporaries": T. S. Eliot, chapter 13, in *Irving Babbitt: Man and Teacher*, ed. Frederick Manchester and Odell Shepard, p. 104.

xiii   lifetime in verifying": Stuart Pratt Sherman, chapter 9, in *Irving Babbitt: Man and Teacher*, ed. Frederick Manchester and Odell Shepard, p. 90.

xiv   definite Protestant creed": René Wellek, "Irving Babbitt, Paul More, and Transcendentalism," in *Transcendentalism and Its Legacy*, ed. Myron Simon and Thornton H. Parsons (Ann Arbor: University of Michigan Press, 1966), p. 191.

xix   *and Romanticism* in 1920: John Middleton Murry, "The Cry in the Wilderness," *Aspects of Literature*, p. 170.

271

xxvi terms of a formula: R. P. Blackmur, "Humanism and Symbolic Imagination," *The Lion and the Honeycomb: Essays in Solicitude and Critique,* p. 147.

xxxiv writes in 1927: T. S. Eliot, "The Humanism of Irving Babbitt," *Selected Essays,* p. 421.

xxxv that of reason": Edmund Wilson, "Notes on Babbitt and More," *The Shores of Light: A Literary Chronicle of the Twenties and Thirties,* p. 456.

xxxvi his central ideas": Paul Elmer More, "Irving Babbitt," *On Being Human,* New Shelburne Essays, 3d ser., p. 29.

xxxviii a great saint!": Paul Elmer More, "Irving Babbitt," *On Being Human,* New Shelburne Essays, 3d ser., p. 42. This essay first appeared in the *University of Toronto Quarterly,* 3 (1934): 129–45; it was later reprinted in *Irving Babbitt: Man and Teacher,* ed. Frederick Manchester and Odell Shepard. pp. 322–37.

What I Believe

4 professor of French: Albert Schinz, *La Pensée de Jean-Jacques Rousseau.*

4 just appeared: *The Meaning of Rousseau,* by Ernest Hunter Wright.

7 the "mucker pose": See "The Mucker Pose" by James Truslow Adams, *Harper's,* November, 1928.

10 able book: *The Ideas of the Fall and of Original Sin* (Bampton Lectures for 1924). See p. 331.

The Terms Classic and Romantic

20 with barbaric: See his *Essai sur le genre dramatique sérieux.*

21 Latin manuscript: Quoted in Grimm's Dictionary.

21 most part fictitious": Ex lectione quorundam romanticorum, i.e. librorum compositorum in gallico poeticorum de gestis militaribus, in quibus maxima pars fabulosa est.

21 extreme, unique, etc.: Perhaps the most romantic lines in English are found in one of Camillo's speeches in *The Winter's Tale* (IV, 4):

> a wild dedication of yourselves.
> To unpath'd waters, undream'd shores.

This "wild dedication" is, it should be noted, looked upon by Camillo with disfavor.

23 have believed," etc.: *Pepys's Diary,* 13 June, 1666.

23   becomes burlesque," etc.: Thomas Shadwell, Preface to the *Sullen Lovers*, 1668.

23   a whining coxcomb": *Spectator*, 142, by Steele.

23   I must paint it: Pope, 2d Epistle, *Of the Character of Women*.

23   early as 1675: Cf. *Revue d'hist. litt.*, XVIII, 440. For the Early French history of the word, see also the article *Romantique* by A. François in *Annales de la Soc. J.-J. Rousseau*, V, 199–236.

24   *Mythoscopia romantica:* First edition, 1698; second edition, 1732.

26   romantic period: Cf. his *Elégie à une dame*.

26

> Mon âme, imaginant, n'a point la patience
> De bien polir les vers et ranger la science.
> La règle me déplaît, j'écris confusément:
> Jamais un bon esprit ne fait rien qu'aisément.
>
> . . . .
>
> Je veux faire des vers qui ne soient pas contraints
>
> . . . .
>
> Chercher des lieux secrets où rien ne me déplaise,
> Méditer à loisir, rêver tout à mon aise,
> Employer toute une heure à me mirer dans l'eau,
> Ouïr, comme en songeant, la course d'un ruisseau,
> Ecrire dans un bois, m'interrompre, me taire,
> Composer un quatrain sans songer à le faire.
>
> [My soul, conceiving, does not have the patience
> To polish verses well and set knowledge in order.
> Order displeases me, I write confusedly:
> A good mind never does anything except with ease.
>
> . . . .
>
> I want to write verses that are not forced
>
> . . . .
>
> To seek out secret places where nothing displeases me,
> Meditate at leisure, dream all at my ease,
> Occupy a whole hour in looking at myself in the water,
> To hear, as in a dream, the running of a brook,
> To write in a forest, interrupt myself, be silent,
> Compose a quatrain without thinking about doing it.]

26   a share": *Caractères*, ch. V.

27   "decaying sense": His psychology of the memory and imagination is still Aristotelian. Cf. E. Wallace, *Aristotle's Psychology*, Intr., lxxxvi–cvii.

28   wins the Heart: *An Essay upon Poetry* (1682).

30   related in all: The French Academy discriminates in its *Sentiments sur le Cid* between two types of probability, "ordinary"
and "extraordinary." Probability in general is more especially
reserved for action. In the domain of action "ordinary" probability and decorum run very close together. It is, for
example, both indecorous and improbable that Chimène in the
Cid should marry her father's murderer.

34   of the three unities: In his *Preface* to Shakespeare.

39   but very concrete: For a similar distinction in Aristotle see
Eth. Nic., 1143 b.

39   and intuition: The Platonic and Aristotelian reason or mind
($\nu o\grave{u}s$) contains an element of intuition.

40   attack on Molière: In his *Lettre à d'Alembert sur les spec-
tacles.*

40   a philistine of genius: *Rousseau contre Molière*, 238.

40   of fine fabling": *Letters on Chivalry and Romance.*

English and the Discipline of Ideas

63   discipline of ideas: I have inserted at this point a number of
sentences from an address that I gave at the Dartmouth ses-
quicentennial celebration on a topic very similar to the
present one, namely, "On Teaching the Intellectual Content
of Literature."

69   regarded as official: The whole plan has since received the
approval of the faculty.

Form and Expression

72   Beauty": For Poe's definition of both beauty and poetry, see
his essay on *The Poetic Principle.*

73   Professor Theodor Lipps: *Aesthetik: Psychologie des
Schönen;* Teile I, II, 1903, 1906.

73   "infeeling": Lipps's process of *Einfühlung* is closely related to
that melting of man into outer objects in a sort of revery
which I have discussed in another chapter. An article on
Lipps and the whole tendency he represents will be found in
the *Edinburgh Review* (Oct., 1908) under the title, "Beauty
and Expression."

73   narrow precepts: Edward Bysshe's *Art of English Poetry*
(Third Edition, 1708) is usually taken to be the extreme expression of this tendency in English.

73   any language": In their metrical experiments, as in so many
other respects, the French symbolists were anticipated by the

German romanticists. Hettner remarks in his book on German romanticism (p. 59) that "the poems in so-called free verse, into which Tieck especially was misled, are absolutely unendurable."

74 work on aesthetics: *Estetica come scienza dell'espressione e linguistica generale*, 1902. My references are to the first edition.

74 to pure expression: *Estetica*, p. 81: "noi possiamo definire la *bellezza* come *l'espressione riuscita*, o meglio, come l'espressione *senz'altro*," etc. [we can define *beauty* as the successful *expression*, or better still, as *simply expression*].

74 his own: *Ibid.*, p. 98.

74 intuitions of sense: *Ibid.*, p. 137 and *passim*.

74 Croce denies: *Ibid.*, p. 68.

74 of the will: *Estetica*, p. 54.

74 upon himself: The first person, according to Signor Croce, who "penetrated the true nature of poetry and art" (*Estetica*, p. 228) was his fellow Neapolitan, Giambattista Vico (1668-1744). In some of his ideas about the spontaneous and primitive Vico may be regarded as a precursor of Rousseau and Herder.

75 aesthetic spontaneity: *Estetica*, pp. 38-41, 147, 465-480.

75 mere logomachy: *Ibid.*, p. 115.

77 life and motion: Κινεῖ οὐ κινούμενον (*Met.*, xii (xiii), 7). The idea is of course found in many other passages of Aristotle.

77 the Middle Ages": *Erstes kritisches Wäldchen* (ed. Suphan), p. 76.

78 they will":

> Non satis est pulchra esse poemata: dulcia sunto,
> Et quocumque volent, animum auditoris agunto.

Pulcher refers in Latin to the formal virtues.

78 form and symmetry: There is still something to be said after Lessing and so many others on the boundaries that are imposed on each art by its own special technique, the material in which it works, its relations to time and space, etc. I am of course approaching the subject from an entirely different angle. Those who are interested in the other avenue of approach will find good material in Ludwig Volkmann's *Grenzen der Künste* (1903), a book that turns to account the conclusions of other recent German theorists (especially A. Hildebrand and A. Schmarsow). Volkmann attacks Rodin (pp. 81 ff.) for confusing at times the standards of painting and sculpture. This impressionistic confusion of painting and sculpture

often resembles the pseudo-classic confusion of the two arts in producing (at least on the eye that is untrained technically) an effect of writhing theatricality.

82   true beauty: For Sainte-Beuve's ideas on this subject, see especially *Chateaubriand et son groupe littéraire, passim.* The first influential application of the idea of the classic age to France is that of Voltaire in his *Siècle de Louis XIV* (Chaps. i and xxxii). Voltaire himself was probably influenced by the Abbé Du Bos, who sets forth the whole theory at great length, translating the inevitable passage at the end of Velleius Paterculus (*Réflexions Critiques,* 2° partie, sects. 12–14).

83   law of force: The humanitarian will of course reply that all this expansion will be sufficiently tempered by an increase in altruism. Unfortunately the evidence is as yet rather scanty that the human nature of the future is going to differ so radically from the human nature of the past. To illustrate concretely, the growth of international good will does not seem to reassure the English entirely regarding the vital expansion of Germany.

85   of baby's bath: I should add that all the admirers of Strauss are not agreed about this describing of baby's bath. The *Domestic* Symphony can scarcely be so interpreted however as to affect my main thesis,—that there is a great deal of expression here compared with the intrinsic importance of what is expressed.

Romantic Love

89   fine ladies": *Confessions,* Livre IV.

90   said elsewhere: *The New Laokoon,* ch. V.

91   to the Virgin: *Franciscae meae laudes,* in *Les Fleurs du mal.*

91   against Cervantes: *Architecture and Painting,* Lecture II. This diatribe may have been suggested by Byron's *Don Juan,* Canto XIII, IX–XI:

> Cervantes smiled Spain's chivalry away:
> A single laugh demolished the right arm
> Of his own country, etc.

92   his *Alastor:* "Nondum amabam, et amare amabam, quaerebam quid amarem, amans amare." [I was not yet in the process of loving, and I loved the idea of loving, and I was looking for something I might love since I was in love with love.]

93   fair feminine face: Cf. Shelley's *Alastor:*

> Two eyes,
> Two starry eyes, hung in the gloom of thought
> And seemed with their serene and azure smiles
> To beckon.

94   Antigone": "Some of us have in a prior existence been in love with an Antigone, and that makes us find no full content in any mortal tie." Shelley to John Gisborne, October 22, 1821.

94   sylphids": *Confessions,* Livre XI (1761).

95   this nature": *Mémoires d'Outre-Tombe,* November, 1817.

95   for his dream: "Je me faisais une félicité de réaliser avec ma sylphide mes courses fantastiques dans les forêts du Nouveau Monde." [I took pleasure in making real my fantastic journeys with my sylphid in the forests of the New World.] *Mémoires d'Outre-Tombe,* December, 1821.

95   containing a sylph": Peacock has in mind *Childe Harold,* canto IV, CXXI ff.

96   any definite object": Rousseau plans to make a nympholept of his ideal pupil, Emile: "Il faut que je sois le plus maladroit des hommes si je ne le rends d'avance passionné sans savoir de quoi," etc. [I would have to be the most clumsy of men if I did not make him passionate beforehand without knowing for what.] *Emile,* Liv. IV.

96   this Sadic fury: Cf. René's letter to Céluta in *Les Natchez:* "Je vous ai tenue sur ma poitrine au milieu du désert, dans les vents de l'orage, lorsque, après vous avoir portée de l'autre côté d'un torrent, j'aurais voulu vous poignarder pour fixer le bonheur dans votre sein, et pour me punir de vous avoir donné ce bonheur." [I have held you on my breast in the middle of the wilderness, in the winds of the tempest, when, after having carried you to the other side of a torrent, I would have wished to stab you in order to fix happiness in your breast, and to punish me for having given you that happiness.]

96   uttered by Atala: The romantic lover, it should be observed, creates his dream companion even less that he may adore her than that she may adore him.

97   and madness: Walter Bagehot has made an interesting study of the romantic imagination in his essay on a figure who reminds one in some respects of Gérard de Nerval—Hartley Coleridge.

97   the philanthropic pose: Don Juan bids his servant give a coin to the beggar not for the love of God but for the love of humanity.

97   the "infinite":

> Demandant aux forêts, à la mer, à la plaine,
> Aux brises du matin, à toute heure, à tout lieu,
> La femme de son âme et de son premier voeu!
> Prenant pour fiancée un rêve, une ombre vaine,
> Et fouillant dans le coeur d'une hécatombe humaine,
> Prêtre désespéré, pour y trouver son Dieu.
>   A. de Musset, *Namouna.*

> [Asking the forests, the sea, the plain,
> The morning breezes, at every hour, at every place,
> For the woman of his soul and of his first vow!
> Taking for betrothed a dream, an empty shade,
> And ransacking the heart of a human hecatomb,
> A priest in despair, to find there his God.]

> "Don Juan avait en lui cet amour pour la femme idéale; il a couru le monde serrant et brisant de dépit dans ses bras toutes les imparfaites images qu'il croyait un moment aimer; et il est mort épuisé de fatigue, consumé de son insatiable amour."
>   Prévost-Paradol, *Lettres,* 149.

> [Don Juan had in him that love for the ideal woman; he traveled over the world, for vexation crushing and breaking in his arms all the imperfect images which he believed for a moment he loved; and he died exhausted with fatigue, destroyed by his insatiable love.]

97   Earl of Peterborough: See Scott's (2d) edition of Swift, XIII, 310.

98   the intoxication?":

> Aimer c'est le grand point. Qu'importe la maîtresse?
> Qu'importe le flacon pourvu qu'on ait l'ivresse?

98   unexpected moments: It has been said that in the novels of George Sand when a lady wishes to change her lover God is always there to facilitate the transfer.

98   *pas avec l'Amour:* "Tous les hommes sont menteurs, inconstants, faux, bavards, hypocrites, orgueilleux ou lâches, méprisables et sensuels; toutes les femmes sont perfides, artificieuses, vaniteuses, curieuses et dépravées; le monde n'est qu'un égout sans fond où les phoques les plus informes rampent et se tordent sur des montagnes de fange; mais il y a au monde une chose sainte et sublime, c'est l'union de deux de ces êtres si imparfaits et si affreux. On est souvent trompé en

amour; souvent blessé et souvent malheureux, mais on aime
et quand on est sur le bord de sa tombe, on se retourne pour
regarder en arrière, et on se dit: J'ai souffert souvent, je me
suis trompé quelquefois, mais j'ai aimé. C'est moi qui ai vécu,
et non pas un être factice créé par mon orgueil et mon ennui."
[All men are liars, inconstant, false, gossipers, hypocrites,
arrogant or cowardly, contemptible and sensual; all women
are faithless, artificial, vain, curious, and depraved; the world
is only a sewer without bottom where most shapeless sea
animals crawl and twist themselves on mountains of slime;
but there is in the world one holy and sublime thing, that is
the union of two of these so imperfect and hideous beings. One
is often deceived in love; often wounded and often unhappy,
but one loves and when he is on the brink of his grave, he
turns around to look back, and he says: I have suffered often,
I have often been deceived, but I loved. It is I who have survived and not an artificial being created by my pride and my
boredom.] (The last sentence is taken from a letter of George
Sand to Musset.) *On ne badine pas avec l'Amour*, II, 5.

99   his earliest years": *Table-Talk. On the Past and Future.*

100   human life": *The Plain Speaker. On Reading Old Books.*

100   their recollection": *The Round Table. On the Character of
Rousseau.*

100   an actual woman: "Aujourd'hui, jour de Pâques fleuries, il y a
précisément cinquante ans de ma première connaissance avec
Madame de Warens." [Today, Palm Sunday, it is exactly fifty
years since my first acquaintance with Mme. de Warens.]

100   reveries: Even on his death-bed the hero of Browning's *Confessions* gives himself up to impassioned recollection:

> How sad and bad and mad it was—
> But then, how it was sweet.

In his *Stances à Madame Lullin* Voltaire is at least as
poetical and nearer to normal experience:

> Quel mortel s'est jamais flatté
> D'un rendez-vous à l'agonie?

> [What mortal ever flatters himself
> On having a rendezvous with death?]

Joubert

116   pernicious being": *Corinne*, 237. My references are to Paul de
Raynal's edition in two volumes (4ᵉ éd., 1866). In the volume

containing the *Pensées,* no numbers are used in the opening chapter ("L'auteur peint par lui-même"). The thoughts are arranged by subjects in the following numbered chapters, which are therefore called "Titres."

117   and goodness": *Ibid.*

117   in English: I am assuming a familiarity with this essay on the part of the reader and have as a rule avoided translating the same *Pensées.*

117   from my pen": *Pensées,* p. 10.

117   intermediary ideas": *Ibid.,* p. 8.

117   the inexpressible": *Cor.,* 20.

117   the clouds": Tit. I, XC.

118   *jeu: Cor.,* 119.

118   mere nothing": Tit. I, XIII.

118   engagement": Tit. I, LXII.

118   the instrument": *Pensées,* p. 8.

119   misfortunes": *Chateaubriand,* II, 138.

119   *Spirit of Laws:* As an example of his courage and good sense see his letter to Fontanes, then Grand Master of the University, in which he protests against the poor pay of teachers and professors (*Cor.* 217).

119   on stilts: Tit. XXIV, V, VII.

119   theatre": Tit. XXXII.

119   for me": *Pensées,* p. 4.

119   of his life": Tit. XVI, LIX.

119   of the future: *Ibid.,* XVII, I.

120   the old ones": Tit. XVIII, LVII.

120   irreligious liberty: *Ibid.,* XVIII, XIII.

120   prejudices": *Pensées,* p. 4.

120   art a child": Tit. XVIII, XX.

120   resolutely traditional: "Aux Grecs, et surtout aux Athéniens, le beau littéraire et civil; aux Romains, le beau moral et politique; aux Juifs, le beau religieux et domestique; aux autres peuples, l'imitation de ces trois-là" [To the Greeks, and particularly to the Athenians, literary and civic beauty; to the Romans, moral and political beauty; to the Jews, religious and domestic beauty; to other people, an imitation of those three] (Tit. XVII, XIII).

120   lamp": Tit. XVIII, V.

120   private ladder: *Ibid.,* XIV.

120   corrupted by it": *Ibid.,* XVI, XIII.

120   of any profit: Tit. XXIV, XXXVIII.

120   his mania": *Ibid.,* XXV.

121   Rousseau": *Ibid.*, L.

121   instrument": Tit. XXI, IX.

121   soul and body": *Ibid.*, IX, LII.

121   full and complete": *Ibid.*, V, LVII.

122   what is abstract": *Ibid.*, XII, VI.

122   special dialect": Tit. XII, XXV.

122   concealing voids": *Ibid.*, XII, XXXII.

122   reasoning shop": *Ibid.*, VI.

122   nothing in them: *Cor.*, 62.

122   of all things": He goes on to say that "la mesure de toutes choses est *l'immobile* pour le *mobile, l'infini* pour le *limité,* le *même* pour le *changeant, l'éternel* pour le *passager,* " etc. [the measure of all things is the *immobile* for the *mobile,* the *infinite* for the *limited,* the *abiding* for the *changing,* the *eternal* for the *passing.*] (*Cor.*, p. 61). For his views of Kant see also *Pensées,* Tit. XXIV, XVII-XIX.

122   sounds and perfumes": Tit. XXI, XXV.

122   about objects": *Ibid.*, XXIII, LXXVII.

123   complementary truth: *Ibid.*, XI, XVIII.

123   *avec des paroles: Ibid.*, XXII, LXXIV.

123   the most harmonious: *Ibid.*, XXII, XXIX.

123   of ideas": Tit. XXI, XXIII.

123   is conducting you": *Ibid.*, XXII, CX.

123   light and serenity: *Ibid.*, XXIII, CVIII.

124   heavenly archetype: Tit. XXI, II.

124   means of bodies": Tit. XX, XLV. Joubert distinguishes sharply between *l'imagination,* an active and creative faculty, the sole intermediary between intellect and spirit, and possessed in a high degree only by the gifted individual; and *l'imaginative,* a sub-rational and passive faculty, that may manifest itself very strongly in children, timid people, etc. See Tit. III, XLVI-LII.

124   imagining them": *Cor.*, 85.

124   be thus veiled: Tit. XI, XXXVI.

124   of life and of art: Tit. IX, V. Cf. Tit. XX, X and Tit. XXIII, CXV.

124   not by frauds": *Cor.*, 125.

124   part of reality: Tit. XI, XXXIX.

124   *voir tout nu:* Tit. XXI, XXI.

125   impulse of sex: I have treated this topic more fully in *The New Laokoon,* ch. V.

125   light and peace": Tit. V, CX.

125   make us chaste: *Ibid.*, CXII.

125   Anacreontic morality": Tit. XXIV, LXVI.
125   die in a swoon": *Ibid.*, LXVII.
125   at them in profile": *Pensées*, p. 2.
125   long white veils": *Pensées*, p. 393.
125   wrote to Molé: *Cor.*, 106 ff. Sainte-Beuve says of this letter that "la psychologie de Chateaubriand y est coulée à fond" [the psychology of Chateaubriand is thoroughly cast in it]. (*Chateaubriand*, II, 396); cf. also *Nouveaux Lundis*, III, 11.
126   *restrained* passions": Tit. XXIII, CXXXI.
126   conscience of the soul": *Ibid.*, XXIII, CXLVII.
126   it is I": *Pensées*, p. 8.
126   form of abundance": Tit. XVIII, LXXXVIII.
126   "there is no literature": *Ibid.*, XXIII, XXIV.
126   an acquired difficulty": *Ibid.*, XLV.
126   love little ones," etc.: *Ibid.*, XXIII, CCXX.
126   *un beau petit livre: Ibid.*, CCXXII.
127   nor touchstone": Tit. XXIII, CXLV.
127   the art of criticism: *Ibid.*, XXIV, LIV.
127   the Abbé Delille: *Cor.*, 251. It is only fair to add that Joubert did not read English.
127   to define adequately: Tit. XVI, L.
128   all that is spiritual": Tit. III, XLIV.
128   his literary perceptiveness: Chateaubriand has a similar combination of qualities in mind when he says more ambitiously that Joubert was a "Platon à coeur de La Fontaine" [Plato with the heart of La Fontaine]. Joubert was, by the way, the first to point out that "Il y a, dans La Fontaine, une plénitude de poésie qu'on ne trouve nulle part dans les autres auteurs français" [there is, in La Fontaine, an abundance of poetry that one finds nowhere in the other French authors] (Tit. XXIV, sect. V, XX)—an opinion since adopted by Sainte-Beuve, Amiel, and Matthew Arnold.
129   would have done": *Cor.*, 257.
129   simply contradict them: Tit. XII, LIV.
129   but asleep!": Tit. VII, LXIII.
129   our lives are made": *L'Evolution créatrice.*
130   delivered from time": "Akappiyo." See *Sutta-Nipāta*, IV, 10.
130   yesterday or to-morrow": Tit. XIII, IV.
130   succession of bodies.): Tit. VI.
130   should remain unshaken": Tit. IX, XLII.
131   thought and written": Tit. XXII, LXXIII.
131   to another intellect": Tit. XXIII, CLXXVII.
131   to be won again!": Tit. XXIII, CLXXXIV.

131   for a short time": Tit. XXIII, CCV.
132   to lodge them: Mes idées! c'est la maison pour les loger qui me
      coûte à bâtir [My ideas! It's the lodging house for them that is
      costly for me to construct] (*Pensées*, p. 10).
132   time to die: Tit. VII, LXXXIX.
132   of a whole book": Tit. XXIII, CCXVII.

Democracy and Standards

138   "I am an Epicurean": *Works* (Ford ed.), X, p. 143.
139   and cultural backgrounds: For example, 41 per cent of the
      residents of New York City are actually foreign-born; if we
      add those whose father or mother or both were born abroad,
      the more or less foreign element in its population amounts to
      80 per cent.
141   but also state rights: He drafted, for example, the so-called
      Kentucky Resolutions (November, 1799).
142   stood for incompatible things: A similar opposition existed, of
      course, between Jefferson and Alexander Hamilton. The *Life
      of Hamilton*, by F. S. Oliver, is to be commended for the clear-
      ness of the insight it displays into the nature of this oppo-
      sition.
142   created a Washington myth: A specially influential book in
      the creation of this myth was the *Life of Washington* (1800),
      by "Parson" Weems.
142   Lincoln and that of Jefferson: Lincoln actually defended
      himself against the charge of having spoken disparagingly of
      Jefferson. See *Works* (Nicolay and Hay ed.), VI, p. 60.
144   liberty of the American Indian: See *Works* (Ford ed.), III,
      p. 195.
144   established by Professor Stuart P. Sherman: *American and
      Allied Ideals* (War Information Series, No. 12), p. 9.
144   ascribes to the Puritan: Strange things have been happening
      to the Puritan conscience of late even in the most authentic
      descendants of the Puritans. Thus Henry Adams inserts in a
      hymn to the Virgin a hymn to the dynamo. The whole concep-
      tion has little relation to mediaeval Christianity and none at
      all to Puritanism. It is, however, closely related to the tend-
      ency of the nineteenth century to see in a sympathy that is
      emancipated from justice the proper corrective of a power
      that is pursued without regard to the law of measure.
145   The multitude: It is estimated that 62,014 statutes were
      passed by our national and state legislatures in the period

1909-13. Some of these laws—for example, those regulating finger-bowls and the length of sheets in hotels—remind one of the minute prescriptions indulged in by the ancient city-states at their worst. Cf. Fustel de Coulanges, *La Cité antique*, p. 266: "L'Etat exerçait sa tyrannie jusque dans le plus petites choses; à Locres, la loi défendait aux hommes de boire du vin pur; à Rome, a Milet, à Marseille, elle le défendait aux femmes. Il était ordinaire que le costume fût fixé invariablement par les lois de chaque cité; la législation de Sparte réglait la coiffure des femmes, et celle d'Athènes leur interdisait d'emporter en voyage plus de trois robes. A Rhodes la loi défendait de se raser la barbe; à Byzance, elle punissait d'une amende celui qui possédait chez soi un rasoir; à Sparte, au contraire, elle exigeait qu'on se rasât la moustache." [The state exercised its tyranny even in the smallest matters; at Locris, the law forbade men to drink pure wine; at Rome, at Miletus, at Marseilles, it forbade wine to women. It was typical that the dress code was invariably fixed by the laws of each city; legislation in Sparta regulated women's coiffures, and that of Athens forbade them to bring more than three dresses on a voyage. At Rhodes the law forbade shaving; at Byzantium it stipulated that anyone who kept a razor in his house would be fined; at Sparta, on the contrary, the law required that moustaches be shaved.]

146   (with very few capital convictions): In 1885 there were 1808 homicides in the United States with 108 executions; in 1910, 8,975 homicides with 104 executions.

146   is reputed to be civilized: "In 1918 Chicago had 22 robberies for every one robbery in London and 14 robberies for every one robbery in England and Wales. . . . Cities like St. Louis and Detroit, in their statistics of robbery and assault with intent to rob, frequently show annual totals varying from three times to five times greater than the number of such crimes reported for the whole of Great Britain. Liverpool is about one and a third times larger than Cleveland, and yet in 1919 Cleveland reported 31 robberies for every one reported in Liverpool." (Raymond B. Fosdick, *Crime in America and the Police*, 1920, p. 18.) Mr. Fosdick ascribes our imperfect administration of justice to our legalism (p. 48) and our sentimentalism (p. 44).

147   his own misconduct: "This is a chain of galley-slaves," cried Sancho, "who are going to the galleys." . . . "Be it how it may," replied Don Quixote, "these people, since they are

being taken, go by force and not of their own will. . . . Here comes in the exercise of my office, to redress outrages and to succor and aid the afflicted." "Let your worship reflect," said Sancho, "that justice, which is the King's self, does no violence or wrong to such people, but chastises them in punishment of their crimes." (*Don Quixote,* Part I, ch. XXII.)

148   he was not a utilitarian: "To be always seeking after the useful does not become free and exalted souls" (*Politics,* 1338b.)

148   ' of scientific discoveries: To suppose, as Bacon did, not only that nature is exhaustible, but that it may be exhausted by the accumulated observations of a number of essentially commonplace specialists is to be wrong at the centre. Cf. *Novum Organum,* Book I, Aphorism CXXII: "My way of discovering sciences goes far to level men's wits, and leaves but little to individual excellence."

149   the divine average: "The American demands a poetry . . . that will place in the van and hold up at all hazards the banner of the divine pride of man in himself (the radical foundation of the new religion). Long enough have the People been listening to poems in which common humanity, deferential, bends low, humiliated, acknowledging superiors. But America listens to no such poem. Erect, inflated, and fully self-esteeming be the chant; and then America will listen with pleased ears." (*Democratic Vistas.*)

149   the principle of union: ". . . the American Soul, with equal hemispheres, one Love, one Dilation or Pride."

152   voters is about fourteen: For a tabulation of these tests see vol. XV of the *Memoirs of the National Academy of Sciences.*

153   embodiment of will: In *Le Droit international public positif* (1920), I, pp. 77 ff., J. de Louter has traced historically the opposition between those who base international law on "jus naturale," conceived as universal reason, and those who incline rather to see in it an expression of will ("jus voluntarium").

154   a consistently imperialistic, people: This consistent imperialism has been traced by H. H. Powers in his volume: *America among the Nations.*

156   in ancient Roman history: See Tenney Frank's *Roman Imperialism,* especially ch. VIII ("Sentimental Politics").

156   the "good old times": As the rural philosopher remarked: "Things ain't what they used to be—in fact they never was."

156   the Romans of his time:

Aetas parentum peior avis tulit
Nos nequiores, mox daturos
Progeniem vitiosiorem.

Carminum, Lib. III, 6.

[The age of our parents, worse than that of our grand-
fathers, has produced us who are still worse, and who will
soon bring forth a progeny still more vicious.]

157   in the Puritan household: Professor G. H. Palmer has written
from his own memories an article on "The Puritan Home."
(*Atlantic Monthly,* November, 1921.)

158   already present in ourselves: Cf. Pascal, *Pensées,* 64: "Ce n'est
pas dans Montaigne, mais dans moi que je trouve tout ce que
j'y vois." [It's not in Montaigne, but in myself that I discover
all that I see in him.]

161   every man is his own Jesuit: Cf. Confucius: "Alas! I have
never met a man who could see his own faults and arraign
himself at the bar of his own conscience."

161   the scrutiny of general terms": See Epictetus, *Dissert.* I, 17.

162   a philosophical occupation: Cf. Joubert on the writings of
Rousseau: "La paresse y prend l'attitude d'une occupation
philosophique." [Indolence takes upon itself the attitude of a
philosophical occupation.]

165   not to renounce Socrates: In his *Life of Christ* Papini not only
attacks Socrates specifically, but bases his whole point of
view on an abdication of the critical spirit.

167   the temporal order: "It was an easier thing to consecrate the
fighting instinct than to curb it. . . . [The crusader] might
butcher all day till he waded ankle deep in blood and then at
nightfall kneel sobbing for very joy at the altar of the Sep-
ulchre—for was he not red from the winepress of the Lord?
One can readily understand the popularity of the Crusades
when one reflects that they permitted men to get to the other
world by fighting hard on earth and allowed them to gain the
fruits of asceticism by the way of hedonism." (Article on
"Crusades," by Ernest Barker, in eleventh edition of *Encyclo-
paedia Britannica.*)

167   heart of genuine Christianity: The predominance of the imperialistic over the religious motif is especially conspicuous in
the fourth Crusade (1202–04).

167   portentous patter of words: Fitzjames Stephen has submitted
this formula to a drastic analysis in *Liberty, Equality, Fraternity.* This book contains also a refutation of Mill's essay on
Liberty.

167   more realistic in temper: This tendency was noted by various
        observers even before the war, for example, by J. E. C. Bodley
        in his essay *The Decay of Idealism in France* (1912).

169   product of the Puritan discipline: If one wishes to measure the
        wideness of the gap between President Eliot's doctrine and
        that of the Puritans, let him read together Jonathan Ed-
        wards's sermon on "A divine and supernatural Light," a bit
        of quintessential Puritanism, and "Five American Con-
        tributions to Civilization."

173   "unwritten laws of heaven": The passage of the *Antigone* (vv.
        450 ff.) needs to be associated with the passage of the *Oedipus*
        (vv. 863 ff.): ". . . laws that in the highest empyrean had their
        birth, of which Heaven is the father alone, neither did the race
        of mortal men beget them, nor shall oblivion ever put them to
        sleep. The power of God is mighty in them and groweth not
        old."

173   a supposed law of "nature": See ch. IV ("The Rights of Man")
        in *The Spirit of the Common Law* (1921), by Roscoe Pound.
        Professor Pound is in sympathy with the second tendency to
        which I refer—the tendency towards what he terms the
        "socialization of justice." His point of view is closely related
        to that of the German Jhering, who may himself be defined as
        a sort of collectivistic Bentham.

174   the materialistic state: "Individuals and families, asso-
        ciations and dependences were so much material that the sov-
        ereign power consumed for its own purposes. What the slave
        was in the hands of his master, the citizen was in the hands of
        the community. The most sacred obligations vanished before
        the public advantage. The passengers existed for the sake of
        the ship. By their disregard for private interests, and for the
        moral welfare and improvement of the people, both Greece
        and Rome destroyed the vital elements on which the pros-
        perity of nations rests, and perished by the decay of families
        and the depopulation of the country. They survive not in their
        institutions but in their ideas, and by their ideas, especially on
        the art of government, they are—

            The dead, but sceptred sovereigns who still rule
            Our spirits from their urns.

        To them, indeed, may be tracked nearly all the errors that are
        undermining political society—communism, utilitarianism,
        the confusion between tyranny and authority, and between
        lawlessness and freedom." (Lord Acton: *History of Freedom
        and Other Essays*, p. 17.)

177   the spirit of the constitution": *Politics*, 1310a. Cf. also *ibid.*,
       1337a.

179   precursors of the elective system: See Herbert B. Adams:
       Thomas Jefferson and the University of Virginia (1888), espe-
       cially ch. IX ("The University of Virginia and Harvard
       College"). Cf. also letter of Jefferson to George Ticknor, 16
       July, 1823. Superficially, Jefferson was friendly to classical
       study; his underlying philosophical tendency (of which his
       encyclopaedic inclusiveness and encouragement of specializa-
       tion are only symptoms) was unfavorable to it.

182   every manner of faction: *Eth. Nic.* 1166b.

182   a shadow in the mist: Cf. Confucius: "The moral man, by
       living a life of simple truth and earnestness, alone can help to
       bring peace and order in the world." "When the men are there,
       good government will flourish, but when the men are gone,
       good government decays and becomes extinct."

184   a will to service: See his *Moral Principles in Education*, p. 22:
       "The child is born with a *natural* desire to give out, to do, to
       serve." (My italics.)

186   with his poison gases: The statement has been made by those
       who should be in a position to know that poison gases have re-
       cently been invented at least a thousand times more deadly
       than any employed during the war.

186   works in his laboratory": *The Socialist Movement*, p. 90.

Madame de Staël

189   society of the time": *De l'Allemagne*, 2ᵉ Partie, c. XV.

189   the little Temple of Taste: Cf. G. Merlet, *Tableau de la Lit-
       térature française, 1800–1815*, III, 21.

189   must fulfil precisely twenty-six rules: *Cours analytique de lit-
       térature générale* (1817), I, 179. Comedy must observe twenty-
       two rules, epic twenty-three.

190   mouthpieces of this opinion: See the whole article in *Causeries
       du Lundi*, I, 371 ff.

190   the tip of his own pen:

       "Nous venons de perdre Geoffroy.
       —Il est mort?—Ce soir, on l'inhume.
       De quel mal?—Je ne sais—Je le devine, moi;
       L'imprudent, par mégarde, aura sucé sa plume."

       [We have just lost Geoffroy.
       —He's dead?—They buried him this evening.
       —From what sickness?—I don't know—I've guessed it;

The imprudent fellow, inadvertently, sucked the tip of
his pen.]

192   wrecks one's life": Letter to Friederike Brun, July 15, 1806.

192   set everything afire": *De la Littérature*, 1ᵉ Partie, c. XX.

192   the most imperious passions": *Discours préliminaire de la
Littérature.*

193   of dignity and glory": *Pensées*, 387 (édition Paul de Raynal,
1866).

194   by her contemporaries: Madame de Staël was supposed to
have portrayed herself in the character of Delphine and at the
same time to have satirized Talleyrand in the character of
Madame de Vernon; whereupon Talleyrand remarked that he
understood she had written a novel in which both he and she
appeared disguised as women.

194   his country and time: "A Londres, un drame intéresse en
faisant haïr les Français; à Tunis la belle passion serait la pira-
terie; à Messine, une vengeance bien savoureuse; à Goa,
l'honneur de brûler les Juifs." [At London, they made a com-
pelling drama out of hating the French; at Tunis, the con-
suming passion was piracy; at Messina, well-savored revenge;
at Port Goa, the honor of burning the Jews.]

195   detach himself from it: *Considérations sur la Révolution
française*, c. XXVI.

196   less than the universe: *De l'Allemagne*, 1ᵉ Partie, c. XVIII.

197   of her whole work: *De l'Allemagne*, 4ᵉ Partie, c. XI.

197   her actual conversation: Sainte-Beuve: *Chateaubriand*, II,
188.

197   by the same wire": *Nouvelle Héloïse*, 2ᵉ Partie, lettre XVII.

197   depth, feeling, wit itself": *De l'Allemagne*, 1ᵉ Partie, c. XI.

197   and not to ridicule": *Ibid.*, 1ᵉ Partie, c. IX.

197   big wig on his head": *Ibid.*, 2ᵉ Partie, c. XXXI.

198   to murder as to gallantry": *Ibid.*, 2ᵉ Partie, c. XV.

198   can make it forget": *De l'Allemagne*, 2ᵉ Partie, c. IX.

198   it should be creative: *Ibid.*, 2ᵉ Partie, c. XIV.

198   know it and admire it": *Ibid.*, 2ᵉ Partie, c. XXXI.

199   to follow his own impressions: *De l'Allemagne*, 2ᵉ Partie, c. I.

199   to particular cases": *Ibid.*, 4ᵉ Partie, c. VI.

199   are worthy of consideration": *De l'Allemagne*, 2ᵉ Partie, c.
XV.

200   (*l'originalité nationale vaut mieux*): *De l'Allemagne*, 2ᵉ Partie,
c. IV.

200   and dexterity they lack": *Ibid.*, 2ᵉ Partie, c. I.

200   to him who exercises it": *Ibid.*, 2ᵉ Partie, c. XXXI.

202   open to our influences": *Annals*, 1804. Carlyle has collected

the passages from Goethe and Schiller that bear on Madame de Staël's visit to Weimar in an appendix to the second volume of his critical essays.

202   chapter in the *Germany:* 2ᵉ Partie, c. XI.

202   of imagination and thought": *De l'Allemagne,* 2ᵉ Partie, c. XI.

205   in Madame de Staël's sense: In this sense Renan says that "le sentiment des nationalités n'a pas cent ans" [the sentiment of nationalities has not a hundred years]. (*Réforme intellectuelle,* 194.)

205   love of his own land:

> "Mon compatriote, c'est homme!
> Naguère ainsi je dispersais
> Sur l'univers ce coeur français:
> J'en suis maintenant économe.
>
> . . . .
>
> Ces tendresses, je les ramène
> Etroitement sur mon pays,
> Sur les hommes que j'ai trahis
> Par amour de l'espèce humaine," etc.
>   (*Repentir.*)
>
> [My compatriot, it's man!
> Not long ago I was dispersing
> This French heart over the universe:
> Now I am economical with it.
>
> . . . .
>
> Those affections, I redirect them
> Exclusively on my country,
> On the men whom I betrayed
> Through love of the human species.]

207   a great cause of uncertainty": *De l'Allemagne,* 1ᵉ Partie, c. II.

207   *à la décision du caractère: Ibid.,* 4ᵉ Partie, c. X.

208   primordial depths of their being: "Charakter haben und deutsch sein ist ohne Zweifel gleichbedeutend, und die Sache hat in unsrer Sprache keinen besondern Namen, weil sie eben ohne alles unser Wissen und Besinnung aus unserm Sein unmittelbar hervorgehen soll" [To have character and to be German doubtless mean the same; and the thing has no special name in our language, because it is considered to proceed immediately from our very existence without any knowledge or reflection on our part] (*Reden an die deutsche Nation,* XII).

208   his country, his age," etc.: *De l'Allemagne,* 4ᵉ Partie, c. V.

208　earth only degrades us": *De l'Allemagne,* 3ᵉ Partie, c. I.

209　as in Italy for example: This Italian influence is perhaps, however, overstated by Texte when he says of her visit to Italy:
"Elle rencontra alors Confalonieri, apôtre de l'indépendance,
et écrivit dans la *Biblioteca italiana* un article retentissant qui
suscita le mouvement romantique italien" [She then met
Confalonieri, apostle of independence, and wrote in the *Biblioteca italiana* a stirring article which evoked the Italian
Romantic movement] (Julleville's *Hist. de la Lit. fr.,* VII,
709–710).

209　literary method and criticism": *Portraits contemporains,* IV,
127.

209　ever appeared in France": *Ibid.,* 232.

209　of the nineteenth century: *Ibid.,* 178.

Buddha and the Occident

225　A symposium: *Les Appels de l'Orient:* Les Cahiers du Mois.
Emile-Paul, Frères, Editeurs. Paris.

226　the lesson of the Orient": *Les Appels de l'Orient,* p. 67.

228　but of Buddha himself: Numerous and intricate historical
problems arise, however, in connexion with the Pāli Canon
and the degree to which it may lay claim to authenticity.

236　answer my question": Kevaddha-Sutta of the Dīgha-Nikāya.

251　Kamakura in Japan: Strictly speaking his is an image, not of
Gotama but of Amitabha Buddha.

BIBLIOGRAPHY

Books by Irving Babbitt

Democracy and Leadership. Boston and New York: Houghton Mifflin Co., 1924. [Indianapolis: Liberty Classics, 1979.]

The Dhammapada. Translated from the Pāli, with an Essay on Buddha and the Occident, by Irving Babbitt. New York and London: Oxford University Press, 1936. [New York: New Directions, 1965.]

Literature and the American College: Essays in Defense of the Humanities. Boston and New York: Houghton Mifflin Co., 1908. [Chicago: Gateway Editions, 1956; Clifton, New Jersey: Augustus M. Kelley, 1972.]

The Masters of Modern French Criticism. Boston and New York: Houghton Mifflin Co., 1912. [New York: Farrar, Straus, and Co., 1963; Westport, Connecticut: Greenwood Press, 1977.]

The New Laokoon: An Essay on the Confusion of the Arts. Boston and New York: Houghton Mifflin Co., 1910.

On Being Creative and Other Essays. Boston and New York: Houghton Mifflin Co., 1932. [New York: Biblo and Tannen, 1968.]

Rousseau and Romanticism. Boston and New York: Houghton Mifflin Co., 1919. [New York: Meridian Books, 1955; Auston: University of Texas Press, 1977; New York: AMS Press, 1978.]

Spanish Character and Other Essays. Edited by Frederick Manchester, Rachel Giese, William F. Giese. Boston and New York: Houghton Mifflin Co., 1940. [With a Bibliography of Irving Babbitt's Publications and an Index to his Collected Works.]

Books and Articles About Irving Babbitt: A Selective List

Aaron, Daniel. "Statement and Counterstatement: Literary Wars in the Early Thirties." *Writers on the Left: Episodes in American Literary Communism.* New York: Harcourt, Brace and World, 1961.

293

Bandler, Bernard. "The Individualism of Irving Babbitt." *Hound and Horn* 3 (1929): 57–70.

Blackmur, R. P. "Humanism and Symbolic Imagination: Notes on Re-reading Irving Babbitt." *The Lion and the Honeycomb: Essays in Solicitude and Critique.* New York: Harcourt, Brace and Co., 1955.

Bush, Douglas. "Irving Babbitt: Crusader." *American Scholar* 48 (1979): 515–22.

Carpenter, Frederic I. "The Genteel Tradition: A Re-interpretation." *New England Quarterly* 15 (1942): 427–43.

Chang, Hsin-Hai. "Irving Babbitt and Oriental Thought." *Michigan Quarterly Review* 4 (1965): 234–44.

Collins, Seward. "Criticism in America: I: The Origins of a Myth." *Bookman* 71 (1930): 241–56, 353–64.

———. "Criticism in America: II: The Revival of the Anti-Humanist Myth." *Bookman* 71 (1930): 400–15.

———. "Criticism in America: III: The End of the Anti-Humanist Myth." *Bookman* 72 (1930): 145–64, 209–28.

Crunden, Robert M., ed. *The Superfluous Men: Conservative Critics of American Culture, 1900–1945.* Austin and London: University of Texas Press, 1977.

Eliot, T. S. "The Humanism of Irving Babbitt"; "Second Thoughts about Humanism." *Selected Essays.* New York: Harcourt, Brace and World, 1960.

———. Introductory Essay. *Revelation.* Edited by John Baillie and Hugh Martin. London: Faber and Faber, 1937.

Elliott, G. R. *Humanism and Imagination.* Chapel Hill: The University of North Carolina Press, 1938.

Foerster, Norman, ed. *Humanism and America: Essays on the Outlook of Modern Civilisation.* New York: Farrar and Rinehart, 1930.

Grattan, C. Hartley, ed. *The Critique of Humanism: A Symposium.* New York: Brewer and Warren, 1930.

Hoeveler, J. David, Jr. *The New Humanism: A Critique of Modern America, 1900–1940.* Charlottesville: University Press of Virginia, 1977.

Hoffman, Frederick J. *The Twenties: American Writing in the Postwar Decade.* New York: Viking Press, 1955.

Hough, Lynn Harold. "Professor Babbitt and Vital Control." *Vital Control.* Forest Essays, 1st ser. New York and Cincinnati: Abingdon Press, 1934.

Jones, Howard Mumford. "Professor Babbitt Cross-Examined." *New Republic* 54 (1928): 158–60.

Kariel, Henry S. "Democracy Limited: Irving Babbitt's Classicism." *Review of Politics* 13 (1951): 430–40.

Kazin, Alfred. "Liberals and New Humanists." *On Native Grounds: An Interpretation of Modern American Prose Literature.* New York: Harcourt, Brace and Co., 1942.

Kirk, Russell. "Critical Conservatism: Babbitt, More, Santayana." *The Conservative Mind.* Chicago: Henry Regnery Co., 1953.

Leander, Folke. *Humanism and Naturalism: A Comparative Study of Ernest Seillière, Irving Babbitt and Paul Elmer More.* Göteborg, Sweden: Wettergren and Kerber, 1937.

———. "Irving Babbitt and Benedetto Croce: The Philosophical Basis of the New Humanism in American Criticism." *Göteborgs-studier i Litteraturhistoria Tillägnade Sverker Ek.* Göteborg, Sweden: Wettergren and Kerber, 1954.

———. "Irving Babbitt and the Aestheticians." *Modern Age* 4 (1960): 395–404.

Levin, Harry. "Irving Babbitt and the Teaching of Literature." *Refractions.* New York and London: Oxford University Press, 1966.

Lippmann, Walter. "Humanism and Dogma." *The Saturday Review of Literature* 6 (1930): 817–19.

Lora, Ronald. *Conservative Minds in America.* Chicago: Rand McNally and Co., 1971.

MacCampbell, Donald. "Irving Babbitt: Some Entirely Personal Impressions." *Sewanee Review* 43 (1935): 164–74.

McEachran, F. "Humanism and Tragedy." *Nineteenth Century and After* 106 (1929): 70–81.

McKean, Keith F. "Irving Babbitt." *The Moral Measure of Literature.* Denver, Colo.: Alan Swallow, 1961.

Manchester, Frederick, and Shepard, Odell, eds. *Irving Babbitt: Man and Teacher.* New York: G. P. Putnam's Sons, 1941.

Matthiessen, F. O. "Irving Babbitt." *The Responsibilities of the Critic.* New York and London: Oxford University Press, 1952.

Mercier, Louis J. A. *The Challenge of Humanism: An Essay in Comparative Criticism.* New York and London: Oxford University Press, 1933.

———. "The Legacy of Irving Babbitt." *Harvard Graduates' Magazine* 42 (1934): 327–42.

———. *American Humanism and the New Age.* Milwaukee, Wisc.: The Bruce Publishing Co., 1948.

More, Paul Elmer. "Irving Babbitt." *On Being Human.* New Shelburne Essays, 3d. ser. Princeton, N.J.: Princeton University Press, 1936.

Morrell, Roy. "Wordsworth and Professor Babbitt." *Scrutiny* 1 (1933): 374–83.

Munson, Gorham B. "An Introduction to Irving Babbitt." *Destinations: A Canvass of American Literature Since 1900.* New York: J. H. Sears and Co., 1928.

Murry, J. Middleton. "The Cry in the Wilderness." *Aspects of Literature.* New York: Alfred A. Knopf, 1920.

Nickerson, Hoffman. "Irving Babbitt." *Criterion* 13 (1934): 179–95.

O'Connor, William Van. "The New Humanism." *An Age of Criticism, 1900–1950.* Chicago: Henry Regnery Co., 1952.

Panichas, George A. "The Critical Mission of Irving Babbitt." *Modern Age* 20 (1976): 242–53.

———. "Irving Babbitt and Simone Weil." *Comparative Literature Studies* 15 (1978): 177–92.

———. "An Act of Reparation." *Modern Age* 24 (1980): 296–303.

Phillips, Norman R. "Positivist Humanism: The Views of Irving Babbitt and G. H. Bantock." *The Quest for Excellence: The Neo-Conservative Critique of Educational Mediocrity.* New York: Philosophical Library, 1978.

Richards, Philip S. "Irving Babbitt: I; A New Humanism." *Nineteenth Century and After* 103 (1928): 433–44.

———. "Irving Babbitt: II: Religion and Romanticism." *Nineteenth Century and After* 103 (1928): 644–55.

Russell, Frances Theresa. "The Romanticism of Irving Babbitt." *South Atlantic Quarterly* 32 (1933): 399–411.

Ryn, Claes G. "The Humanism of Irving Babbitt Revisited." *Modern Age* 21 (1977): 251–62.

Shafer, Robert. "The Definition of Humanism." *Hound and Horn* 3 (1930): 533–56.

Spingarn, J. E. "Notes on the New Humanism (1913–1914)." *Creative Criticism and Other Essays.* New York: Harcourt, Brace and Co., 1931.

Sypher, Wylie. "Irving Babbitt: A Reappraisal." *New England Quarterly* 14 (1941): 64–76.

Tate, Allen. "Humanism and Naturalism" ["The Fallacy of Humanism"]. *Reactionary Essays on Poetry and Ideas.* New York: Charles Scribner's Sons, 1936.

Vivas, Eliseo. "Humanism: A Backward Glance." *T'ien Hsia* 11 (1941): 301–13.

Warren, Austin. "Irving Babbitt." *Yearbook of Comparative and General Literature* 2 (1953): 45–48.

———. "Irving Babbitt." *New England Saints.* Ann Arbor: University of Michigan Press, 1956.

————. "The 'New Humanism' Twenty Years After." *Modern Age* 3 (1958–59): 81–87.

Wellek, René. "Irving Babbitt, Paul More, and Transcendentalism." *Transcendentalism and Its Legacy.* Edited by Myron Simon and Thornton H. Parsons. Ann Arbor: University of Michigan Press, 1966.

West, Rebecca. "Regretfully." *Ending in Earnest: A Literary Log.* Garden City, New York: Doubleday, Doran and Co., 1931.

Wilson, Edmund. "Notes on Babbitt and More." *The Shores of Light: A literary Chronicle of the Twenties and Thirties.* New York: The Noonday Press, 1967.

ACKNOWLEDGMENTS

For introducing me to Irving Babbitt's work and thought I owe much to Austin Warren, my friend and friendly critic, who spurred me on, in conversation, letters, and print, to pursue a more systematic study of Babbitt's ideas.

To Mrs. Esther Babbitt Howe, Babbitt's daughter, and to her husband, Dr. George F. Howe, I am indebted for their personal kindnesses to me. To Mrs. Howe and to her brother, Edward S. Babbitt, I am grateful both for encouraging my work and for granting to me permissions rights for the reprinting of Irving Babbitt's copyrighted writings contained in this book.

To J. David Hoeveler, Jr., who read an earlier draft of the manuscript, I am obligated for suggestions he made concerning not only the selection and arrangement of Babbitt's writings but also ways of strengthening and shaping my Introduction.

I wish to thank Dr. David S. Collier, indefatigable editor of *Modern Age: A Quarterly Review,* for his continuing interest and championing of my critical mission.

Professor Leonard Lutwack, my colleague, kindly lent me a copy of his master's thesis, "New Humanism and American Literary Criticism" (Middletown, Connecticut: Wesleyan University, 1940), with its helpful bibliography, without which much time would have been lost in my hunting down some important bibliographical items.

For her untiring assistance in preparing the manuscript, I am greatly indebted to Mary E. Slayton.

For painstakingly editing my Introduction and headnotes, I am, as always, much indebted to Martha E. Seabrook.

For their various forms of support of my work I want to thank A. Owen Aldridge, Milton Birnbaum, Douglas Bush, Thomas D. Eisele, Harold Flavin, D. W. Harding, Richard B. Hovey, Shirley Strum Kenny, Folke Leander, Harry T. Levin, Sergei Levitzky, John F. Lulves, Jr., Charles D. Murphy, Fotini D. Panichas, Nathan M. Pusey, Claes G. Ryn, Eliseo Vivas, René Wellek.

INDEX

Index of Names

Abélard, Peter (1079–1142; French medieval philosopher), 102

Acton, Lord (John Emerich Edward Dalberg-Acton, first Baron Acton) (1834–1902; English cultural historian), 3, 66

Adams, John (1735–1826; second president of the United States, 180

Adams, John Quincy (1767–1848; sixth president of the United States), 142

Adams, Henry (1838–1918; American historian, scholar, man of letters), xxv

Addison, Joseph (1672–1719; English critic, poet, essayist), 27

Alarcón, Pedro Antonio de (1833–91; Spanish novelist, diplomat, journalist), 218

Ammianus Marcellinus (330?–?400; Latin soldier and historian), 44

Amory, Blanche (lover of Arthur Pendennis in Thackeray's *The History of Pendennis*), 53

Ananda (sixth century B.C.; Buddha's favorite disciple), 253–54

Anaxagoras (500?–428 B.C.; Greek philosopher who believed in a dualistic universe), 238

Antigone (the elder daughter of Oedipus and heroine of Sophocles' *Antigone*), 94

Aphrodite, 90

Aquinas, Saint Thomas (1225–74; Dominican philosopher and theologian, greatest figure of scholasticism), 3, 52

Archilocus (714–676 B.C.; Greek poet, satirist), xi

Aristotle (384–322 B.C.), xi, xxviii, xxix, 3, 16, 21, 29–32, 36, 39, 52, 63, 65, 69–71, 74, 76–78, 84, 86, 91, 101, 107–9, 111, 127, 129, 131, 148, 158, 160, 175–77, 179, 181–82, 185, 204, 224, 231, 255

Arnold, Matthew (1822–88; English poet and critic), xi, xxv, xxxviii, 44, 57, 82, 86, 103–17, 138, 163, 226, 236, 237, 252

Asoka (third century B.C.; Buddhist emperor of India), 228–29, 246, 254–55, 261–62

Asquith, Lord (Herbert Henry, first earl of Oxford and Asquith) (1852–1928; British statesman, Liberal party leader, prime minister, and first lord of the treasury), 169

Atala (titular heroine of Chateaubriand's *Atala*), 96

Augustine, Saint (354–430; early Christian church father and philosopher), 3, 10, 92, 235, 241

Aulnoy, Madame Marie d' (1650–1705; French baroness, writer of fairy tales), 212, 215

Averrhoës (1126–98; Spanish-Arabian philosopher, influential in

301

Index of Titles

Other Books by George A. Panichas

Adventure in Consciousness:
The Meaning of D. H. Lawrence's Religious Quest

Epicurus

The Reverent Discipline:
Essays in Literary Criticism and Culture

The Burden of Vision:
Dostoevsky's Spiritual Art

The Courage of Judgment:
Essays in Criticism, Culture, and Society

Mansions of the Spirit:
Essays in Literature and Religion (editor)

Promise of Greatness:
The War of 1914–1918 (editor)

The Politics of Twentieth-Century Novelists (editor)

The Simone Weil Reader (editor)